CONTINUAL PERMUTATIONS
OF ACTION

COMMUNICATION AND SOCIAL ORDER

An Aldine de Gruyter Series of Texts and Monographs

Series Editor

David R. Maines, Wayne State University

Advisory Editors

Bruce Gronbeck • Peter K. Manning • William K. Rawlins

David L. Altheide and Robert Snow, **Media Worlds in the Postjournalism Era**

Joseph Bensman and Robert Lilienfeld, **Craft and Consciousness: Occupational Technique and the Development of World Images** (*Second Edition*)

Valerie Malhotra Bentz, **Becoming Mature: Childhood Ghosts and Spirits in Adult Life**

Jörg R. Bergmann, **Discreet Indiscretions**

Herbert Blumer, **Industrialization as an Agent of Social Change: A Critical Analysis** (*Edited with an Introduction by David R. Maines and Thomas J. Morrione*)

Dennis Brissett and Charles Edgley (*editors*), **Life as Theater: A Dramaturgical Sourcebook** (*Second Edition*)

Richard Harvey Brown (*editor*), **Writing the Social Text: Poetics and Politics in Social Science Discourse**

Norman K. Denzin, **Hollywood Shot by Shot: Alcoholism in American Cinema**

Irwin Deutscher, Fred P. Pestello, and H. Frances G. Pestello, **Sentiments and Acts**

Bryan S. Green, **Gerontology and the Construction of Old Age: A Study in Discourse Analysis**

Pasquale Gagliardi (ed), **Symbols and Artifacts: Views of the Corporate Landscape** (paperback)

J. T. Hansen, A. Susan Owen, and Michael Patrick Madden, **Parallels: The Soldiers' Knowledge and the Oral History of Contemporary Warfare**

Emmanuel Lazega, **The Micropolitics of Knowledge: Communication and Indirect Control in Workgroups**

Niklas Luhmann, **Risk: A Sociological Theory**

David R. Maines (*editor*), **Social Organization and Social Process: Essays in Honor of Anselm Strauss**

Peter K. Manning, **Organizational Communication**

Stjepan G. Meštrović, **Durkheim and Postmodernist Culture**

R. S. Perinbanayagam, **Discursive Acts**

William K. Rawlins, **Friendship Matters: Communication, Dialectics, and the Life Course**

Dmitry Shlapentokh and Vladimir Shlapentokh, **Soviet Cinematography, 1918–1991: Ideological Conflict and Social Reality**

Anselm Strauss, **Continual Permutations of Action**

Jacqueline P. Wiseman, **The Other Half: Wives of Alcoholics and Their Social-Psychological Situation**

CONTINUAL PERMUTATIONS
OF ACTION

Anselm L. Strauss

ALDINE DE GRUYTER
New York

About the Author

Anselm L. Strauss, Emeritus Professor and Founder of the Department of Social and Behavioral Sciences, University of California, San Francisco, is widely known for his theoretical writings. Among his notable books are *The Discovery of Grounded Theory* (Aldine, 1969), written with Barney Glaser; *Mirrors and Masks* (1958); and *Negotiations* (1978).

Dr. Strauss's research has been mainly in the areas of the sociology of work, occupations, and professions, and in the sociology of health. Apart from the titles cited, he has also published numerous other books and journal articles.

ALDINE DE GRUYTER
A division of Walter de Gruyter, Inc.
200 Saw Mill River Road
Hawthorne, New York 10532

This publication is printed on acid-free paper ☺

Library of Congress Cataloging-in-Publication Data

Strauss, Anselm L.
    Continual permutations of action / Anselm L. Strauss.
        p.   cm. — (Communication and social order)
    Includes bibliographical references (p.   ) and index.
    ISBN 0-202-30471-X (cloth). — ISBN 0-202-30472-8 (pbk.)
    1. Action theory.   2. Social interaction.   I. Title.   II. Series.
    HM24.S773   1993
    302—dc20   93-4075
                                                                                CIP

Manufactured in the United States of America

10 9 8 7 6 5 4 3 2 1

To

the Memories of
Alfred R. Lindesmith
and
Fred Davis
Close Friends and Intellectual Companions

"[T]he very nature of the investigation . . . compels us to travel over a wide field of thought crisscrossed in every direction. The . . . remarks in this book are, as it were, sketches of landscape which were made in the course of these long and involved journeyings. The same or almost the same points were always being approached from different directions, and new sketches made."

L. Wittgenstein—Preface to *Philosophical Investigations*

Contents

PART II

Acknowledgments

Three friends to whom this book owes most, in inception and commentary, are more than mentioned in the introduction. They are Juliet Corbin, San Jose State University; Fritz Schuetze, University of Kassel, Germany; and Hans-Georg Soeffner, University of Hagen, Germany. Also Adele Clarke and Leonard Schatzman, University of California, San Francisco and Leigh Star, University of Illinois, read the manuscript with infinite care and gave the benefit of their scrutiny and additional valuable ideas. To Berenice Fisher, New York University, and Elihu Gerson of Tremont Institute, I am also grateful for their useful commentary.

I am similarly grateful to the many publishers who have kindly consented to allow me to extract quotations from my own earlier works and from the works of others. In specific, the following passages are used with permission of the copyright holders:

The passage on the conditional matrix on pages 61–64 is taken from A. Strauss and J. Corbin, *Basics of Qualitative Method,* © 1990 by Sage Publications, Inc., by permission of the publisher.

The two case studies of Algerian youths accused of murder of a European schoolmate on pages 75–76 are taken from F. Fanon, *The Wretched of the Earth,* © 1968 by Grove Press, Inc., and used by permission of Grove Atlantic.

The passage on the sociology of work on pages 94–95, and the earlier passage on the intractability of medical work for a rationalistic framework on pages 83–84, are both taken from A. Strauss, S. Fagerhaugh, B. Suczek, and C. Wiener, *The Social Organization of Medical Work,* © 1985 by the University of Chicago Press, by permission of the publisher.

In addition, I acknowledge briefer citations throughout the text from these publishers and copyright holders, among others: JAI Press; Bantam, Doubleday, Dell; the Museum for African Art; Jossey-Bass, Inc.; the University of California Press; Random House, Inc.; Viking-Penguin; Yale University Press; Phaidon Press Limited; Stanford University Press; Prentice-Hall; The Center for Dewey Studies (Southern Illinois University); Northwestern University Press, and MIT Press.

In a volume like this, so many other voices speaking contemporaneously or from one's past have entered that I would be puzzled how to acknowledge them all. Hopefully, they will recognize themselves if they should happen across this book. Particularly, too, I want to thank David

Maines, Wayne State University, the editor of the series in which this book appears; as friend, colleague, and editor he has added to the book's clarity and readability. And as always, my wife Fran showed her usual great patience for this all too absent-minded professor.

Foreword

In his evaluation of the resurgence of Pragmatism in the human sciences, Richard Bernstein expressed the view that Pragmatism was ahead of its time. I think the same has been true of symbolic interactionism.

These two closely related perspectives, one philosophical and the other sociological, have placed human action at the center of their explanatory schemes. It has not mattered what aspect of social or psychological behavior was under scrutiny. Whether selves, minds, or emotions, or institutions, social structures, or social change, all were conceptualized as forms of human activity. This view has been the simple genius of these perspectives—one based on the ability to recognize the obvious—but ironically it also has been their biggest problem. Scholars such as Thomas, Park, and Blumer, listening carefully to the likes of Dewey, Mead, and James, insisted without qualification or apology that sociological domains and social facts were created, maintained, and changed through action. In the course of that insistence, however, they committed the great sociological sin of placing the causal arrow in a direction opposite to that which was in the ideological and administrative interests of a discipline in its institution-building phase. That is, the proposition that "human action causes social structure" was not as convenient or useful as the one asserting that "social structure causes human action."

Anyone who has paid any attention at all to the history of sociology is aware of, or may actually still believe, the stereotypes and myths surrounding interactionism that grew up in response to the perspective's ill-timed proposition. There are signs, however, that sociology may be catching up with the interactionists. For example, many of sociology's more visible and active social theorists are busy proposing one form or another of action theory. Whether called structuration, rational choice, neo-functionalism, ritual chains, or conversation analysis, or whether in the hands of Giddens, Coleman, Hechter, Collins, or Alexander, the underlying proposition is that human activity is the phenomenon that must be theorized. Further, and relatedly, advanced quantitative analysts, such as those using event history or event structure analysis, now propose that it is social process that ought to be studied and that events rather than variables are the proper unit of analysis. These three ideas—theorizing action, studying social processes, and placing events at the base of analysis—clearly have been at the heart of Pragmatism and have been among the cornerstones of interactionist sociology since its inception in the early work of the Chicago School. Not surprisingly, of course, a bifurcation of consciousness pervades this trend toward interactionism, since these new theorists and researchers seem largely unaware that they are advocating core tenets of interactionist thought. Sorokin might not turn over in his grave at the thought of this situation, but were he alive, he might be moved to add a few more examples to *Fads and Foibles* under the sections on amnesia and the new discoverer's complex. Nonetheless, it is good that sociology in general is coming to take these matters more seriously, if for no other reason than that the field has never had any viable alternative.

It is probably obvious why I have first written of sociology before writing of *Continual Permutations of Action.* Anselm Strauss has always taken ideas pertaining to action and process seriously. Now, at the urging of some of his colleagues, he has herein made explicit the theory of action that has implicitly guided his research for roughly forty years. It goes without saying that Anselm accepts the proposition that action—or (to use the gerund he prefers) *acting,* or even better, *interacting*—causes social structure. He lays the basis for this idea in the nineteen assumptions he articulates early in the book—assumptions, by the way, that elaborate and make clearer Blumer's famous three premises of symbolic interactionism. But those are only the starting point. The task Strauss put before himself, I think, is how to keep the complexity of human group life in front of the researcher/theorist and simultaneously articulate an analytical scheme that clarifies and reveals that complexity. With these two imperfectly related issues before him, Strauss outlines an analytical scheme of society in action. It is a scheme that rests not on logical necessity but on research and observation, and the concepts he uses are proposed because they do a certain amount of analytical work.

Strauss hints at the idea that his action theory is a generic one. True to his Pragmatist and Chicago roots he rejects all dualisms, and with them the validity of micro versus macro phenomena. Accordingly, he sees both individuals and collectivities as capable of acting. Following Dewey, he theorizes action as ongoing, and recognizes that if action is to be continuous, it must intrinsically involve temporality and consciousness. Such involvement is organic; that is, temporality and consciousness are basic mechanisms through which continuities are produced. Strauss thus places great emphasis on the concepts of work, trajectory, biography, and symbolization—not so much, I believe, because he is an interactionist (although that, too) but because his research tells him to theorize action along those lines.

Ongoing action, however, occurs in contexts; more precisely, it creates contexts that then become the situations of acting. Strauss theorizes the properties of situations as "conditional matrices" that give form, direction, and, to some extent, fate to activity. These matrices contain structural conditions, such as divisions of labor, resources, and institutional mandates, which are part and parcel of the articulation of lines of action. They contain the structures of routine activity and serve as hosts for the obdurate character of societal life. Instances of these matrices are illustrated in Anselm's discussions of social worlds and arenas, in which he clears the path for the analysis of intercontextual relations.

But he asks more of us in his theorizing of the relations between action and context, as expressed in his concept of "processual ordering" and the insistence that we focus more explicitly on variation and emergence. Routine and change are part of one another, Strauss argues, and in either case, they are at least partly a function of their being symbolized as routine or change. Social worlds are heterogeneous and, at any given point, imperfectly formed. Obdurate conditions may restrict choice, but those conditions must be *defined* as restrictive to be restrictive. Events conventionally regarded as completely settled may later be revealed as "mirrors mirroring mirrors," as he so evocatively writes. Ambiguity is persistent and persistence is ambiguous. All in all, the theoretical import of what Strauss has to offer here goes well beyond that implied in "negotiated orders" because of his sharper focus on what I would call the soft dialectics of human group life.

As I have been finishing the last part of these reflections on Anselm Strauss's book, I have also been paging through a new issue of a journal frequently read by sociologists. One of the articles contains the term "robust action," in its title, and in its abstract stresses the view that in order to understand state formation, analysts must focus on the conditions of peoples' actual lives rather than on totalizing institutions. I am fully prepared to believe the article, but right now it punctuates for me that the authors' conclusion has always been the interactionist starting point. And that fact reflects back to me how extraordinarily advanced Strauss's action theory actually is. All of us would be well advised to take *Continual Permutations of Action* very seriously, if only to help poor old Sorokin avoid having to add another chapter to his book.

David R. Maines

Introduction

If it had not been for repeated, and separate, urging by three of my closest friends and intellectual communicants, I would never have embarked upon this book. That sentence may strike you as suitable for a footnote of acknowledgment, but not for an opening line in a serious book on social theory. You would be wrong, for the story of their insistence is part of a biographical and theoretical story that I shall tell. My purpose will not be to dwell on personal narrative as such but to give enough of it as is necessary to understand more fully the theory of action that will be developed in these pages.

Why a book on a *theory* of action? Most American sociologists would probably associate this topic—if it meant anything at all to them—with Parsons or Weber. Exactly this was my initial response when two Germans, Fritz Schuetze and Hans-Georg Soeffner, each attempted to convince me that embodied in my writings was a unique theory of action. Although interested in substantive aspects of my writings, they were more deeply attracted by my way of studying and thinking about action and social reality. I did not myself believe it to be unique or novel, for reasons to be more fully described below; nor did I understand why they characterized my approach to research and theory as a theory of action. Yes, action of course—or interaction, as I prefer to think of this—but theory? In my reading of science, theories arise from the study of events: They vary in scope and abstractness; they are provisional, incomplete, require verification and qualification; they have a life of potential usefulness but having contributed to the movement of a science they vanish or become incorporated in newer theories. So what did my European friends mean when they said my implicit theory of action was so effective and that I should write about it?

Further, each argued that the greater significance of my writings could be missed by readers (ironically, I was missing it myself) because they read me only as a researcher into substantive areas, or as a theorist about certain general areas like negotiation or status passage—but not for some-

1

thing still more general. "Indeed," said Schuetze, "some of your best ideas are in your subordinate clauses." Both critical friends argued that running all through my publications was an implicit but never quite spelled out view of action/interaction, and that it should be made explicit.

For about five years I stalled—how to do what they urged? Not that I was inordinately modest; it was just that all of this had been said in dozens of different ways and publications. Also, most of these writings reflected a theorist who did research in order to ground his theories, or theoretical interpretations, upon data. I rarely felt comfortable merely theorizing without fairly direct contact with data. Also I have coauthored (with Barney Glaser, 1967) a style of analyzing data (grounded theory) that advocates continuous contact between theorizing and data collection. Hence the stances of a lifetime mitigated against taking up my pencil or pen (I still write with those before turning to the word processor) and composing one more book. The task was neither daunting nor did it seem unimportant; it just did not come easily, despite the hours upon hours already spent discussing sociological issues with my German colleagues. What stirred me into final motion was that another colleague, Julie Corbin (1991), recently had written a review of my intellectual biography for a festschrift (Maines 1991). Her paper about my writings is so persuasive about the place of action/interaction in them that I had no option other than to put this book on my agenda—before one of them perhaps wrote their own version of it.

All of this account has been written, you may think, with unseemly levity, but I am dead serious about its relevance to the contents of this book. To suggest its relevance initially, I move next to a discussion of the Pragmatist philosophy origins of my position on action/interaction.

PRAGMATISM AND CHICAGO
SOCIOLOGICAL INTERACTIONISM

As early as 1896, John Dewey laid down his basic strategy vis-à-vis action, in an influential and long-lived paper, "The Reflex Arc Concept in Psychology." Attacking an early version of stimulus-response psychology, his essential argument was this: It is incorrect to assert that a stimulus external to an organism elicits a response. Quite the reverse: Organisms need not be set into motion, for any stimulus must play into whatever is the ongoing activity, so that the response elicited is the result of an interaction between the two.

Dewey soon elaborated this basic position, eventually making a very clear and systematic statement of it in *Human Nature and Conduct* (1922), a book probably read by most Chicago-trained sociologists in that decade and by many even in later years. His elaborated version was really a scheme about ongoing continuous *acting*. (The more static contemporary term *action scheme* does not convey this active quality, but for convenience sake in this book I may occasionally use this term instead of the *theory of action* or of *acting*.)

Dewey's scheme embraced the following ideas: Acting is ongoing, as is the experiencing that is integral to it; action is mainly routine; interrupted routine action, by some sort of blockage that is usually environmental or situational in source, precipitates mental processes that involve a review of imagined options, the making of choices among them, and leads to the reorganization and continuance of action. Transformation though inter-action—of lines of action, objects, environment, self, and the world—is central to this theory of action.

As is generally recognized, there was a direct connection between University of Chicago interactionist sociology and philosophic Pragmatism. The sociologists absorbed some of the philosophers' assumptions—especially those of Dewey and later of G. H. Mead—building them into their sociological versions of philosophic principles. I will begin, then, by discussing this conjunction of traditions, emphasizing only those aspects of each that pertain most directly to my subject: action/interaction.

Mead (1932, 1934, 1938) added very significant elements to Dewey's formulation, which was after all rather schematic and left open a great many issues. Mead was the first to begin this filling in of important conceptual detail, and knew it; the Chicago-trained and later Chicago-derived sociologists are still filling in the Deweyian framework but make few citations to this, since that framework is so much a part of their basic assumptions about society and social behavior. (For a longer discussion of these points see Strauss 1991.)

Mead's contributions are well known, so probably it is only necessary to mention several that are most directly related to my central topic. These include his formulation of stages of the act, his radical conception of the temporal and complex and potential flexibility of any act, his elaboration of social interaction and of multiple perspectives of the actors, his detailing of self as process including self-reflection and the interplay of the I and the Me, his greater emphasis on the body in action, his elaboration with more specificity of "mind" as mental activity, and his development of a crucially important perspectival view of temporality and interaction.

Pragmatism's action scheme went hand in hand with a determinedly antidualistic position (no separation of body-mind, real-ideal, value-fact), including the argument that truth arises out of interaction, is enacted rather than discovered. [See the philosopher, Addelson (1990) for a clear statement about this.] This pits this action and process–oriented philosophic tradition, which had a firm belief in scientific modes of thinking, against positivistic forms of science as well as against a priori interpretations of social life. Chicago interactionism would inherit these perspectives also.

The action scheme was self-consciously applied by Dewey and Mead in a multitude of directions and areas of life: education, science, social and political reform, art, morals, religion. So they provided philosophical statements of the nature of society, and in Mead's case the universe (as known by humans) itself. Chicago interactionists are still treading, in sociological ways, some of the same paths but with little or no awareness of their Pragmatist assumptions, nor particularly of the distinctive Pragmatist theory of action.

CHICAGO SOCIOLOGY AND ACTION/INTERACTION

Early Chicago sociologists like W. I. Thomas and Robert Park, and even a later generation including Everett Hughes, did not call themselves interactionists, but from our contemporary vantage point of course they were. (Herbert Blumer coined the term *symbolic interaction* in a 1937 paper titled "Social Psychology," but not all sociologists working in this tradition accept that term for themselves.) Thomas and Park came by their sociological interactionism largely through contact with the Pragmatists: Thomas with Dewey, who was his colleague at the University of Chicago; Park by way of undergraduate classwork with Dewey at the University of Michigan, and later work with William James at Harvard University. Neither sociologist seems to have been particularly influenced by their colleague Mead, who not only taught in a neighboring department but was also teaching social psychology to some of their students, especially to Park's in the 1920s.

In general, these two men and their students developed concepts and styles of research that were consonant with Pragmatist perspectives and assumptions about action/interaction. Some of Park's central topics even derived from or overlapped with Dewey's: community and public opinion, for instance. I do not mean to imply that their sociology was entirely consistent with or used all of the elements of Pragmatism, but most of it certainly was consistent with that philosophic tradition. They had, of course, their own ways of putting Pragmatism to use; they were not philosophers but sociologists who had their own work to do. In hindsight, some of this work, I believe, consisted in taking the basic Deweyan action scheme and filling in what the philosopher had left implicit. (By implicit, I am not suggesting either that Dewey deliberately left things implicit, or that he recognized the need to fill in his conceptualization to make it additionally useful or useful for purposes different than his own.) As a philosopher he had no need to sociologically elaborate this scheme; rather he used it in the service of philosophy [especially in developing a logic (1938a) and in his reform interests (especially education (1916, 1938b) and public affairs (1927, 1935)]. Dewey was not centrally concerned with the same substantive issues as the sociologists; hence he did not attack certain sociological problems that would have added relevant sociological detail to the original scheme. Such additional conceptualization by sociologists has come about because the world we have lived through since the 1920s is so changed—new events and phenomena have precipitated new kinds and areas of sociological research that have added to the Dewey-Mead versions of the Pragmatist theory of action.

NARRATIVE: AUTOBIOGRAPHICAL DETAIL
AND COLLECTIVE BIOGRAPHY

My intellectual autobiography can be interpreted as that of someone who has devoted himself to further working out the sociological implications of the Pragmatist/interactionist action scheme. Of course it is much more than that, but certainly this is a major ingredient in my work. The developmental story of this ingredient is worthwhile for the light it may shed on the nature and evolution of this action scheme. It should be evident from the foregoing pages that my relationship to this tradition is not unique, but discussing it can serve as a springboard to the next chapters.

As an undergraduate at the University of Virginia, I studied and talked about sociology with Floyd House, who in his graduate years had studied principally with Park. House assigned a textbook written by Dawson and Gettys (1929), two other students of Park, patterned after Park and Burgess's famous *Introduction to the Science of Sociology* (1921), which probably had been read by every graduate student in the Chicago department during the 1920–1940 period. House's reading assignments also included a book about immigrant experiences, *Old World Traits Transplanted* [the authors listed were Park and Miller (1921), though the book was actually written by W. I. Thomas] and various articles by Park, mainly on race relations. Also assigned were sections of Thomas and Znaniecki's *The Polish Peasant in Europe and America* (1918–1920) and Dewey's *Human Nature and Conduct* (1922). (I bought copies of them and read avidly, especially Dewey's book.) Since House himself was reading Dewey's most recent book, *Logic: the Theory of Inquiry* (1938a), I absorbed much of that too, or at least as much as I seemed to understand; that is, the nontechnical but important theoretical sections.

As a graduate student at the University of Chicago, I was quickly introduced by Blumer to Mead's *Mind, Self and Society* (1934). As a consequence I fell under the charismatic spell of both men but more directly of Blumer, for he had built also upon the Park-Thomas-Dewey thinking in which I had already been steeped. Meanwhile, I had swallowed an idealized ideological version of science—I was to be a *scientist*, sociological variety! My generation had grown up with a roseate picture of the scientific creator, exemplified by Paul de Kruif's *Microbe Hunters* (1926), books about famous scientists like Eve Curie, and fictionalized in Sinclair Lewis's bestseller, *Arrowsmith*.

So picture to yourself a graduate student, terribly naive about most of the world and its happenings, but resonating to the combined harmonies of Pragmatism and interactionism, eager to become a research scientist by using their tools, fully confident that these would work easily and effectively. In this I was fortified by doing a master's thesis under Blumer, which was a critique of the amorphous, confused, and confusing theoretical literature on "attitudes" and of the very narrow view of attitudes that undergirded their "measurement." Note that I was already embarked on a close look at action per se, for attitudes could only make sense as preparatory to action.

Once out of graduate school and teaching, I began a study of daydreaming. It did not turn out well because nothing in my training had prepared me for successfully analyzing the daydreams that my students reported to me. Yet the important point was that, without thinking about the relationship of this phenomenon to any theory of action, I put whatever interpretations I made into an action framework, analyzing daydreams in terms of such categories as "anticipatory daydreaming" (in which actors worked out in advance through scenarios how they might act in given situations) and "retrospective daydreams" (in which actors replayed performances that displeased or dismayed them, trying to work out how these could have turned out better). It was not that I denied daydreams could be idle, playful, or merely expressive, but I was focusing on their relation to action.

So this young sociologist began with the Pragmatist/interactionist tradition, but like anyone with similar training who has intellectual ambitions, then had to make it his own; had to use it on his own materials; use it in a personal way; apply it to new substantive areas; update its ideas; and add to the common ideational tradition—all without suffering undue constraint through too strict adherence to the masters' teachings. Moreover, since Pragmatism represented a radical critique of other philosophical positions, including prominent ones of the day, it should come as no surprise that later Chicago interactionism would produce people who were be highly critical, although appreciative of some elements, with respect to alternative traditions like structural-functionalism, "dogmatic" Marxism, "positivistic" and process-poor survey research, and also of culture and personality anthropology, ethnomethodology, sociobiology, and some forms of psychoanalysis but especially the biologically rooted ones. (Today Chicago-derived interactionists resist postmodernism, at least in its more extreme versions, seeing these as unreasonable, misleading, or destructive to creative thought.) In short, a Chicagoan could become eclectic, but many did not.

Reading the autobiographical account thus far, you might get the impression that this novice sociologist had a firm grasp of the Pragmatist action scheme and was explicitly following through on its logic. Nothing of the sort! Like other Chicagoans, I was focused on doing research on particular phenomena, using a general framework inherited from intellectual forefathers.

As noted by commentators on the Chicago sociology tradition, its practitioners were empirically oriented, although generally the faculty and students were also interested in making theoretical interpretations of their data. Park and Everett Hughes ([1962] 1971), his student, were especially gifted at theorizing: although doing little firsthand research, they directed students' theses and fashioned brilliant theoretical interpretations of the resulting cumulative data. However, they had no interest in exploring or extending their own *philosophical* underpinnings; consequently neither did their students, who were receiving straightforward messages about the necessity for doing "good" empirical research before effective social reforms could be mounted. The many theses, papers, and monographs published from 1920 (and even before) through the 1940s reflect this belief and commitment. From the perspective of other sociological traditions, the Chicagoans might have looked as alike as the proverbial peas in a pod; nevertheless, considerable individual differences existed among them regarding their research interests and areas of specialization, even differences in their research styles and differential reliance on one or another set of research procedures. Yet they all recognized that they shared a certain perspective, summarized in standard phrases like how important when collecting data it was to get (also, but not necessarily exclusively) "the subject's point of view" (through interviews, life histories, and field observations).

Their commonality was also reflected in a general suspicion of speculative or highly abstract theory. Ironically, it was a now little remembered Chicagoan (E. B. Reuter), editor of an important series of sociological volumes during the 1930s, who recommended publishing a manuscript submitted by Parsons, titled *The Structure of Social Action* (1937)—a book little appreciated or cited by Chicagoans. Ironically also, this book was used by graduate students of my generation as a source of information when studying for qualifying examinations, which were likely to include questions about Durkheim and Pareto. We had little patience for Parsonsian "grand theory," nor have Chicagoans since. Some students recognized (although the recognition didn't much matter to us) that Parsons's premises—wrong ones of course—were different, such as the need to explain social change rather than assume its occurrence and so the need to track and explain its specific directions. The Parsonsian theory of action was spelled out in this book, but I do not recollect any of us paying particular attention to this.

In short, the Chicago faculty, students, and graduates mainly confined themselves to developing substantive theory, and only occasionally attempted, like Blumer (1937, 1969), to extend the abstractions of a Dewey or a Mead. However, Park, Hughes, and Blumer also wrote higher-order theory of more generality, but always grounded in substantive materials. Yet interest in general theory among the Chicagoans was a rarity, and stylistically perhaps best exemplified by Hughes, whose style of presenting it was so indirect that his brilliance was seen by most students and contemporaries as merely a production of penetrating insights and very useful concepts. This misreading and underestimating of his intent and accomplishment is reflected in the lack of general theory written by his students, including those who contributed to the Hughes festschrift (Becker, Geer, Riesman, and Weiss 1968). In the Hughes-Park line of descent, Howard Becker perhaps is the follower most concerned with developing and applying general theory.

In my first writing and research, I followed a restricted range of theoretical implications resident in Mead's writings. My first book, *Social Psychology* (1949), written with Alfred Lindesmith, also a Chicagoan, was not concerned with action/interaction as such—it assumed it—but spelled out the implications of language for perception, memory, socialization, self conceptions, interaction itself, and a number of other phenomena—all of this in explicit opposition to behavioristic explanations or eclectic mixtures of psychology and sociology that predominated in social psychology during that era.

Shortly after returning to teach at Chicago in 1952, there was a crystallization in my sociological life. I will outline what happened in greater detail there, since my intellectual development then began to depart from the usual Chicago pattern—at least as I came to see it later. Two or three years before leaving Indiana University for Chicago, I had begun to define the social psychological components of Chicago sociology as being insufficiently "social organizational," and to feel my way back to its more structural side as well as to the structural side of social anthropology. In conversation around this time with a functionalist sociologist, I criticized his work and others like him for using a commonsensical and oversimplified social psychology, arguing that a combination of sophisticated social psychology and social organizational theory was needed.

When I arrived back at Chicago, I found that Hughes and his current and recent students were carrying out fascinating research on occupations, professions, and work, and I soon began a trial study in this mode. Then, when beginning to write *Mirrors and Masks* ([1959] 1969), I began with a version of Pragmatist-derived social psychology but increasingly and deliberately fused it throughout the book with a social organizational (structural) approach. In that book I emphasized the fluidity and complexity of interwoven individual and collective identity, the significance of contingencies and of potentially blurred organizational boundaries, the range in scope of organizational and interactional forms, and the need to bring personal and collective histories into sociological explanations. Structured process and the wedding of macro and micro (in today's terminology) levels of analysis run all through *Mirrors and Masks*. Underlying every page of the book is Chicago's action scheme (as later interpreted here), although I was completely unaware of this at the time. I only sensed that what I was writing was in touch with "reality out there." Like Blumer throughout his life (cf. 1969) I supposed then that Pragmatism/ interactionist assumptions represented reality itself, rather than useful assumptions about the world of individual and collective action. Chicago ways of expressing this were to write about "behavior" and "interaction": I was typical in expressing this propensity.

Perhaps it may convey the same meaning to admit that I have never had a program of long-term research, and certainly then had no vision of extending or deepening the Dewey-Mead action scheme as such. That would have seemed, if I would have thought of it, as a philosopher's job, not a sociologist's. Any programmatic evolution along this line was completely unintended and until rather recently quite unrecognized. The pattern of my development was to move from one research project to the next. Increasingly this was done in a cumulative manner, guided both by emerging questions and concepts that had precipitated out of my previous studies.

If I had a program then, it was only to follow Blumer's urgent advice that sociologists needed to close the yawning gap between an abundance of empirical data (mostly descriptive or at a low level of abstraction) and speculative theory (distant from data). His view made sense to me. It appealed to me as a "scientist"—science meant theories, not just data collection and scanty interpretation of them; science also meant theories that were developed by creative investigators through interaction with data—not by "armchair theorists." Besides, we sociologists had no extensive body of grounded theory from which theorists could deduce propositions that could be tested, as in physics, by a host of experimentalists. Each of us had to be both data collector and theorist, and the connection between data and theory should be firm and explicit.

The main aim of this interweaving of personal and institutional intellectual biography has been to underscore the implicit acceptance by Chicago interactionists of the Pragmatist theory of action. This is true whether they have been students at Chicago, or students of their students. As argued in more detail elsewhere (Strauss 1991), if one looks closely at Chicagoans' publications in terms of their assumptions about interaction, there seems little doubt of the continuing Pragmatist influence. Yet nowadays they are not necessarily familiar with Dewey's writings, and although probably most have read *Mind, Self and Society* during graduate years they do not, I suspect, necessarily recognize in Mead a *systematic* theory of action. Yet the Dewey-Mead theory translates silently into their sociology. Often they make explicit use of Pragmatist terminology like *process,* and assertions about the inseparability of individual and society. It is only that they do not note the action scheme underlying these items. For instance, here is David Maines acknowledging an intellectual indebtedness to his graduate mentor, Robert Habenstein, who in turn was a student of Hughes and Blumer in the late 1940s. (Habenstein has only recently retired from thirty years of teaching at the University of Missouri.)

> [A]mong the many lessons I learned from [him] were that persons and groups are never completely separable, that social life is best seen as a process, and that genuine knowledge is obtainable but only after a hard fight with obdurate realities. 1991, p. 7)

So, in sequential order: from Thomas and Park through Hughes to Habenstein to Maines, and presumably to the students of Maines—substantially the same sociological stances and terminology.

I do not say this is the only valuable sociological stance and terminology: I say it has been typical for over seventy years. This has been my own stance too. Since it is a familiar one, it is easily recognizable in source and style. Here, for instance is a bit of Maines's characterization of my writing: "two outstanding features of Strauss's work are its conceptual coherence which has centered on the interplay of structure and process and its application to a wide array of substantive and theoretical areas"

(191, p. 6). (Maines's characterization did overlook the "identity" theme.) Nobody that I am aware of, except the three friends mentioned earlier (two are German, the third is an ex-student) has written about action—or rather a theory of action—as central to my writing. [However, Elihu Gerson clearly recognized its Pragmatist sources and at least fifteen years ago urged me to write another book like *Mirrors and Masks*. So in a sense did Leonard Schatzman, who urged writing more general theory rather than yet another substantive one. Isabelle Baszanger (1992) in her introduction to a French translation of my writings recently has highlighted the centrality of action in them.]

A SLOW RECOGNITION

Next I will describe briefly my slow recognition of the significance of the Pragmatist-derived action scheme that is deep in my thinking. Why this slow dawning if I knew the Pragmatists' views so well? My reasoning about this question doubles back to the previous discussion of the data-theory dialogue in research. Keep in mind the particular significance of this dialogue for me. (Here, the European readers of this book will probably say, "How very American!") But also imagine this researcher-theorist looking at a variety of substantive areas and theoretical issues: identity, urban symbolization, the symbolization of mobility, psychiatric ideologies and the organization of psychological care, work organization in hospitals for care of the dying and also for pain management, the complexities of types of medical work in high-technology hospitals, the management of chronic illness in a variety of settings, status passages, negotiation, the division of labor, social worlds, and policy arenas. Aside from the specific "findings" of these studies, their products included an array of concepts such as negotiated order, trajectory, awareness context, sentimental order, articulation, and those associated with social world processes, arena processes, and work processes. In all of this, I was well aware of the Pragmatist heritage, but phrased it much as in Maines's characterization of me—and to state the point only once more, not at all in terms of action theory but of either substantive or formal theory.

A decade ago there came a time of increased self-reflexivity, after a deliberate review (with Berenice Fisher, 1978, 1979) made of writings by Mead, Thomas, and Park, followed by my close look at their followers Hughes and Blumer, and prominent contemporary interactionists like Becker (1970), Freidson (1976b), Goffman (1963), and Janowitz (Burke 1991). (Leave aside whether the latter two were "true" interactionists.) What we were aiming at in these reviews was to discover the main "deep" intellectual problems that appear over and over again in each man's publications, how these problems were answered, and the contradictions—and tensions they led to—in their answers. Another aspect of our study was attempting to understand elements of intellectual biography that might lie "behind or below" the sociological problems that persistently concerned these scholars. For instance, a major theme in Janowitz's writing is the instability or fragility of the social order. [See the selection of his writings, by Suttles and Zald (1985).] So how can order be maintained in the face of this potential threat? The latter sentence would seem to be the core of his personal biography rather than purely sociological concern.

However, I have no intention here of telling deep biographical tales about myself. My intent rather is only to indicate an increasing reflexivity about the consistency of stance and problem in my publications. The consistency it seemed to me derived from a wholehearted acceptance of basic Pragmatist premises (at least what seemed basic), and being convinced of their immeasurable value as guides in a variety of researches—though note that I say guides, *not* answers.

Also, at my intellectual core perhaps is the sense that—however naive you may think this—the world of social phenomena is bafflingly complex. Complexity has fascinated and puzzled me much of my life. How to unravel some of that complexity, to order it, not to be dismayed or defeated by it? How not to avoid the complexity nor distort interpretations of it by oversimplifying it out of existence?[1] This is, of course, an old problem: Abstraction (theory) inevitably simplifies, yet to comprehend deeply, to order, some degree of abstraction is necessary. How to keep a balance between distortion and conceptualization?

But what relevance has this last page or so of apparent digression to my growing appreciation of the significance of the Pragmatist/interactionist theory of action? My answer is that grounded theory methodology, as developed in close and equal collaboration by Barney Glaser and me (1967), evolved out of this sense of complexity that we shared; in this instance, the complexity of interaction and interactional forms that we were studying as played out in the care of dying patients. [The immediately preceding study of psychiatric ideologies (Strauss et al. 1964) was virtually a grounded theory study, but only implicitly so.] After having reviewed the premises and problems of Mead and the Chicago interactionists, and gazed thoughtfully for some time at my cognitive navel, I began to comprehend the links among complexity, action/interaction, and the research methodology that we had fathered. It did not take very much, thereafter, for Fritz Schuetze and Hans-Georg Soeffner, and later Juliet Corbin, to convince me that a theory of action might lie at the heart of my sociology.

So we have come full circle to the first sentence of this introduction, and can no longer delay looking at action itself. Yet, before turning to this, there is one last point to be mentioned. Just as the Pragmatist philosophers were determinedly antidualist, so also have Chicago interactionists been steadfastly opposed to certain dualisms expressed in other sociological positions. From the beginning, the interactionists talked of the unbreakable linkage between society and the individual, and this meant they did not give primacy either to macro- or microlevels in analysis and explanation. Both were necessary. As in Robert Park's conceptualization of collective behavior and social movements (see Hughes 1951, 1952a, 1955), they did not, except analytically, separate social stability and social change; nor, as in the terminology of Thomas and Znaniecki (1918–1920), separate except analytically social organization and social disorganization or attitude and value. Perhaps this is why Hans-Georg Soeffner could say to me that on a number of important current issues, or dimensions, my position was neither "this nor that" but in some sense both—neither all process nor all structure, but both; neither all rules nor no rules, but both; and neither all macro nor all micro, but both; and so on. An elaborated theory of act*ing*, descending in the line of heritage from Dewey and Mead, needs both to preserve its antidualism and sociologically to make the most of this stance—and *explicitly*.

Please note that, in this book, though I will usually refer to a theory of action, you should regard action and acting as synonymous: So this particular interactionist theory of action should automatically be translated by you as a theory of *acting*.

ASSUMPTIONS, AND THEORIES OF ACTION

If a theory of action is not actually a theory in the usual scientific sense of the term, why exert the energy to develop one? Of what use is it, either for research or for "real" theorizing? In large part, this entire book is meant as an answer to those questions. For impatient readers, however, a brief preliminary answer is that any action theory consists of a set of assumptions and related conceptualization. Both pertain not only to (1) action and interaction but to (2) action and interaction in relation to a host of phenomena, and to (3) phenomena found at any level of organization, from the most macroscopic to the most microscopic. In Chapter 1, "An Interactionist Theory of Action," I will assert that such a theory is capable of thoroughly informing sociological perspectives so that one "automatically thinks interactionally, temporally, processually, and structurally, as well as in the relatively complex ways ensured by the sociological assumptions built into this theory of action." Explicitness of assumptions and a systematic formulation, elaboration, and presentation of them is my principal goal in this volume.

This is *an* interactionist theory of action. It stands in contrast to many other explicit or implicit action theories. All researchers and social theorists necessarily make assumptions about action and interaction, whether or not they are aware of this, and their assumptions and the related conceptualization greatly affect their conclusions, interpretations, modes of explanation, procedures, and sometimes surely their choice of what phenomena to study. There should be no debate that any set of assumptions and concepts about action and interaction is more "truthful" than any other—that is not the issue. Like any other set, some are more useful for some—and probably for many more—purposes than are others.

Reading this book, not a few readers will disagree either about the kind of social universe I envision that ought to be studied and explained, or the assumptions (in part or perhaps in large part) that might be made to usefully study that universe. I have no quarrel with that reading of this book. At the very least, however, I would hope such rejections would make readers more aware of and explicit about their own theory of action, and its strengths and weaknesses for the work that it supports.

As a brief but telling example, consider the position of perhaps the most celebrated founder of survey research, Paul Lazarsfeld, in a paper written in 1958 (though not published until 1972), "Historical Notes on the Empirical Study of Action: An Intellectual Odyssey." In this semiautobiographical sketch he drew conclusions about action and interaction that are very different than those I advocate, and that are still assumed—perhaps mostly implicitly—in "mainline" survey-derived research today. A theory of action, he argued, requires both action and "mutual modification": "A kind of conceptualization is needed that looks at the human being as a goal pursuing entity whose activities are modified by his socii" (1972, p. 101). Happily he joins this need for conceptualization with the need for empirical research that "will flow into the theory of action *which so far is still unfinished business*" (p. 101, italics in original). However, because Lazarsfeld was reacting against the German intellectual tradition of *handlung* [my dictionary—*The Random House Dictionary of the English Language* (Stein and Urdang 1991)—translates this as "act(ion), deed"], exemplified for him by Max Weber, he dismissed or at least missed the historical, symbolical, and macrosocietal thrust of that Weberian tradition and of course that of the Pragmatists and interactionists.

Contemporary mainline sociology in America and elsewhere, derived in large part from survey and functionalist traditions, simplifies complexities of social phenomena drastically, and mostly leaves implicit the underlying action assumptions of its research and theorizing. In the post–

World War II period, Lazarsfeld's research methods profoundly influenced sociologists everywhere—only yesterday a young Japanese (not an interactionist) complained in correspondence to me about the continuing influence in Japan of Lazarsfeld-style survey methods. This Lazarsfeldian history adumbrates a central theme of this book, that an interactionist theory of action should support—undergird—the kind of sociological research and theory that can capture intricate aspects of human existence, ones that survey and/or functionalist approaches slight or even quite leave out of consideration.

To continue now with my interrupted argument: What I most hope for from this book is that those who are closer to me in general perspective will be prompted by reading it to become more perceptive about their own set of assumptions and related concepts. They certainly need not accept or utilize all of mine, as long as they are clear and explicit about what they choose and reject from the (systematic) smorgasbord I put before them. Generally speaking, neither critics nor partial appreciators of Pragmatism and interactionism have adequately grasped some basic assumptions of those that contravene their own. [See the special issue, edited by Shalin, of *Symbolic Interaction* (1992b), containing discussions of Habermas's work; and also Shalin (1992a). See also the excellent "Why Pragmatism Now?" by Rochberg-Halton (1987).]

To turn now to the book itself: It can be read as if written on several levels. It can be read literally as a presentation of a type of theory of action, or as my interpretation of what is useful in the Pragmatist tradition, some—but only some—of which got incorporated into the Chicago interactionist tradition. The substantive chapters (3 through 11) can be read as representing implications of my theory of action that I believe have not yet been sufficiently developed within any interactionist tradition. In a way, then, those same chapters can be thought of as variations on the main theme of the theory itself. Or of course they might be only read for content, if their topics are of interest but others skipped. To add one more possibility: You might suspect that in writing those substantive chapters I also had at least slightly hidden purposes, one of which is an implicit critique of certain alternative theoretical approaches to the same topics. If so, you would be correct. I have kept the critiques mostly implicit, reasoning that explicit criticism was not the purpose of this book. Perhaps a more accurate characterization is that the book offers a consistent although not directly confrontational argument against alternative perspectives on the same issues, some of them of recent vintage and others either more traditional or updated versions of traditional perspectives.

In Chapter 1, which follows, I present the assumptions in this particular version of interactionist theory of action (acting).

NOTES

1.   While editing the manuscript for this book, I was reading Thomas Alexander's enlightening and carefully researched *John Dewey's Theory of Art, Experience, and Nature* (1987). After only six pages, these lines jumped out at me: "From the start, Dewey was intensely concerned to develop a philosophy which would treat experience in all its richness, complexity and ambiguity without forcing it into some sort of reductionist scheme." I certainly do not claim to be the scholarly equal of Dewey, but in light of my deep indebtedness to his thought it is not surprising to find this resonating similarity.

PART I

Chapter 1

Assumptions of a Theory of Action

[W]e are confronting a universe marked by tremendous fluidity; it won't and can't stand still. It is a universe where fragmentation, splintering, and disappearance are the mirror images of appearance, emergence, and coalescence. This is a universe where nothing is strictly determined. Its phenomena should be partly determinable via naturalistic analysis, including the phenomenon of men [and women] participating in the construction of the structures which shape their lives.

—A. Strauss, "A Social World Perspective"

CONTRASTS

What kind of a theory of action might fit the nature of the universe assumed in the quotation above: a world that is complex, often ambiguous, evincing constant change as well as periods of permanence; where action itself although routine today may be problematic tomorrow; where answers become questionable and questions produce ultimately questioned answers?

First of all, such a theory of action calls for specificity about the dimensions of action that need to be included in the total gestalt of the conception of "action." If we were psychologists or psychiatrists, our dimensions of action might be different. If we were a different kind of sociologist, making other kinds of assumptions, the chosen dimensions might be different also. Understand that whichever ones are chosen will have crucial implications for your sociology and mine.

As a striking illustration, consider the differences between how two influential thinkers, Talcott Parsons and George H. Mead, conceived of acts and action. For Talcott Parsons's views I will quote the summary statement by Alfred Schuetz (1932; see Grathoff 1978, p. 12) in a paper titled "Parsons' Theory of Social Action: A Critical Review." I will follow each summary point with my own commentary. It is not necessary to assume that Schuetz has correctly interpreted Parsons, though I think he has; the point is rather to see the kinds of elements or dimensions that might go into thinking about a sociological scheme about action.

"(a) The act implies an Agent, an 'actor.'"

"The": one; single. "Act," not action; connotation perhaps of brief duration, brief action. "An agent": one person, or collectivity—group, organization?—who engages in the act. "An" actor: one; single. In sum: one bit of action, carried out by one individual or a collectivity.

"(b) The act must have an 'end,' a future state of affairs to which the process of action is oriented."

"[M]ust have an end": teleological. Also, "an" or one. Also, perhaps specific? But also, act as means: thus, a means-end scheme.

"[A] future state of affairs": Act has temporal aspect. Faces forward over some unspecified stretch of time.

"[T]he process of action": Act is a process. Does this mean stages, steps, changing over time, or just unfolding?

"[F]uture state of affairs to which . . . is oriented": image or projection of the way things will be. Probably also means will be as a consequence of the act? Anyhow, an image/projection of future state and an act to reach it, or else cannot reach it. Act, as noted above then: a means to that future end.

"(c) The act must be initiated in a 'situation' which in turn is 'analyzable' into two elements: 'conditions' of action over which the actor has no control, and 'means' over which he has control."

"[I]nitiated in a 'situation' which . . . is analyzable into two elements." His definition of the situation seems limited to only one dimension: control or no control. Why does he so limit this?

"(d) The act involves a certain mode of relationships between these elements, a 'normative' orientation of action."

I am uncertain exactly what is meant, except it seems clear that again he has restricted his definition of the act to "a certain mode of relationships between these elements." It is important, then, to note this specificity and this restriction.

Contrast this Parsonsian view of action with that of G. H. Mead. We are in a different world entirely, breathing a different sociological atmosphere. Here is Mead at the very beginning of his lectures in *Mind, Self and Society* talking about action:

"Social psychology studies the activity or behavior of the individual as it lies within the social process: the behavior of an individual can be understood only in terms of the behavior of the whole social group of which he is a member, since his individual acts are involved in larger, social acts, which go beyond himself and which implicate the other members of the group." (1934, pp. 6–7)

Even when studying individuals [Mead was talking about social psychology rather than society (sociology) in this part of his lectures], Mead does not talk of isolated, individual actions. An individual's actions are, in Mead's frequent terminology, thoroughly "social." After birth, the infant begins to become socialized, its acts are a part of the flow of "group" activity. The latter precede the individual's actions and will continue afterward. So both individual and collective activity have historical dimensions as well as future ones. Moreover, from his discussion we can also see that, along with its temporal features, this activity embodies moral, biographical, symbolic, and even perhaps aesthetic properties.

Actions are in effect *interactions* between and among group members, *not* simply an individual's actions or acts. Mead uses the word *conduct*, implying meaning—given to it by everyone involved. Elsewhere, as we know, Mead emphasizes multiple meanings for the same actions that derive from the multiple perspectives of the interactants. (These include, along with the temporal, the moral, biographical, and aesthetic.) We also know that he elsewhere emphasizes how individuals engage in self-reflection (thinking) before, during, and after their overt action.

BASIC ASSUMPTIONS OF A THEORY OF ACTION

What *would* be the basic assumptions of a sociological theory of action? The Pragmatist philosophers, including Florian Znaniecki in his early philosophic treatise, *Cultural Reality* ([1919] 1983), certainly did not develop their common theory of action as a service to sociology. Rather, it was designed to combat competing philosophic positions like idealism, realism, and materialism; to attack dualisms, including a separation of mind and body, and of individual and society; to address the nature of reality and human relationships to it; to elucidate the characteristics and functions of reflective thought; and to better understand the creative processes happily granted to humans as a favored species. These are specifically philosophical issues, not immediately sociological ones, albeit the stands taken on them most assuredly affect the kinds of sociologists that we become.[1] Philosophic tasks, however, are not identical with sociological ones.

In the next pages, a number of assumptions on which an effective sociological action theory will rest are suggested and discussed. This list of assumptions is based both on my interpretation of the Dewey-Mead perspectives, and development of this interpretation through a series of research projects. As mentioned earlier, my research projects were not guided by any explicitly formulated theory of action. However, now it is clear that a list of assumptions about action and interaction obviously derived from Pragmatism have run like a red thread through my research. In different studies, particular assumptions are more leaned upon than others, but the total list seems to be what I have assumed generally.

Few of them will appear strange or novel to interactionists, and some are so much part of sociological tradition that the commentary on specific ones can be scanned with no loss of understanding of the overall presentation. Interactionists operate with many of these assumptions when carrying out research, but have not necessarily adopted all. The list is offered not as dogma but as a set of suggestions designed to enhance sensitivity toward sociological phenomena and to increase the sociological awareness that I myself treasure. Of course, all of the assumptions are not necessary for carrying out particular research studies, but the entire list makes for a more powerful theory of action. Although these assumptions are designed to capture the nature and details of the social universe described at the outset of this chapter, you need not be an interactionist to find such a conceptualization of action useful. Usefulness is the operative criterion here, not truth.

DEFINITIONS

Working definitions of action, interaction, and an act are needed first.

Action: though expressed in the English language as a noun, is actually a verb—"to act." It has two dimensions. *Acting overtly* is the dimension most frequently taken as synonymous with action. Overt action can be observed by other people. However, *acting covertly*, or reflectively, is also an aspect of action. It cannot be observed by others (although body cues may suggest it), but of course it can be reported by the actor.

Interaction: is acting, by an individual or collectivity, toward others who are not necessarily aware of this action. The others may not be present, may be dead, may be imaginary, or in some way may be cultural others (heroes, celebrities, models for the actor, etc.). If alive, the others may in turn act toward, or respond to, the actions of the first actor. There can be no interaction without persons, groups, or organizations acting; just as there is virtually no acting, at least after very early infancy, where action is divorced from interaction.

Reflexive interaction: is the interplay of an actor (person, group, organization) acting toward some aspect of the actor's self. Mainly, we social scientists conceive of this as internal, and when done by persons as covert action. It can, however, be expressed visibly in actions, say, by hitting one's head angrily when missing an easy tennis shot or preening before a bedroom mirror. Reflexive action by organizations is, of course, observable at least by its own members.

An act and *to act*:   will be used in this book (although only rarely) as the common English equivalent of any of the above—of acting, interacting, or reflexive interacting. Thus, "it was an unjust act" is a judgment made of some interaction, including an act by oneself as in "I (we) acted unjustly."

An actor: will be the agent of an action—a person, a group, an organization, or other social unit.

A LIST OF ASSUMPTIONS

Now for the list of assumptions of this interactionist theory of interaction. Some of them overlap, but for the sake of clarity they will be noted and discussed separately. The well-recognized and accepted ones will receive scant attention; fuller commentary will be reserved for the less obvious.

Assumption 1.   *No action is possible without a body:*   That is, the body is a *necessary condition* for action; but as a concept "body" can be a very rich one, embracing multifaceted actions toward body and bodies as *object* including complex *body processes*. This multifacetedness is only deceptively a matter of individuals with bodies, for collectivity is intrinsic to this individuality. (See Chapter 4.)

Martha Graham, the celebrated dancer and choreographer, when asked in her eighties how she felt about no longer being able to dance, answered that at first it was very difficult and her self-regard suffered, but that now she views her beautiful young dancers as extensions of herself, dancing her dances for her.

The first phrase of this assumption, about body as a condition for action, is so patently banal that social scientists implicitly assume it, but few follow through very far on its implications. Since a number of those implications for interaction will be discussed in Chapter 4, this first assumption will only be touched on here summarily. Keep in mind, however, that it is not the body itself that is central but aspects of the body in their relationships with interaction. Everything about the body, sociologically conceived, turns around those relationships including both the suffering and conversely the joy they may bring.

The body is a condition for means of interaction since none can occur without a body or bodies. With these, actors can perform, present themselves, and their interactions can be judged with respect to performance and appearance, during and after the interactions. These three modes are central to interaction and the body is necessary to them.

Bodies can also be acted toward as objects. However, it is not the body as such that acts toward itself or others' bodies (or a part of itself or the others), but actors with selves and identities who direct actions toward bodies as objects. When actions affect someone's body, change some aspect of it physically (or "mentally"), then this altered body part or system will constitute a new condition affecting further actions.

If the dualism of distinguishing between mind and body is rejected, then one can see that mental activity is also a bodily function, and in addition that every action involves mental/body activity. It is only an artifact that body and mind get separated, whether in common speech or social science discourse. (Dualism is "A system or theory which asserts a radical duality or twofoldness of nature, being or operation." (Funk and Wagnalls 1935).)

Willed, or voluntary, action arises as a possibility because of self-reference. Actors with selves initiate the interaction, at the same time giving commands to the bodies that will be and are agents in the interaction. Even routine interaction represents willed action. Although these may be automatically carried out, done without self-consciousness, they are still self-referential and willed.

A variety of "body processes" serves to enhance, promote, denigrate, destroy, maintain, or alter performances, appearances or presentations. It is through these processes that much of the shaping of selves, identities, biographies, and even changes of body occur. The body processes include protecting the body, abusing the body, training the body, shaping the body, presenting the body, symbolizing the body. This concept of body processes underlines the multifaceted aspects of the otherwise deceptively singular noun *body*, which deceptively masks collectivity even in acts by individuals.

Assumption 2. *Actions are embedded in interactions*—past, present, and imagined future. *Thus, actions also carry meanings and are locatable within systems of meanings. Actions may generate further meanings, both with regard to further actions and the interactions in which they are embedded.*

Mirrors and Masks began with a discussion about the crucial relevance of classifying objects for action: "[T]he direction of activity depends upon the particular way that objects are classified" ([1959] 1969, p. 21). Classifications are components of language, and while individuals can invent classifications, of course they do this through the instrumentality of language itself. (*Classification* really means *to classify*—an act itself.) This theoretical approach to action links action to meaning, but does so in conjunction with the linking of actions to interactions. Acts are not bits of uninhabited activities, even those of a Robinson Crusoe alone on his isolated isle or a hermit in his desert cave. Acts are directed at oneself, persons, organizations, at societal rules and legal regulations, at valued goals, and so on. They can be made in terms of images of past interactions and in a sense made toward those interactions, as well as to imagined future interactions—even those occurring after one's demise. Looked at more analytically, even face-to-face interaction between two actors is unlikely just to involve the two actors but also what they bring into the situation by way of respective interactional histories, imageries, and meanings. "The interactional situation is not an interaction between two persons merely but a series of transactions carried on in thickly peopled and complexly imaged contexts" (p. 56).

There is nothing new in such statements and certainly when social scientists do their research they assume this embeddedness of action in interaction and in systems of meaning. Yet the rare theorists who write about action per se (such as Weber, Schuetz, and Parsons) tend to begin with *the* act, with a separate island of action; not with the assumption that interaction is the prior, central concept, nor with the assumption that to separate action from interaction is an analytic artifact. Of course, a person or an organization does act, and may expect or at least receive counteracts toward this act, but these respective actions are embedded in a network of interactions, including in those that have temporally preceded their acts. This is precisely what Mead was assuming in the passage quoted and commented on early in this chapter: "his individual acts are involved in larger, social acts, which go beyond himself and which implicate the other members of the group" (1934, p. 7). After the acts are carried out, further interaction is stimulated, which in turn generates further meanings for past acts. All of this has been said clearly by the Pragmatists, and most sociologists assume this in their research, sometimes explicitly saying so.

Assumption 3. *During early childhood and continuing all through life, humans develop selves that enter into virtually all their actions and in a variety of ways.*

Paradoxically, Japanese beliefs helped the Nisei assimilate . . . the willingness to endure . . . an acting out of a Japanese proverb . . . : The nail that sticks up gets hammered down. . . . [A]ny wonder that the next generation would inherit, instead of Japaneseness, a sense of shame? (Mura 1991, p. 218)

This assumption is necessary for all the remaining assumptions although most obviously for those such as pertain to self-evaluation, meaning/symbol, and perspective. Most social scientists, quite like laypersons, assume that humans have selves. A vast technical and multidisciplinary and frequently dissonant literature bears on "the self"—including its nature, sources, structure, functions, developmental course, degree of stability, and changeability, and its relation to personality, identity, culture, and society. For my purposes, I will only use the term *self* in the most general and commonsense way. Mead's ideas (1934) about self as process are usable as a general framework, but of necessity must be concretized and made more complex when used in research enterprises.

Experientially we all recognize a self "in" our actions and those of others: a self that can be made an object (as of scorn or admiration) by oneself or others; a self that can be divided (experiencing tugs in opposing directions); and something that is called a "self-conception" or "self-image"; also we refer to someone as "self-conscious," and to the fact of possession by using linguistic forms like "my" and "mine" and "his" or "hers" or "theirs." Furthermore, it is impossible to imagine human emotions like shame, guilt, anxiety, or joy without self-processes; nor can it be overlooked that people have a general sense of themselves as coloring all of their actions—or "not me, not characteristically me" when startled by an unexpected action of which they are later ashamed.

Consciousness of self within interaction is highly variable, ranging from the most explicit to the barely explicit or hardly noticed. This complexity of actions embodying self is captured nicely by Kurt Riezler's poetic statement: "The Me can mean many things; the Me of yesterday, today, or tomorrow, or the Me of everyday, the Me in the particular action or situation, or the Me in all actions or situations" (1950, p. 80).

In sum, except in our reflex reactions, we have to take our selves and those of others into account, both in everyday action as well as in research when interpreting or analyzing data. Even in some reflex reactions—like those that occur when crossing terrain defined as dangerous—more than a little of the self can be involved.

Assumption 4. *Meanings (symbols) are aspects of interaction, and are related to others within systems of meanings (symbols). Interactions generate new meanings and symbols as well as alter and maintain old ones.*

The . . . front page story about a prostitute raised all the profound public policy questions . . . a working hooker who almost certainly was an AIDS carrier [a huge issue] exemplifying the classical conflict between public health and individual rights. (Shilts 1987, p. 510)

As adumbrated in the foregoing section, meanings are linked in symbolic systems. If I say "home" then connotations immediately embed the respective nouns in sets of meanings: home, house, domesticity, stability, and other meanings suggested by the dictionary itself. Your imagery of home may certainly not be the same as mine, but it will just as certainly be linked with image after image. Because symbolic systems seem to be just that—systems—and because they are so widely shared, and because they are often believed to be true and perhaps often also believed by some people *not* to be true but constraining: because of all of that, symbolic systems are easily and widely reified. Yet all of this symbolizing was created by interaction and just as surely will be re-created over and over again. A theory of action should put symbolizing (a *verb*) into the heart of interaction, as being generated and regenerated during courses of action. The universe is symbolized and resymbolized: again, note the verbs and the implied process. (Symbolizing and symbols are discussed further in Chapter 6.)

Assumption 5. *The external world is a symbolic representation, a "symbolic universe." Both this and the interior worlds are created and re-created through interaction. In effect there is no divide between external and interior world.*

Man lives in a symbolic universe . . . [He does not] confront reality immediately; he cannot see it, as it were, face to face. . . . Instead of dealing with things themselves man is in a sense constantly conversing with himself. (Cassirer 1944, p. 25)

The gist of Cassirer's statement is that humans cannot know reality as such. Mere mortals can only know the world out there in some constructed sense. "Social constructionists" assert, or more accurately assume, that the constructed world is the only world humans can know, and that researchers must discover the constructions of the people they are studying in order to understand the how, why, and wherefore of their interactions. The Pragmatists more specifically asserted that relationships established between actors and objects were constructed through interactions, that is, they were enacted and repeatedly reenacted. This was done not merely through thought processes but through repeated overt interaction and discovery of its consequences. The changing conditions bearing on interaction, whether "within the heads" of individuals or between individuals, lead in turn to changing objects, meanings, and social universes.[2]

Also, the Pragmatists asserted the unity of collective and personal/

individual interaction. The implications of this nondualistic position are highlighted by such phenomena as the joint collapse of social orders— like the breakup of command socialism in Eastern Europe—and the variable personal effects that range from a sense of joy, of freedom, to anxious and threatened identities. In recent years, the newspapers reporting on this region of the world almost daily reflect the twin phenomena of personal and collective loss of social universes along with some happier reconstructions of social orders and personal identities. Perhaps I should add that while individuals certainly do invent new meanings, they do so only in connection with extant ones—even if in revolt against them. Most meanings are collective, if only in the sense that those developed by individuals need to be taken up, ratified, and evolved further in communities of action, otherwise they die with the individuals who invented the meanings. The communities may be as small as families of direct descent, but they must be communities.

The Pragmatist and Chicago interactionists had and have a clear stance toward what Alfred Schuetz (1966) called second-order (or the analyst's) interpretation of first-order (or natives') interpretation of reality. This stance is quite different than some versions of postmodernism, which having discovered that scientists—both physical and social—also construct realities, have turned (when sensible) to developing methods for locating the observer's observational position and (when not sensible, in my opinion) to cease reporting on any other world than their own private, if carefully noted, experiences with the people under study. By contrast, George Mead ([1932] 1980a, pp. 161–75; 1982, p. 6) addressed the issue in philosophic terms, in the language of "objective relativism," taking into account the inevitability of multiple perspectives and the necessity through ongoing discourse to choose provisionally among them, or combinations of them, through observation or testing of their consequences. Significantly, his view is echoed in contemporary sociological translation by a young interactionist, a close observer of physical scientists at work, as she attacks a version of postmodernism that denies any kind of objectivity. Joan Fujimura writes:

> [T]wo suggestions for future work in the sociology of science. . . . First, rather than focusing on finding the ultimate form of representation or undermining our representations, we should encourage new voices to speak, to make their own representations, and to address representations made by others. . . . Further, since we do not have one fundamental method to be exalted over all others, I would like to encourage and generate a *profusion* and *diversity* of methods, theories, and "facts." That is, I would like to see *other perspectives, new perspectives* in the sociology of science. We also need to regard "interests" as empowering those voices. I use Dewey's (1920: 194–95) concept of interests here. . . . If truth [as shown; in studies of

science] is negotiated order (temporally and spatially located), we need to understand which perspectives are not included in the final product and how they were eliminated during the processes of negotiation. Making scientific representations and artifacts is a collective process, as our studies have shown. (Fujimura 1991, pp. 22–23)

Later she reaffirms the Pragmatist/Chicago interactionist faith infallible, because provisional, science: "[W]e *can* make decisions about what is a better or worse science and sociology in more *finite* terms. . . . I agree with Dewey (1927) . . . that scientific and political discourse is continuous" (p. 24).

In short, even scientists must negotiate their constructions of reality, must claim no final picture of it, need to discuss and negotiate and debate their provisional constructions—and yet must act on them, being directed in their action by their tentative constructions, and must judge their consequences. Insofar as one accepts something like this Pragmatist/interactionist stance, then social science can proceed in what can be anticipated as increasingly sophisticated ways, as well as with increased self-awareness of this vital interactional process itself.

Assumption 6. *Actions* (overt and covert) *may be preceded, accompanied, and/or succeeded by reflexive interactions. These actions may be one's own or those of other actors. Especially important is that in many actions the future is included in the action* (cf. Mead 1938, pp. 3–25, on "stages in the act").

For commentary on this sixth assumption of a theory of action, I will quote a few passages from *Mirrors and Masks*. Implementation of these points can be found in my own research, as well as in that of many other investigators.

To say that [human beings] use language is to say that they must evaluate the past, the present and the future. Regardless of how any society's vocabulary may cut and order temporal flow, past and future impinge upon and influence action in the present. The human experience of time is one of process: the present is always a "becoming"; it is always coming up, as the future moves toward us, or it is moving away as present action recedes into the past. . . . An action can be evaluated immediately after its performance—so immediately that it feels subjectively as if evaluation and action occurred simultaneously. . . . During a sequence of action I may guide and change my course by making evaluations of immediately past actions. When the sequence, or entire act is finished, I may . . . sum up what transpired and how it turned out.

The evaluation of recent performances is frequently necessitated by the fact that they surprise even the actor. . . .

An act performed is, in a certain sense, never finished, unless it becomes quite forgotten. Most acts, of course, are forgotten, but the very possibility of recollection permits re- evaluation.

The act or person being judged is an "object." Any [person] can be both, simultaneously; having acted, he may make his act an object of scrutiny. He may take as many different stances toward it as his vocabulary permits, just as own act may be his object of scorn, denial, discount, blame, attack, shame, disapproval, a yardstick for further endeavors, a cross to bear, a sign of personal brilliance, or anything else that he has the capacity to view it as. And if he should acquire new terminology through new group participations, he will inevitably reassess certain of his past acts—and himself—in the new terms. . . .

The reappraisal of past acts and the appearance of surprise in present acts gives [humans] indeterminate futures. . . .

All of this is equally true of groups that have histories. The temporal spans of group life mean that the aims and aspirations [and I would now add "visions"] of group endeavor are subject to review and recasting. Likewise past activities come to be viewed in new lights, through reappraisal and selective recollection. . . . History, whether that of a single person or of a group, signifies a "coming back at self" (Mead 1936, p. 69). ([1959] 1969, pp. 31–34)

Assumption 7. *Actions are not necessarily rational: Many are nonrational or, in common parlance, "irrational." Yet rational action can be mistakenly perceived as not so by other actors.*

rational . . . I. a. 1. Possessing the faculty of reasoning. 2. Conformable to reason; judicious. 3. Pertaining to reason; attained by reasoning. (Vizetelly 1935, p. 945)

She was blind with love—acted quite like Madam Bovary. (Anonymous)

Rational action is made possible by self-reflexivity. To those who take purposeful action for granted—and the number of social scientists who do so is legion—it seems otherwise. Yet as the Pragmatists and interactionists generally assumed, a closer look will show that this self-reflexivity is involved. We all understand that not all action or interaction is thoroughly rational, logical, carefully thought out, or clearly conceived. Much is impulsive, spontaneous; also some of it gets out of control, as in mass or individual panic or as may happen to loyal spectators when their team scores a winning touchdown. Actions of whose sources the actor is unaware are likely to be less than completely rational. Yet actions that are carefully reasoned, thought out in advance, may well be assessed by others as nonrational and even as crazily irrational. The observers are likely to attribute motives that the actor if privy to them will reject, unless ultimately persuaded that his or her (or they if a collectivity) self-attributed reasons for acting were not the "real ones." (Motives and motive attributions are discussed in Chapter 6.)

Assumption 8. *Action has emotional aspects: To conceive of emotion as distinguishable from action, as entities accompanying action, is to reify those aspects of action.*

> The men were sluggish in obeying his order, and the lieutenant called for his "tech/sergeants" to supervise the work. When no one responded, he became very angry and screamed, "What's the matter with you tech/sergeants? Don't you know when you're being called?"
> The undertaking came to a standstill. Everyone turned around to see what was happening. Then, to their dismay, he pointed his finger accusingly at T/4 Yamada, who was standing just a few yards away. The sergeant was stunned; he stood mute, staring about helplessly. The others had difficulty controlling themselves, and before long some burst out laughing. It seemed incredible, but the lieutenant was apparently unfamiliar with the various grades of sergeants! . . . The men were utterly disgusted.
> For the rest of that week all NCOs who held the rank of T/5 were addressed in mock respect as "tech/corporal." (Shibutani 1978, p. 119)

There is a tendency both by laypersons and social scientists to distinguish between emotions and action, thus implicitly denying a crucially significant attribute to action. This translation of an adverb (emotional) into a noun (an emotion, or emotions) is easy to understand, for many languages include routine ways of referring to "emotions"—anger, anxiety, joy, and so forth—as if these were entities. This tendency to reify is perhaps furthered by commonplace phrases like "he was in an emotional state" and "he felt an enormous anger rise up in himself." Also, English speech makes remarkably easy the use of the noun *emotion*, when we may not at all intend to reify. Such reification, though, complicates the difficulties of understanding the complexities of interaction. Just as there is no interaction without symbolizing, there is little without "accompanying emotions."

Routine behavior, of course, or actions in which there is minimal self-involvement, carry virtually no emotional freight. Let the routine be brutally interfered with or repeatedly disturbed, and let self-involvement rise above the minimum: Then even an outside observer to the person or collectivity will see the rise in emotional temperature "of" the next actions.

As suggested by the preceding quotation in which an army scene was described, "emotions arise" in relationship to social situations (whether real or imaginary), and cannot be comprehended in their specificity without reference to the symbolizing that is transpiring, and also require self-reflexivity to properly be regarded as characteristically human. Interaction with others (again, real or imaginary) is necessary for (emotional) action. An implication of all of this is that people who have been socialized in different cultural settings may act in seemingly identical ways, but the emotional aspects of their acts may greatly differ. It is therefore no surprise that actors of different social class, ethnicity, nationality, gender, or any other biographically influential social unit should evince differences in their emotionality.

Assumption 9. *Actions are characterized by temporality, for they constitute courses of action of varying duration.* Various actors' interpretations of the temporal aspects of an action may *differ*, according to the actors' respective perspectives; these interpretations may also *change as the action proceeds.*

> *Act* is single, individual, momentary; *action* a complex of *acts*, or a process. . . . (Vizetelly 1935, p. 14)

> I am stuck and time is stuck within me. . . . Now time has no dimension, no extension backward or forward. I arrest the past, and I hold myself stiffly against the future; I want to stop the flow. (Hoffman 1989, p. 11)

One major property of any action is duration. While an action may be brief, more likely it will have some measure of temporal extension. Among the most interesting are those of long duration, including projects, programs, and other long-term sets of acts that add up to the total course of action. Iago would recognize himself in that last sentence, but so would the founding fathers of the United States. In a certain sense, the creating of the American constitution, which took a considerable but not an unduly long time to finish, has still not been completed as a collective action, nor will it be unless abandoned or the nation ceases to exist. For social scientists, the courses of action are among the most important actions because they are the most challenging to study and most consequential for societies, organizations and other collective units, and for their members as well. As will soon be emphasized, these temporal courses are replete with contingencies, changes of projections and plans, even of the original goals. Furthermore, the various actors' interpretations of the temporal aspects of an action may differ, according to the actors' respective perspectives. These interpretations may also change as the action proceeds. Indeed, Mead ([1932] 1980a, esp. pp. 171–72) argued that perspectives necessarily embraced the temporal—or in our terminology, temporality would be written into any interpretation of an action qua object.

Assumption 10. *Courses of interaction are definable into sequences,* sometimes classified into stages or phases. Definitions arise out of identical or shared *perspectives* or must be *negotiated.*

Course: n. *1*. The act of moving onward. . . . *2*. The way passed over, or the direction taken. *3*. A sequence of connected motions, acts, or events. . . . *4*. Line of conduct. (Funk and Wagnalls 1935, p. 276)

Actors often talk about connected events or acts as a "sequence." The idea is that "things follow each other." This connectedness is sometimes referred to in terms of stages or phases. In these commonsense conceptualizations, actions are linked with "forward motion" over time, and causality is sometimes explicitly associated with the later actions owing their existence to preceding ones.

These in vivo conceptualizations yield to researchers important and possibly crucial clues to actors' interactions and worlds. However, if a researcher's classifications of sequence actually match those of the actors, then it is necessary to guard against having gone native, though this may not actually have happened. Also, the social scientist may not find it useful or necessary to classify sequences into phases or stages.

Analytically, also we must be careful to guard against the assumption that because action always moves on it always moves forward. Reversibility is always potential, whether precipitated by contingent events or reviewing/rethinking the interactional course. [On reversibility, see Strauss, Fagerhaugh, Suczek, Wiener (1985) for courses of illness; and Callon (1991) concerning technoeconomic networks.] Again, what is defined as reversibility or re-reversibility, or indeed any sequence, is something that *is* defined. Agreement on such definitions arises either out of the identity or sharedness of perspectives or must be negotiated.

Assumption 11.   *Means-ends analytic schemes are usually not appropriate to understanding action and interaction.* These commonsense and unexamined social science schemes are much too simple for interpreting human conduct.

"No," Yakovlev replied, "Yes and no. There was a clear-cut understanding that what had to be overturned—the authoritarianism, the command-bureaucratic economic system. It was clear that democracy had to be developed, but in what amounts or how? That plan didn't exist. It was clear that we had to return to Lenin's theory that people should rule their affairs. But how could that be done, in what stages? That, of course wasn't there at the beginning. There was one thing, and the most important: that society would have to radically change its nature—what we call 'renewal.' But we had to find the instruments along the way, in the process of transformation: in politics, the economy, culture, the law, *glasnost*, and democracy. And it turns out those instruments are very important—no less important than the overall concept." (Smith 1990, p. 561)

The actions that interest social scientists are not the relatively momentary, infrequent, or inconsequential, such as the swatting of an annoying

fly, or random and relatively aimless movements. The actions that interest us generally are patterned, repetitious, and meaningful to the actors
themselves. "Acts are teleological" is the usual but not at all accurate way
of referring to such actions; that is, actions are directed at goals. As for
courses of action, generally it is believed that these can scarcely be thought
of as courses unless in some sense directed toward goals.

However, the phrase *in some sense* conceals considerable ambiguity.
Many and possibly most goal-directed actions cannot be explained by a
simple means-end scheme, because of the many complexities that attend
them. A theory of action must capture these complexities as well as the
more straightforward course of action.[3]

Those complexities can be quickly conceptualized by considering some
dimensions, first of goals and then of means, that affect the form, direction, attainability, and other characteristics of interactional courses. Goals
may vary along such dimensions as the following:

single	multiple
consensus on	dissensus on
old	new
clearly imaged	unclear
specific	not specific
unchanging	changing

As for the means employed to reach projected goals, their dimensions
may include the following:

clearly perceived	not clear
small number	large number
familiar	unfamiliar
specific	not specific
easily achievable	not easily achievable
cheap	costly
easy to evaluate	difficult to evaluate
consequences known	consequences unknown
consensus on	dissensus on

Translated into sets of conditions for interaction, these dimensions
quickly clarify why some interactional courses are characteristically
highly uncertain and others are rigidly institutionalized or ritualistic. A
Hopi rain dance ritual operates under conditions mainly found on the left
side of the goals-means list. But Yakovlev's description of planning for a
new Soviet Union could not possibly be honestly described otherwise,
given the dimensional conditions (right side of the list) bearing on planning under the uncertainties characterizing that tormented region today.

Aside from ritualistic and unpredictably evolving interactional courses, the list of dimensions gives cues to their other variations. Here are a few of the many possible ones. First of all, many courses have no clear-cut goals. The actors begin without a clear goal or goals, and may not (or cannot) formulate them for some time. Indeed, sometimes they keep their goals purposely very general, even ambiguous, open-ended. This is often done by creative artists and scientists who wish to be surprised by a better end than they might otherwise envision. They wish to seize upon and make something of whatever unpredictable events may occur along the way in order to reach the rather ambiguous general goal of a better artistic (scientific, or perhaps commercial, industrial, or even personal) product than might now be conceived.

Second, even when action is instituted with a specific goal projected, nevertheless over time something happens to this imagined goal. In some way it gets changed or modified. At the least, it gets slightly altered, or is joined by unanticipated secondary goals. At the other extreme, a projected aim can be totally abandoned, perhaps now perceived as not feasible or as totally wrong, misleading, harmful—even redefined as misguided and evil, as when someone has undergone religious conversion. Additional alterations are possible of course; for instance, the dissolving of the original goal into several. Another possibility is that the aim is retained but narrowed in scope.

Furthermore, when the interactional course involves multiple actors, they may sooner or later discover misunderstandings about their respective conceptions of a supposed common set of goals. What to do now? Separate? Negotiate, merging the goals into a compromise conglomerate of aims? The possibilities are varied, depending on conditions that are affecting the course. This last sentence brings us to the next assumption of our theory of action.

However, let us first consider still another difficulty that besets a simple means-end scheme for explaining action. Even when a goal is clear, the effective means to it may not be known, as in creating an industrial product for the market when it is not yet known how to produce the product, let alone do so efficiently and cheaply. Some presumedly effective means will be discarded. Others may have to be discovered or stumbled upon. Moreover, sometimes means lead to a more exciting venture than the original conceived end, becoming perhaps a major end itself. The new end might generate acts that lead to radical new means and considerable alteration of the newly conceived end itself.

There may even be surprises in carrying out strictly prescribed rituals, so that improvised acts may be necessitated; while relatively routine interactional courses, like a normally uneventful drive to work, may tomorrow entail some very inventive measures—so that the driver can reach his or her office at all, let alone on schedule. Nevertheless even immensely large and nonroutine projects, providing they have fairly definite and agreed upon aims—such as placing men on the moon and thereby "beating the Russians"—may attain those aims even when many of the instruments to those ends have still be developed and may be frequently changed over the course of the project.

So our theory of actions must be capacious enough to take into account both the routine interactions and the more problematic or changeable ones. (Routine and problematic interactions will be discussed below and in Chapter 8.) Also, it must take into account types of interaction that ordinarily the various means-ends analytic schemes do not: namely, those associated with "sheer" play, sometimes virtually ungovernable building-up of a case of collective laughter, spontaneous embraces, chatter at a cocktail party, a couple's expressions of shared delight or relief that an expensive dinner was well worth the money, and self-interaction like playful fantasy or drifting off into past memories. In this book, I will not much address these kinds of phenomena, but this particular interactionist theory of action does apply to them. All of these remarks relate directly to discussion of the next assumption.

Assumption 12. *Contingencies are likely to arise during a course of action. These can bring about change in its duration, pace, and even intent, which may alter the structure and process of interaction.* (This is sometimes referred to as "emergence.")

> May the men who are born
> From my time onwards
> Never, never meet
> With a path of love-making
> Such as mine has been!
> (Hitomaro, ca. 700 A.D., in Van Doren 1939, p. 36)

My dictionary defines "contingency" as "a contingent event, a chance, accident, or probability, conditional on something uncertain" (Stein and Urdang 1981, p. 316). This definition is only partly useful for my purposes, since although it suggests range of probability or expectation, it touches neither on source nor degree of significant impact on action.

There are two major classes of contingencies. The most obvious consists of conditions ordinarily considered as "external" to the course of action, such as changes in economic, political, cultural, organizational, physiological (sickness), geological (earthquakes), or climatic (rain) conditions that may directly or indirectly affect aspects of the course. Analytically speaking, these seemingly external conditions can be regarded as part of the action itself, providing that they can be shown to have some influence "on" changing the action. Indeed, if the actors themselves perceive these kinds of conditions as relevant to their actions ("I lost my job because the company laid people off in the recession"), whether or not the perceptions are accurate, then these can certainly affect a course of action.

Such conditions may even be anticipated, and if so then their impact may be reduced by foresight, planning, and other aspects of the actor's action scheme. To the extent that anticipatory images are accurate and that anticipated corrective action is as effective as imagined, then the contingency should not alter the next actions. But for many expected contingencies (an unanticipated recession), there are no surefire procedures to successfully counter such contingencies.

A less obvious source of powerful contingencies is the course of action itself. Its constituent acts have many unanticipated consequences, some of which may be highly consequential for next acts. That is, the consequences become conditions. This simple point seems difficult for some people to grasp, perhaps because they do not understand that a course of action, even a brief one, entails process. Contingencies, both externally and internally derived, relate to the Pragmatist/interactionist nondualistic stance of action being variously routinized or nonroutinized, that is, neither completely undetermined or determined. (For the preceding points see especially Chapter 8; also Star 1983).

Among the processual consequences are those that affect the actors, who after all are implicated in the action itself. At the very least, actors "change their minds," but they also become different persons, their identities having undergone more or less of a sea change during the extended course of action.

Assumption 13. *Interactions may be followed by reviewals of actions, one's own and those of others, as well as projections of future ones. The reviewals and evaluations made along the interactional course may effect a partial or even complete recasting of it.*

We do not necessarily change our minds about past acts, but we may; some acts, deemed important, may be reassessed many times over, as one gets new orientations or new facts. (Strauss [1959] 1969, p. 32)

Recollect that earlier I noted that a generic feature of the human condition is the reviewing and forecasting of actions: one's own and those of others. This accompaniment of overt action is an additional source of contingencies for the recasting of interactional courses. This gyroscopic source for the shaping and reshaping of courses is immensely significant.

Any action, except one that is brief or believed of no importance, is likely to get reviewed and evaluated: whether in part or whole, occasionally or frequently, informally or formally, covertly or overtly. This will lead to judgments about maintaining the course or changing various of its aspects. It is not only the overt action that is being evaluated, but also what Dewey (1934) calls the "experiencing" and "undergoing" that occurs during and following the overt acting. Evaluation and reevaluation is made also about what is known or guessed about others' experiencing and undergoing. So interactants are making judgments of both overt action and interior accompaniments of the action, along the entire course of interaction, as being: successful, unsuccessful; efficient, inefficient; pleasant, unpleasant; harmful, dangerous, beautiful, sinful, etc.. Thereby goals as well as means are open to being altered, action changed in midstream in some regard. This is what gives interactional courses an additional potentially open-ended, flexible character.

Do not assume, however, that such reviewals and reevaluations are necessarily made with full self-awareness, or as a species of rational clearheaded thought. There are other types of thought processes, among them daydreaming. But as daydreaming is a complicated phenomenon, it may take various forms: for example, anticipatory daydreams in which interactions are tried out as if they were possible scenarios; and daydreams that replay past scenes to see what went wrong behaviorally and why, or to check out if in fact one acted well in them. Flashes of association can open up unexpectedly frightening projections that call into question specific means and even the wisdom of pursuing a given goal.

These kinds of inner, subjective processes are integral to interactional courses, and also to much interaction of shorter duration. While sociologists seem to have assumed these subjective processes, they have scarcely noted and rarely studied specifically their implications for interaction. These less tangible processes of "thinking," I am convinced, are necessary to making decisions about future interaction that involves social relationships, since it is difficult to imagine many future actions and "scenes" or scenarios without images, just as in thinking about the past, we often add some species of cognitive imagery to pure recollection of past interactions and scenes. (Thought processes such as daydreaming are discussed in Chapter 5.)

Long after a course of action is physically complete, or is regarded as complete by one or other participant in it, there may be additional reviewals, as well as belated projections of "what if I (we) had. . . ." In this sense, the interactional course may not yet have been totally finished, and indeed may be reopened after additional events. A striking example is Hedrick Smith's characterization of millions of Soviet citizens who, having lived unquestioningly and loyally under Stalin, now confront devastating revelations about the despotism and cruelty of his regime. "'When we argue about Stalin, it's not just about the past, it's about the present.

We have a part of Stalin in all of us. Stalinism is the living past, and the worst poison is here,' he said, pointing at his head" (Smith 1990, p. 131).

Assumption 14. *The embeddedness in interaction of an action implies an intersection of actions. The intersection entails possible, or even probable differences among the perspectives of actors.*

> In a recent paper Star and Griesmer (1989) [have used] an "ecological" approach framed in terms of understanding science as collective action from the viewpoints of all the actors and worlds involved, and thereby avoid the preeminence of any one actor. The ecological approach is based on views which prevailed at the University of Chicago during the first half of the twentieth century and became embedded in the pragmatist perspective in philosophy and the symbolic interactionist school in sociology. It has only recently been used to study science. [It] focuses on the multiple translation efforts through which scientific knowledge is constructed by standing in several positions in order to present multiple perspectives. All actors are simultaneously attempting to interest others in their concerns and objectives. The final (or temporary) outcomes of these efforts are constructed through the processes of negotiation, articulation, translation, triangulation, debating, and sometimes even coercion through "administrative persuasion" by members of different social worlds as actors attempt to install their "definitions of the situation" . . . as the different worlds intersect. (Fujimura 1992, p. 172)

It is impossible to carry out a course of action of much duration or complexity without actors interacting with each other. Actors may be intent on pursuing their own courses of action, or they may be engaging in a shared course of action. Both forms of interacting involve the *intersection* of respective actions.

Intersection carries the likelihood of discrepancy among the perspectives that individual or collective actors bring to the course of the interaction. Moreover, the likelihood that all will continue to share exactly the same perspective during a common course of action is unlikely, especially if the course is of much duration. Besides, even while cooperating in a common interactional course, each will simultaneously be engaged in pursuing other lines of action. Moreover, differences among perspectives lead to differential stances on the various dimensions of goals and means. Consequently, a great deal of communication and a playing out of interactional processes (especially negotiation and persuasion, but also education, manipulation, and possibly coercion) are necessary to maintain a common interactional course.

A central implication for sociological research of the Pragmatists' writings about differential or multiple perspectives of actors is that the stances of "all" the major participants in an interactional course need to be understood, and brought into the analysis. Of course the major participants need first to be discovered; they are not always obvious, even to the others.[4] Even as I am writing those sentences, a striking if somewhat extreme instance of this is occurring: Iraq and over twenty-five countries are poised on the point of war, but meanwhile both overt and covert negotiations are going on to prevent warfare. We can imagine that at least that many countries' diplomats are operating behind the scenes, and from different perspectives, since what is to the interest of the American president is not necessarily seen as such by the heads of government of twenty-five other nations. Probably only historians some years hence, with governmental archives finally available, will be able to piece together the courses of action that prevented or failed to prevent warfare.

So it is important to keep in mind the *paradoxical* nature of cooperative action. For such action to take place—whether it is enormous or tiny in scope, lasting or only relatively temporary in duration, immensely significant or insignificant in its consequences—at least two interactants are necessary. When they are from or represent different social worlds, then inevitably somewhat different perspectives can be enhanced. Yet in this intersecting, the interactants have to work together or there will be no cooperative action. Obviously their differences can pose difficult problems for them. They can also pose methodological and analytic problems for a researcher who wishes to understand the success or failure of their interaction, as well as for a theorist who is attempting to probe the nature of action in general. Intersection I conceive of as primarily a social world process, and a complicated one. (It will be discussed when examining the concept of social worlds, in Chapters 9 and 10.)

Assumption 15. *The several or many participants in an interactional course necessitate what Blumer termed the "alignment" (or "articulation") of their respective actions.*

> [A] joint action cannot be resolved into a common or same type of behavior on the part of the participants. Each . . . necessarily occupies a different position, acts from that position, and engages in a separate and distinctive act. It is the fitting together of those acts ánd not their commonality that constitutes joint action. . . . Their alignment does not occur through sheer mechanical juggling. . . . [T]he participants [must] fit their acts together. (Blumer 1969, p. 70)

Blumer's well-known views of the necessity for alignment of actions suggests another assumption of a useful theory of action. The multitude of sequential actions involved in any interactional course requires a constant aligning (lining up) or articulation of these actions (Strauss 1985, 1988). The necessity for this can be seen, for instance, even during simple projects such as two couples deciding to meet for dinner at a restaurant. What day? What hour? Where? Not there, it's too far or too expensive or too formal, so why not at another place? A complex project like the ascent of Mount Everest by a team involves thousands of acts that need to be articulated in order to carry it off.

What is involved in aligning all these acts? Blumer has supplied an insight about the centrality of alignment to a theory of action. A more developed theory requires a statement and study of the mechanics of articulation. These mechanics include both interactional processes and work processes. While the interactants themselves see certain strategies as necessary to arrive at their goals, from the researcher's perspective these strategies constitute interactional processes. They include negotiation, persuasion, manipulation, teaching, the threat of coercion and perhaps actual coercion (Strauss 1978). Without one or more of these, the sequential acts that constitute any interactional course cannot be articulated. Also involved are several "work," or "action," processes including the making of commitments, the dividing up of work, and the supervising of action (Corbin and Strauss 1988, 1993; Strauss 1988). (These points will be discussed further in Chapter 3.)

Assumption 16. *A major set of conditions for actors' perspectives, and thus their interactions, is their memberships in social worlds and subworlds. In contemporary societies, these memberships are often complex, overlapping, contrasting, conflicting, and not always apparent to other interactants.*

This is a theme about which I have written a fair amount (Strauss [1959] 1969, [1961] 1976, 1982, 1984, [1978] 1990a, [1978] 1990b; Strauss et al. 1985; see also Shibutani 1955), so little will be said concerning it here. The main point is that in contemporary societies the activities and interactions within social worlds and subworlds profoundly shape their members' perspectives. Yet few of us belong to just one or two social worlds; we are likely either in the course of a lifetime or at any one time to belong to several. Participations "within all these social worlds involve various generalized commitments, beyond the more specific and easily discernible commitments, to agencies, institutions, organizations, cliques, and specialties associated with the social world" (Strauss [1959] 1969, pp. 162–63). Multiple memberships in social worlds that variously are discrepant, overlapping, or consonant lead to complexities of perspective that in turn become conditional for commitment and action. These memberships are not always visible to others, either because actors are deliberately concealing them or they are simply not known to others. Yet the memberships may be entering into the interaction, perhaps being only discovered or revealed over a long course of interaction. Interactions within and among organizations are also shaped by the social world (and subworld) commitments of their members: Some organizations are conglomerates of differential social world membership, and few organizations are composed only of persons who act in terms of only a single social world/subworld commitment. (Chapter 7 takes up some of these points in more detail.)

Assumption 17. *Other conditions bearing on interactions can be thought of in terms of a conditional matrix, ranging from broader, more indirect conditions to narrower and more directly impacting ones. The specific relevance of conditions can be analyzed by means of tracking conditional paths.*

A strong stand against dualisms (individual-collective, mind-body) was incorporated into early Chicago interactionism when Pragmatist assumptions were adopted. Another antidualism that interactionists made central to their position was the refusal to separate determinism and antideterminism. The Pragmatists had emphasized that humans were active in shaping their environments, their ways of living, and the evolution of their cultural values—*but* this shaping occurred within the constraints of their extant physical and cultural environments. Consequently, in Chicago-derived interactionist writing to this day, there is no great strain between recognizing constraints on action while also emphasizing that actions cannot possibly be completely determined by economic, cultural, biological, ideological, political, etc., conditions. Interactionists also bring microconditions into their analyses.

What nowadays are termed macro- and microconditions were with clear intent brought into early Chicago sociology. Priority was given to neither set of conditions. Rather the research thrust was to follow their interplay—or at least get both sets into the explanations of phenomena. [Thomas and Znaniecki spell this out in their *Polish Peasant in Poland and America* (1918–1920), exemplifying it in the distinction and interplay between "values" and "attitudes"—values referred to structural conditions and attitudes to interactional ones.]

Directly related to these points is the Chicagoans' general tendency to be both structural and processual in their theoretical explanations. When writing about, say, race or ethnic relations, Thomas and Znaniecki, Park, Hughes, Blumer, and later Killian all pay attention not only to social structure (the rules of racial etiquette, the color line, demographic features of immigration) but to process—even to discerning phases of historical development of race or ethnic relationships. It is for this reason that Barney Glaser and I coined the term *structural process* (1968, pp. 239–42) to capture both sides of the equation, a concept that since then has been fairly widely used. Chicago-derived contemporary sociologists continue to think and explain in these nondualistic ways, and to take exception to frankly deterministic explanations and to explanations that give priority either to macro- or microconditions.

The analytical importance of these points for a theory of action is that an analyst needs carefully to trace and establish linkages among specific patterns of interaction under study. Some conditions only indirectly affect particular interactions, and do this through their impact on more directly impinging conditions.

Over the years of my research, like many other researchers I have struggled with how to *discover* and then *establish* these conditional influences. More recently, with the collaboration of Juliet Corbin, I have developed a methodological procedure termed *conditional matrix* and a more specific procedure for tracing *conditional paths*. These procedures do not at all guarantee explanatory success, but have proven an effective check on loose causal thinking and a reminder of what to "check out." The procedures are not esoteric—presumably any researcher can learn to use them and perhaps become skilled in their use. (See Chapter 2 for a detailing of these procedures.)

Assumption 18. *A useful fundamental distinction between classes of interactions is between the routine and the problematic. Problematic interactions involve "thought," or when more than one interactant is involved then also "discussion." An important aspect of problematic action can also be "debate"—disagreement over issues or their resolution. That is, an arena has been formed that will affect the future course of action.*

[O]ne man's routine of work is made up of the emergencies of other people. . . . In many occupations, the workers or practitioners . . . deal routinely with what are the emergencies to the people who receive their services. (Hughes [1962] 1971, pp. 316, 346)

Most interactions are routinized. Actions and counteractions are expectable; often repeated; governed or guided by rules, regulations, standardized procedures, agreements, or understandings. Without routines, SOP (standard operating procedures), conventions (Becker 1982, pp. 28–35, 40–46), and other forms of relatively patterned interactions, social order would be impossible. Yet given the many contingencies affecting human life, there is also a tremendous amount of problematic interaction—not entirely directed by rules and regulations, not entirely in all its elements expectable, let alone completely routinized.

In Dewey's action scheme (1922), routine ("habit") was a central feature; when it broke down action was disrupted and so deliberation/ reflection was called into play to get action moving again. Dewey was primarily concerned with the role of thought processes in the reestablishment of a course of action, in short, with the process of moving from routine to problematic action, and ultimately into effective routine action again. This interplay is basic to any theory of action, but of course the Dewey scheme is far too simple. With more than a single actor, Dewey's principal analytic term *deliberation* would have to be supplemented with *discussion*. Moreover, even well-established routines are not necessarily like deeply grooved channels through which action passes: There are slight differences in each situation encountered, and built in anyhow are considerable amounts of "local knowledge" that actors bring into play in carrying out routine action. (See especially Gasser 1986.) Also, faced with problematic situations, with questions about what actions to take, debate also enters the process whereby previous elements of action are related to new elements. The novel can only be conceived of in relation to the old, so the latter is likely to enter after debate into the former in complex ways, and perhaps in ways invisible to the actors themselves. (See Chapter 8 on routine and nonroutine action.)

The debate over the problematic, whether about goals or means of projected interaction, carries an implication that the contingent nature of human interaction leads to the phenomenon of "arenas." While this term has been used mainly as a reference to "policy arenas," there is no need to so restrict it. Arenas come into existence at every level of interaction, from the most microscopic (the internal debates of a single actor) to the most macroscopic (as in debates over national issues). At all levels, generic arena processes characterize these debates (see Chapter 10). Here it is enough to recognize that these processes are important components of a theory of action, and that they relate to interaction from the most collective to the most individual. In combination with interactional and action processes, they are central to "social order," which I believe is principally a complex "negotiated order" (see Chapter 11).

Assumption 19. *Also, problematic interactions frequently bring about a process of identity change that entails some degree of suffering and strangeness toward the selves of individuals or collectivities.*

> My mother's [ten-year physical] suffering grew into a symbol. . . . [In response a] somberness of spirit . . . settled over me that was to make me stand apart . . . keep [me] forever on the move, as though to escape a nameless fate seeking to overtake me. (Wright, 1945, p. 87)

> I held my life in my mind . . . each day, feeling at times that I would stumble and drop it forever. . . . My days and nights were one long . . . continuously contained dream of terror, tension, and anxiety. (p. 222)

It is common to theorize that blocked action in which the identity is involved will mainly result in frustration. When, however, the individual's or collective's identity is more deeply involved, some degree of suffering is likely; and when it is very deeply affected then great anguish, loss, or destruction of significant aspects of identity will characteristically occur. Certainly, the end product of this process may finally be—as when therapy is experienced as successful—a more integrated and "improved" identity. (This process will be discussed more fully in Chapter 2.)

A FINAL COMMENT

The theory of action sketched and somewhat elaborated in these chapters is to the best of my knowledge free of assumptions about dualisms. In the writings of the Pragmatists we can see a constant battle against the separating, dichotomizing, or opposition of what Pragmatists argued should be joined together: knowledge and practice, environment and actor, biology and culture, means and ends, body and mind, matter and mind, object and subject, logic and inquiry, lay thought and scientific thought, necessity and chance, cognitive and noncognitive, art and science, values and action.

Chicago interactionist sociologists absorbed this aspect of Pragmatism. Thomas, Park, and their students, notably Hughes and Blumer, also adopted nondualistic and sometimes explicitly antidualistic stances toward specifically sociological issues. Some of those stances are not unique to this tradition, being shared by other schools of thought and inquiry. You too may share their antipathies or rejections of certain dualisms. For example, making a distinction between society and the individual, or between structure and process, or macro- and microlevels of analysis, or deep structure and surface behavior; and perhaps most basic of all, between reality that must be discovered and social scientists as the discoverer of reality. Extreme determinisms whether biological, cultural, economic, technological, and so forth are also instances of dualities; they divide the world into essential forces and derived effects.

Chicagoans endlessly indicate their antidualistic or nondualistic positions. For instance: "The social and technical are a 'seamless web,' co-constructed and mutually embedded" (Clarke 1991, p. 139). Or again, a researcher can assert that participants in Western culture experience ambivalences and subjective tensions over dichotomies (youth versus age, masculinity versus femininity, work versus play, license versus constraint) but these dualities are given an embracing and subtle sociological analysis by the author that is in no way captured—goes native—by the dualities themselves (Davis 1991, pp. 106–7). Chicagoans express an underlying epistemology either explicitly or implicitly.

Many other social science traditions assume one or more fundamental dualisms. Frequently these come in sets or clusters. For instance (to paraphrase), there is a reality out there (say, social structure) that must be discovered (by the investigator) through rigorous (say, field methods). Conversely, since reality is constructed (even by highly trained investigators), it is senseless to speak of finding the truth rather than through proper methods (say, deconstructive) to examine what representations have been expressed by the investigator-writer and through what particular rhetorical techniques. You may not agree with my characterizations of such positions, but that is not the point. Rather, the preceding passages were intended to emphasize that both dualistic and antidualistic positions have profound implications for theorizing and research.

NOTES

1. E. G. Jaco makes a similar kind of assertion when he says about Znaniecki's *Cultural Reality*, in an editorial introduction to its reprinting: [Znaniecki] "has provided the necessary philosophical foundations for the entire discipline of sociology. And the cross-fertilization of ideas and theories of Mead with Znaniecki provide a profound intellectual challenge to sociology that no serious sociologist can ignore!" ([1919] 1983, p. ix)

2. The Pragmatists would have appreciated Latour's recent efforts (1988a, 1988b) to call attention to the important role of technology as a set of objects and embedded in systems of meaning and action within interactions.

3. Some years ago, Znaniecki leveled a devastating critique at means-ends schemes; unfortunately the book in which it appeared was never very widely read, though happily it has recently been reprinted ([1919] 1983). See also John Dewey's extensive treatment in *Human Nature and Conduct* (1922).

4. Feminist social scientists are demonstrating that many of women's "invisible actions" have remained invisible to—mostly male—social researchers.

Chapter 2

An Interactionist Theory of Action

Theory, n. . . . a particular conception or view of something to be done or of the method of doing it: a system of rules or principles
—Stein and Urdang, *The Random House Dictionary of the English Language*

Trajectory, n. . . . the path described by a body moving under the action of given forces
—Stein and Urdang, *The Random House Dictionary of the English Language*

Sociology . . . is fundamentally about between-ness. What is between people, between one time and another, one place and another, people and things. It is strictly anchored for this reason in what Mead called the specious present—it is never really there, but always in the future or the past. Its always studying something that's escaping. At least our kind of sociology is.

But between-ness, just like the white spaces in a poem or the frame of painting, is not nothing. It has a shape, a pattern. Like silences.

Trajectory is one way of capturing the between-ness without leaving the specious present, of noticing the pattern and the shape.

But beware!

Between-ness is an elusive and fragile thing to describe. Even though it's the most robust and necessary thing in the world to experience.

—Leigh Star, personal communication after reading this chapter

---

If the preceding chapter had been subtitled "Pragmatist Philosophic Assumptions Translated into Sociological-Interactionist Ones," then this one might appropriately be subtitled: "The Next Step in Translating a Pragmatist Philosophical Theory of Action into an Interactionist Sociological One." Having shown how Pragmatism is translatable, it is then reasonable to develop a sociological theory of action that *embodies* the totality of those sociological assumptions and puts them faithfully and *systematically to use.* I will consider in a moment, what "use" might mean.

Before launching into this chapter, I will note briefly several points to be developed in this complex theoretical chapter. To begin with, the set of assumptions discussed in the preceding pages can be systematically embodied in a *theory of action.* This means that this theory is grounded in research activities rather than, as in most theories of action, constructed mainly through a logical working out of presuppositions. That research and its analysis have led me to distinguish among types of action.

At the heart of this theory of action is the concept of "trajectory," which has informed many of my own studies. This concept represents processes that I believe are central to any interactionist theory of action, and to understanding crucial features of human life and institutions.

I will develop also the point that this theory of action constitutes a general perspective that can be useful for guiding studies of the courses of action taken by diverse phenomena and the interactions taken by interactants as they attempt to shape those courses. Nevertheless, studies of specific phenomena should not merely apply the theory, including its trajectory conceptualization. Local concepts that are relevant to the phenomena must be "discovered." This theory of action helps the researcher to organize and understand the interactions that are specific to the phenomenon under study.

INTRODUCTORY REMARKS

As remarked earlier, most social scientists and certainly most sociologists do their writing and research without resorting or referring to any theory of action. Some do not even have an image of such a theoretical construct; or they associate it, with negative connotations, with the less empirical writings of Max Weber or with such names as Alfred Schuetz or Talcott Parsons. (In the candid phraseology of Fred Davis, a well-known sociologist, in answer to my question, What does a theory of action mean to you?: "I have no views on it other than that I always thought it a Parsons neologism, i.e., his own way of pretending he was 'getting the actor back in' when in fact he was not.") Such views raise a question that begs for immediate answer. What is the use of this type of theory that seems more speculative or at least quasi-epistemological than truly data-grounded and data-tested theory? What are its purposes? I cannot answer precisely for theories of action other than my interactionist one, which I believe can contribute to two kinds of interrelated social science activities.[1]

Theory and the Range of Actions

The first is directed at understanding the entire range of human actions, of which there are so many that the dictionary scarcely can refer to them all. That is, an interactionist theory of action should address action generally *and* be applicable to specific types of action, so that in effect the theory can also help us to understand the incredibly variegated panorama of human living. Life may be more than action and interaction, but surely they are so central to our lives that sometimes I am amazed at how this crucial part of our existence gets overlooked as a theoretical concern by social scientists.

It follows that a theory of action should not be so abstract or speculative as to distance us from understanding the concreteness of "real life" and of "life in general." Reading some theories of action, it is easy to get lost in their abstractions and in dense commentaries directed toward points made by other theorists; so that after reading these writings it takes a leap of imagination to become immersed again in events, happenings, situations, and the problems, passions, and struggles of actual people, and their institutions and other collectivities.

An interactionist theory of action can help guide us to informed observations and reflections about action, whether individual or collective. It does this by enhancing sensitivities to what otherwise might be overlooked; it raises astute questions about action that might not be raised; and it can minimize becoming captive to overly simple explanatory models, or doctrines, that are claimed as interpreting or explaining human life and behavior. (Their number has been and is legion.) In using a theory of action, social scientists need not engage in competition with the profound descriptions of and commentaries on the human comedy by a Balzac, a Rabelais, a Dickens, or a Dostoevski, and in our day by a Faulkner. Yet we need a theory of action that at least will enable us not to ignore the range of individual, institutional, and societal interaction addressed by these great novelists.

Perhaps I can add specificity to my discussion by referring to contemporary sociological debate over the place of the human body in sociological theory. There is increasing criticism, both scholarly and ideological, directed at the absence or slighting of the body's role in the writings of both past and present social theorists. The following lines give the sense and coloration of one aspect of the critique:

> In attempting to establish the analytical foundations of sociology, Weber, Pareto and Parsons took economics and law as models for the formulation of the basic notions of actor, action, choice and goals. Consumer choice, which in principle could have produced a theory of the embodiment of the social actor via the idea of consumer needs and wants, remained largely

underdeveloped in economics and sociology. . . . [S]ociology, partly by
evolving theoretically along the notion of rational economic action, never
elaborated a sociology of the body. . . . [T]he body . . . was either allocated
to other disciplines (such as biochemistry or physiology) or it became part
of the conditions of action, that is, an environmental constraint. The body
thus became external to the actor, who appeared, as it were, as a decision-
making agent. (Turner 1991, pp. 7–8)

Building on but also criticizing the "action theory of the body" developed by the author of the above quotation, Bryan Turner, still another
sociologist (Frank 1991) offers an alternative "nonfunctionalist" one. I am
not actually interested here in detailing this debate about the how the
body relates to individual and collective action. Yet, I cannot forbear
remarking that advocates of the body not unsurprisingly sometimes take
extreme positions, making the body *the* central or basic building block in
understanding everything in which a social scientist might be interested.
My own stand, as the previous chapter makes clear, is that body and
body processes are essential to understanding and studying human action, but they ought not preempt the conductor's baton; they are simply
a crucial part of the orchestra. Yet the critique of past and contemporary
social theory, including theories of action, as being relatively empty of
reference to human bodies is accurate. Insofar as that is true, such theories
miss or slight vital elements of the human drama. (See Chapter 4 for an
elaboration of these points.)

So also do theories or approaches that omit or underplay self-reference;
or follow the widespread Cartesian practice of separating subject and
object (Grathoff 1970), making the "reality" out there something to be
explored and discovered by the scientist; or give predominant determi-
native force to a single source (culture, technology, social class, genes);
and so on. In other words, the assumptions on which they rest are either
radically different or at least in part somewhat different than those that lie
behind my Pragmatist-derived and interactionist theory of action.

I do not claim that this particular theory can, in its social science functions, rival the grasp of human affairs by great novelists (or by
Shakespeare!), but the stakes riding on a more modest claim are sizable.
Some of the evidence for it rests on the analyses of materials presented in
the remaining chapters of this book, and how much these will stimulate
your imagination as well as suggest research directions to you.

Research and the Theory of Action

That last phrase touches on a second purpose for this interactional
theory of action. The theory has been developed in and through research,
so I am confident that it can suggest significant research areas and research problems, and also provide guidelines for approaching these. A

theory of action that is not oriented toward research in this particular era would be of only academic significance. Earlier theories of action were formed and proffered in different eras of history than ours. Weber ([1922] 1957) devised his during a period of discipline building, with the intent of giving a firmer foundation and more legitimacy to sociology. Parsons published his theory of action in 1937, as part of his effort to bring European theoretical perspectives to the too empirically oriented and noncosmopolitan American sociologists. Meanwhile Schuetz (1966), an immigrant from Austria living in New York, was avowedly attempting by building on Bergson and Husserl to give epistemological depth to Weber's theory of action. He did this at least in part to convert an otherwise erring generation of sociologists, including Parsons himself, as their brief correspondence during the early 1950s reflects (Grathoff 1978).

I read the present era as one in which the post–World War II political-social-economic and demographic order is in radical breakup and transformation. You may not agree with this social diagnosis. However, if you do agree that research should address social issues—and not merely arouse the appreciation of your disciplinary colleagues—then you will understand that a theory of action ought to have research implications. Your choice of such a theory may lie elsewhere, but at least consider the validity of this second of its purposes.

This research purpose cannot be taken for granted, as perhaps most readers do, because it is quite possible to propose a contemporary theory of action with no research purpose whatever. For instance, one of the advocates of body-oriented action theories has done just that, substituting other purposes for a theory of action: "Researchers have and will proceed well enough without [such] an analytic theory." Rather it "is proposed such a theory should function only as a prerequisite to the theorist's orientation to the mass of fragmented materials that the study of the body presents" (Frank 1991, p. 210). Thereby, one can more accurately define the current boundaries of "an ethics of the body" (p. 210). Not surprisingly, another author who also advocates a body-oriented "sociology of action" suggests two other purposes for "such a theory." It "should first of all enable us to account for the effects of social structures on agency, and at the same time provide a critique of extant social structures" (Lash 1991, p. 276). Its additional aim: "in such a theory the body should possess some positive, libidinal force" (p. 276). The emphasis in much of the writing on the body and the related theory of action is on the theory's critical function and far less, if at all, on its linkages with evolving research.

WORK, A MAJOR FORM OF ACTION

It is not my intention to explore all the different kinds of action in this book. Rather, I choose to focus on those with which my own research has mainly been concerned, including one universally important form of activity: *work*.

Implicit in the Pragmatist theoretical action scheme is the idea of *work*—imagining, trying out, assessing actions or lines of action involves "working things out," to use a common phrase. Work is entailed in the process of unblocking the blocked action, and moving along into the future. This action scheme has affected my theorizing about work insofar as it has long been an influence on me. I will discuss work briefly now, but more extensively in the next chapter and at least implicitly throughout the entire volume.

Studies in the sociology of work, earlier as well as now, are not focused on the social mechanics of work—work as interaction—but rather on gender, class, occupation, professional and other determinants of work, and the consequences of work on these. Research on work carried out within the Chicago sociological tradition pertained not so much to the mechanics of work as such as to several other matters: especially to work and occupations, work relationships, work and careers, and work and organizations. Only a few publications examined the details of work itself (cf. Dalton 1954; Freidson 1976). Eventually, no doubt because of my Pragmatist assumptions, I began to look directly and closely at work as such, rather than in more traditional "Chicago" ways. This led eventually to studying such phenomena as the division of labor; the articulation of work; various of the work processes (like monitoring and assessing safety); the interactional processes as related to work; and to types of work, including biographical and "sentimental" work; forms of work that characterized "negotiated orders," social worlds, and "arenas." (All of these are discussed or at least touched on in this book.) That focus on work as interaction also became linked with a rather persistent concept, "trajectory," that ran through most of my research writing, which provides the central theme of this chapter, along with the work associated with any trajectory.

TRAJECTORY AND RELATED CONCEPTS

Apropos of this concept and its relation to an interactional theory of action, I will note another bit of personal history. I became aware of my continued use of certain sociological assumptions, and how they functioned in my research, at about the same time as I realized something else. For many years, in a succession of studies, my colleagues and I had been using and developing this concept. As various phenomena were explored more deeply or new ones examined, it seemed to become more complex, more elaborated, and enriched. The concept, central to these successive studies, had developed, so to speak, almost a life of its own. It was steadily evolving. This, despite my care not simply to apply it in every study, and skeptically to hold off commitment to its use until late in each study. The concept nevertheless ended by "earning its way," as my colleague Barney Glaser would say, into what I believed were genuinely grounded studies (cf. Glaser and Strauss 1965, 1968; Strauss and Glaser 1970, 1975; Fagerhaugh and Strauss 1977; Strauss et al. 1985; Fagerhaugh, Strauss, Suczek, and Wiener 1988; Corbin and Strauss 1988). As I continued to think about my translation and development of the pragmatist action scheme, I very slowly and with some surprise concluded that this elaborated conceptualization of trajectory was the central concept in my sociological, interactionist theory of action. I realized also that it embodied all of the assumptions of a theory of action that were discussed in the preceding chapter.

There has perhaps been some ambiguity in my coauthors' and my use and development of the concept of trajectory. As will be seen, it refers to a course of action but also embraces the interaction of multiple actors and contingencies that may be unanticipated and not entirely manageable. The Pragmatist scheme and my trajectory version of it seem not necessarily to distinguish between two courses of action. The first is rather straightforwardly rational in the sense that many projects are planned, carefully worked out, though sometimes as complex as putting the first man on the moon. However, a course of action can be directed at managing an evolving set of problems that are so unanticipated, difficult, and in extreme cases so "fateful" that control of the course of action is threatened and even rendered virtually impossible. A simple example is when a physician thinks he or she has a made a clear diagnosis of a patient's illness and puts into action a clearly planned treatment. However, then problems arise—both anticipated and unanticipated but neither very manageable—and continue to arise and even to multiply, with increasing numbers of resources (drugs, tests, diagnoses, personnel) and amount of work entering into the evolving course of interaction (Strauss et al. 1985). Sometimes this trajectory turns into a "cumulative mess" (Strauss et al. 1985, pp. 160–81) in which each set of actions produces unanticipated consequences that add to the complications both of the illness itself and the "messiness" of work relationships among the personnel, and the articulation of all the work involved in managing "everything" is made more complex and more difficult. It is this second form of trajectory (the more "fateful" kind) that has been central to much of my own research.

To be more exact now, I shall use *trajectory* in two ways: (1) the course of any experienced phenomenon as it evolves over time (an engineering project, a chronic illness, dying, a social revolution, or national problems attending mass or "uncontrollable" immigration) and (2) the actions and interactions contributing to its evolution. That is, phenomena do not just automatically unfold nor are they straightforwardly determined by social, economic, political, cultural, or other circumstances; rather, they are in part *shaped by the interactions* of concerned actors. Some phenomena do not change for long periods of time, but then we need to know how interactions of concerned actors have contributed to that stability. This central concept of trajectory gives life and movement to studies of phenomena and the related interactions; it forces one to view interactants as active in attempting to shape the phenomena. Over time, as the interactions continue they and the actors themselves are affected by different combinations of structural and interactional conditions. These are outcomes of previous interactions and also of external influences bearing on the interactions.

Like any theory, this very general theory of action—presumably pertinent to all kind of actions and interactions—has more than one concept. Besides the central one of trajectory, it not only has subsidiary concepts but includes the relationships among them. Both will be described below.

SUBCONCEPTS

To this major ordering concept, trajectory's subconcepts pertain to dimensions of the course of the particular phenomenon under study, conditions pertinent to interactions and strategies bearing on the shaping of the course, or consequences of how interactions and strategies have affected that course. Several of the subconcepts developed in the specific researches by co-workers and me will be touched on here. Assuredly more would evolve from additional studies made of phenomena different than those we have studied.

Trajectory phasing represents the researcher's conceptualization of phases, in accordance with changes in the interaction occurring over time "around" the phenomenon as it evolves. Analytically, these phases are properties of the sequence of interactions.

The interactants themselves often develop conceptualizations of phases too; these then may affect their next actions and interactions, as when illness moves into a "they are dying" phase (Glaser and Strauss 1968). Also, when a phase is viewed as desirable, then people are likely to attempt to prolong it, or if the phase is viewed as undesirable, even painful, as with a phase of economic depression, there may either be an attempt to reverse it or those affected are counseled (or counsel themselves) to "wait it out until it disappears." The concerned parties may differ in their conceptualizations of phase, so that there are consequences for their interaction and perhaps for their perceptions of movements of the course into a new phase. None of this should escape the researchers' keen eyes, as they make their own analytically directed classifications of phase.

Trajectory projection stands for a vision of the expected course of interaction perceived as needed to shape action with regard to the phenomenon. If the course is clearly outlined, has precise ends, and is of short duration, then the means-ends scheme may be sufficient to account for the course of action. However, in courses not affected by those conditions, the projections are very likely to change. This is not only because of external contingencies that impinge on the course, but also the appearance of internal contingencies in the form of consequences of interaction that then are taken into account by one or other of the interactants.

In other words, a trajectory projection is *not at all* an "end" or "goal" to which action and interaction are directed as a "means." (I cannot emphasize this point too much; see the discussion in Chapter 1.) As G. H. Mead (1938) noted, the "end" affects (as a condition) the formation of a line of action, *but* taking overt action is likely to bring about changes in the end. In Dewey's (1922) terminology, there is an interplay of "ends in view" and flexible means over the course of action.[2]

As for *the* end or goal, we should not conceive of a trajectory projection as having a single one or as independent of other ends or goals. Those indeed contribute to a context of conditions that affect the course of interaction through the actors' shaping of their respective actions with respect to the phenomenon. Actors may or may not share projections; in either case there are consequences for their respective actions and for the overall interaction among the actors. Furthermore, we—the researchers— should not think of their projections as only looking forward in time: Built into them are individual and perhaps collective memories and experiences that enter into the visions of future action.

Trajectory scheme refers to the plan consciously designed to shape interaction as desired, given the content of a trajectory projection. Designed by whom? The answer must be specifically related to particular situations and their circumstances. Understandably these vary greatly according to numbers of actors, their statuses, and their relative influence and power. Also, the trajectory scheme can have various properties—defined by the actors themselves—along certain dimensions: detailed to vague, probable to improbable, and successful to unsuccessful. The trajectory scheme is essentially envisioned as an overall strategy that when acted on becomes translated into actual actions. Because these are deliberate, an actor will be well aware of them. Other actors too may become aware of the strategic character of these actions and the thinking that lies behind them. So in response they take what they believe are appropriate counteractions: opposing, supporting, and so forth. Again, there can be much disagreement, whether recognized or not, among the participants to the evolving course of interaction. Also, again, the trajectory scheme may be revised over time, even while being enacted, with spontaneous or after the fact reviewals of the results of the actions. The revisions may range from none to a great many; and different participants may revise their own versions at different pace and in different terms. Again, as with the trajectory projection, these trajectory schemes are embedded in contexts of a plurality of other schemes envisioned by other actors.

All of this necessitates that the researcher catch as fully as possible the relevant, sequential, *and* multiple conceptualizations of trajectory scheme and related contextual changes. Quite as important, the researcher should realize that there is an *organization* of strategies, otherwise the participants would not use terms like *plans* and *planning* nor would their more immediate conceptualizations of future action deserve the term trajectory *schemes*.

Arc of action is the researcher's concept for the cumulative action and interaction that has taken place in attempts to shape the course of the phenomenon, as perceived by the researcher looking backward from the present time. The actors' projections of the trajectory, and for some the explicit recognition of the arc of action, affect their actions and interactions through a recasting of trajectory schemes and even trajectory projections. Therefore, these become a condition for future action, whether the actions become deliberately altered or judgment is made to continue "on course."

As actors ourselves, we know that such acts of looking back and reviewing may be both internal to an actor as well as involve bringing other actors into awareness of these reviews and their resulting conclusions. The interactional game can get further complicated however—aside from differential assessments of an arc of action by different participants in the evolving interaction—because one actor can deceive the other(s) as to his or her review. These reviews have other pertinent properties, like frequency and self or other blaming. Also they may or may not become discussed or debated by any or all of the interactants. Again, researchers must do their best to capture much of this complexity or their interpretations will be faulty.

Reciprocal impact refers to the potentiality for consequences of interaction to become, in their turn, conditions that affect further interaction, which then produces further consequences. To express the reciprocal impact of conditions and consequences in these terms is merely to make explicit what had been implicit in the concepts discussed just above.

Trajectory management represents the entire process by which the course of the phenomenon is shaped by the actors, through all of its phases and perhaps subphases, by the carrying out of a trajectory scheme. Issues of influence and power come into sharp relief here, as do differences in modes of action chosen and of preferred interactional styles. There is also the probability that many actions will be spontaneously taken, sometimes surprising to all the interactants. Any of them may then respond spon-taneously or deliberately.

Once again, researchers must attempt to catch this interactional com-plexity, or at least as much of it as they can within the constraining conditions of their particular studies. If they follow the interactionist theory of action outlined here, they must not be committed beforehand to some version of determinism, for this will mislead their interpretations of the interactional course under study and will result in their missing im-portant aspects of it. Quite aside from conceptual precommitments of any kind, they need anyhow to be wary of and attempt to guard against tendencies to selective perception that flow from their own professional or personal assumptions.

In this regard, there is an additional theoretical and methodological point. In many evolving courses of phenomena and their associated in-teractions, no single actor guides or manages the total course. In trajectory management, there is no deus ex machina. The interactants are all at-tempting to shape the course or some part of it with respect to constraints within which each is acting. Yet some interactants may be much more influential or display more power in shaping either the entire course or its phases. If one interactant were to completely dominate the entire course, then we would not be discussing interaction but some sort of command structure—something that occurs in a blueprint, "on paper," in planning but rarely in actual execution no matter how dominated from above. This is especially true if the interaction course is anything but of the briefest, and most are not.

The clear implication is that one or several interactional processes may be going on and simultaneously among the various interactants. As will be noted below, these processes include negotiation, persuasion, educa-tion, manipulation, and coercion or the threat of coercion. In effect, unless coercion is continuously resorted to, then a negotiated order (negotiation plus the remaining interactional processes) will obtain, whereby interac-tants must come to terms with the goals and actions of each other (Strauss 1978; Maines 1982). I repeat, so as not to be misunderstood, that this does not mean that all interactants are equal in power or influence in their attempts at shaping the trajectory as they would wish if they had com-plete control over the constituent interactions.

ADDITIONAL SUBCONCEPTS

Biography

The subconcepts just discussed are paralleled by five others that per-tain to biographies (identities over time) of actors, whether individual or collective, as conceptualized both by the researcher and by the interactants themselves. These conceptualizations pertaining to biographies have their source in interactants' *involvement* in courses of interaction. True, their involvements, or commitments, may be quite different but there must be some measure of involvement. There may be even minimal involvement (that of a garage mechanic fixing a car as compared with that of its owner) yet the potential exists for enhancement or damage to any participant's self-regard. When a trajectory is collective, with many actors being involved, then the interactional sequence, including the identity aspect of it, is likely to be quite complex.[3] The biographical phenomena to which these subconcepts refer are conditions that affect the trajectory and also consequences of action and interaction.

Just as there is trajectory phasing, there is *biographical phasing*, that is, phases in the development of a biography in association with an evolving course of the phenomena. The remaining biographically related concepts are *biographical projection, biographical scheme, arc of biographical action*, and *biographical management* (Corbin and Strauss 1988).

Biographical projection refers to what the actor perceives will happen to his or her or its identity. Biographical scheme refers to plans to shape that perceived future. The arc of biographical action refers to the perceived accumulation of action and interaction with reference to the interactant's identity. Biographical management is the attempt to shape what happens to identity over the course as it evolves.

Body

That bodies are related to biographies is unquestionable, since those of infants mature and later age, eventually to die. A social scientist need not overreact to biological determinism, rejecting versions of it on scholarly, ideological, or moral grounds, to admit that at least our species' requirement for food and liquid must be met. Beyond that, humans assuredly act passionately, expressively, have dreams and daydreams, so that to quibble over the assignment of these "essentially" to body or mind would frankly be to succumb to a dubious mind-body dualism. Humans also engage in complex acts of remembering. Without a rich texture of memories, a loss that happens after drastic strokes or other brain damage, humans lose their capacities to do more than function in the present and perhaps also the proximate future. So integral to the concept of trajectory is explicit reference to bodily matters. (See Chapter 4 for discussion of these.)

Interactional and Action Processes

It is useful to conceptualize the evolving interaction as carried out *and* shaped through two kinds of processes: *interactional* and *action*. The first has been touched on already. It should be mentioned that terms for interactional processes, such as negotiating or manipulating, will tend to evoke in you various strategies taken by interactants, who indeed view them as strategies, but from an analytic viewpoint they constitute processes. It is not difficult to see that a great deal of interaction (but certainly not all) consists of just these kinds of processes. They are characteristic of interactions from the most macroscopic (negotiations between nations) to the most microscopic (negotiations about the detailed carrying out of a task even while it is being performed).

The *action processes* are those which characterize various forms of action, whether work, play, collective fantasying, or lovemaking. Examples of such processes as they appear, let us say, in work interactions are the "articulating" of tasks; the "resourcing"—that is, obtaining and maintaining resources; the "division of labor"—that is, dividing up work into tasks; the "decision making"—deciding who does what tasks, when, where, and how; the "performing" or actual carrying out of tasks; the "motivating," or the generating and maintaining of rewards (or threatening of punishments); and the "supervising"—the overseeing and evaluating of task performance. For these action processes to proceed, interactional processes will be entailed; but again the interactants view the latter as strategies to get the work done.

Orders: What Is Shaped

Another useful concept is that of *orders*. These are analytic abstractions that summarize what, with regard to an evolving phenomenon, the actions and interactions are directed at shaping. For instance, there is a *spatial* order: how objects are arrayed in given spaces; how actions take place or are supposed to take place in certain spaces; the symbolism associated with various spaces. There is a *temporal* order that pertains to such matters as the scheduling, pacing, frequency, duration, and timing of actions. There is a *work* order: this refers to how work is conceived of, set up, maintained, reconceived, rearranged. There is a *technological* order, easily seen if one thinks of action that requires machinery or equipment or other "hard" technology; but technological order is equally characteristic of any kind of action—there are always at least procedures that constitute significant "soft" technology. Also there is an *informational* order pertaining to the flow of information among the interactants. This includes type of information, amount, who sends and who receives, and how the information is passed. I will mention just two additional types. *Sentimental order* refers to such matters as moods, motivations, organizational climates, and interpersonal relationships. These too will be shaped through deliberate or implicit interactional strategies, and in turn provide conditions affecting later interactions. There is also the *moral order*, which refers to norms and rules and agreements that pertain to ethical values and issues. Perhaps an *aesthetic* order can be added, referring to proper style, or appropriately aesthetic standards as conceived by actors. These several constructs are essentially sets of major conditions that become related to each other in the researcher's analysis in conditional/consequential ways. As such, elements of each can be conditional for those of other sets.

The degree of success at trajectory management—at shaping the course of the phenomenon and its associated interactions—is likely to be phrased by the actors in terms of one or more combinations of these orders: for example, success at attaining desired interpersonal relationships, or gaining appropriate technological resources to carry through to a project goal, or control over a reasonable scheduling so that "something can really get done right."

Elements of these orders can be disrupted by broader structural conditions as well as by conditions that arise during the sequence of interactions. In order for interactants to shape the sequence and the associated phenomena to their satisfaction, they will work out strategies to restore essential elements of a disturbed order. Of course, interactants may differ in their definitions of the degree of disturbance, the elements that are awry, and the specific strategies that should be carried out.

A CONDITIONAL MATRIX

Conditions of varying scope or scale affect interaction, interactional processes, work processes, and other details of trajectory unfolding. A conditional matrix, previously referred to as Assumption 17, and its corresponding diagram are *ways of conceptualizing, discovering, and keeping track of the conditions* that bear on whatever phenomenon—*as defined by the researcher*—and its associated interactions that are under study. This is especially true when the trajectory is very complex. Then it is helpful to think both graphically and conceptually in terms of a conditional matrix. While its actual use is complicated, I have found that this mode of analysis is essential to carrying out the research implications of this interactionist theory of action. At the end of the extended quote below, some additional remarks and a warning will be appended.

To describe the matrix and the conditional path analysis associated with it, I quote from a previous publication (Strauss and Corbin 1990, pp. 162–71; see also Strauss 1988):

> The conditional matrix may be represented as a set of circles, one inside each other. . . . In the outer rings stand those conditional features *most distant* to the action/interaction; while the inner rings pertain to those conditional features bearing *most closely* [in the analysis] upon an action/interaction sequence.
>
> Conditions at all levels have relevance to any study. Even when studying a phenomenon that is clearly located at the inner part of the matrix—the action/interaction level—the broader levels of conditions will still be relevant. For example, participants in any interaction bring with them attitudes and values of their national and regional cultures, as well as their past experiences.
>
> To maximize the generalizability of the matrix as an analytic tool, each level is presented [here] in its most abstract form. *The researcher needs to fill in the specific conditional features for each level that pertain to the chosen area of investigation.* Items to be included would thus depend upon the type and scope of phenomenon under investigation. Specification of conditions may come from the research itself. Or they may come from the [technical] literature and experience: Then they would be considered provisional until data indicate their relationship to the phenomenon. . . . [E]ach condition within the matrix possesses the properties of time (through temporality) and place (location within the matrix). Also, one can study any phenomenon at any level of the matrix. For example, one might study world hunger, or hunger within a community, or organizational decision making, negotiations between countries, chronic illness in individuals, AIDS as a national problem, professionalism among nurses . . . and relationships between arenas of debate within a community. . . . Regardless of the level within which a phenomenon is located, that phenomenon will stand in conditional relationship to levels above and below it, as well as within the level itself. . . .
>
> [The general features of the matrix levels are as follows.] The outermost level may be thought of as the international level. It includes such items as [international]: politics, . . . values, philosophies, . . . international problems and issues like [the earth's] environment.
>
> The second level may be regarded as the national level. Its features include [national]: politics, governmental regulations, culture, history, values, economics, problems and issues.
>
> Next . . . the community level, including all of the above items but as they pertain to the community. Each community has its own demographic features that give it singularity.
>
> [Next is] the organizational and institutional levels. Each will have its own structures, rules, problems and histories.
>
> Still another circle represents the suborganizational, subinstitutional level. This would include the peculiar features of a part of the city, hospital ward, or sublocation within a larger location, where the study is taking place.

Then . . . the collective, group, and individual level. This level includes biographies, philosophies, knowledge and experiences of persons and families, as well as those of various groups (special interest, professional, and scientific).

[Then] the interactional level. By interaction we mean people doing things together or with respect to one another in regards to a phenomenon (Becker 1986)—and the [various forms of] action, talk, and thought processes that accompany the doing of those things. Even things done alone, like managing an illness, require interaction in the form of self-reflection, and contact with others to obtain medical supplies, counsel, and sometimes support. Interaction is carried out through [various] interactional processes. . . .

Finally, reaching the center of the matrix [is] action: both strategic and routine. This level represents the active, expressive, performance form of self and/or other interaction carried out to manage, respond to, and so forth a phenomenon. Action is carried out through action processes [most notably "work"]. These [action processes] combine with interactional processes. . . . For example, the term "division of labor," which refers to an action process for the carrying out of . . . work, involves much more than different people doing different tasks to some end. . . . This process also encompasses [interactional processes] to arrive at and maintain a division of labor and accomplish its associated tasks.

[We turn next to the procedure of tracing conditional paths.] Tracing paths involves tracking an event or incident from the level of action/interaction through the various conditional levels [downward and upward] to determine how they relate. This is done in order to directly link conditions and consequences with action/ interaction.

[Why is tracing conditional paths important?] Often, the presentation of a study begins or ends with descriptive lists of conditions that pertain to the phenomenon under investigation. That is, the author locates a phenomenon in a set of historical circumstances and events, or explains what conditions in a general sense relate to the phenomenon. This description gives us a background for understanding something about the context in which the given phenomenon is located or why it occurs. Yet, often, we are left only with this very general image, for no attempt was made to connect the specific conditions to the phenomenon in question, through their effect on action/interaction. Nor does the author systematically relate consequences back to the next action/interactional sequence. . . .

To trace a conditional path . . . begin with an event, incident, or happening, then attempt to determine why this occurred, what conditions were operating, how the conditions manifest themselves, and with what consequences. You determine the answers to these questions by systematically following the effects of conditions through the matrix. What levels were passed through? With what effects?

This procedure of tracking conditional paths can be demonstrated through an example. One day while observing a head nurse at work on a medical unit, the researcher noted the following incident. A physician came onto the unit to make rounds, and while doing so she wished to check the colostomy of one of the patients. She asked the team leader, a nurse who was accompanying her on the rounds, for a pair of size six sterile gloves—a relatively small size. The team leader checked in the unit's storage area but the smallest available size was a seven. She offered these larger gloves to the physician, who refused them. This posed a problem for the team leader. Not knowing what to do, she turned to the head nurse. The latter explained to the physician that there were no size six gloves on the unit, suggesting the larger ones be used. Again, the physician refused. Now the head nurse was faced with the problem of locating the size six gloves. First, she called Central Supply, but was told that gloves of this size were temporarily in short supply, because of a large demand for gloves created by the AIDS epidemic. Therefore gloves were being closely monitored by a designated person, who presently was attending a meeting. The head nurse would have to wait to obtain the gloves until after the meeting. Meanwhile, the physician was getting very impatient. Consequently, the head nurse began to telephone other units, eventually locating a pair of size six gloves in the recovery room. She went to fetch them. The physician was finally able to proceed with the medical procedure. All of this interaction took about thirty minutes of the head nurse's valuable time.

Analyzing this incident, the researcher notes that work is interrupted because a needed resource in the form of a supply is missing. To keep the flow of work going, the head nurse will have to locate this resource: a pair of gloves. But the researcher is forced to ask: Why is finding these particular gloves so problematic? After all, gloves are not controlled substances, like drugs, to be kept under lock and key. What's happening to make this so, in this hospital, at this time? Following through with this question, the researcher—beginning with the interrupted action—traced the following conditional path. (The phenomenon under investigation was "work flow" as related to patient care at the organizational level.)

(a) We begin with action, which was interrupted because the needed resource was lacking. (b) Next . . . move to the interactional level of the conditional matrix. The head nurse had attempted unsuccessfully to persuade the physician to accept the larger gloves. The physician had been adamant in her refusal. The head nurse then contacted central supply; here too she attempted to persuade, but was unsuccessful. Finally, she was able to persuade one of the other units to loan her some gloves. (c) Next . . . move to the individual level of the matrix. Another physician may have accepted the larger gloves, but this one refused. Her hands were small. So physical size plays some part in the refusal. (d) Then . . . the suborganizational level of hospital ward, where the work occurs. Gloves were in short supply on the unit. Only a few limited sizes of sterile gloves were available. Why? Because they were being used so much. Why? Because of newly published national guidelines on infectional control. To protect themselves and other patients, health workers were being asked by the National Center of Communicable Diseases to wear gloves when working on patients in a manner that might involve contact with their body fluids (since the patients might have AIDS. . . .

(e) . . . gloves are in short supply within the hospital. To insure that each unit has an adequate supply for its respective type of work . . . gloves are kept under lock and key, and given only according to need. (f) Next . . . the community level . . . the supply of sterile gloves here is also limited, for in this community many hospitals and nursing homes are following the same national guidelines. This brings us to production, distribution, and supply of sterile gloves within the community [where] local suppliers were caught unprepared for the demand. (g) Now . . . move to the national level where the new guidelines originated, and ask "why?" here we can trace the situation back to the current perception of an AIDS epidemic. So, [the researcher] can show a relationship between AIDS and the work on a hospital unit by tracing upward through each of the conditional levels. Each level is more distantly removed from the problem at hand, yet in a wider sense contributes to it. . . .

Tracing conditions in this manner is quite different from saying that "AIDS is having an effect on hospital work," but leaving it to the reader to figure out how this effect actually occurred. Since we are studying how head nurses keep the flow of work going, we are interested in showing how the available resources . . . bear significantly on their abilities to maintain work flow. . . .

Now this illustration refers to a rather minor incident, and one whose conditional path is relatively easy to trace. Of course, a researcher would not want to trace every incident . . . would chose only those incidents that seemed especially pertinent to the central phenomenon under investigation. Thus, in [such] a study of work flow that was focused at the organizational level, a researcher might trace only those conditions and consequences pertaining to the repeated problems that were slowing down or interrupting work flow; or conversely, those that were serving to keep the work flow smooth.

While the concept of conditional matrix and the associated procedure of tracing conditional paths were designed as research tools, they are meant also to protect researchers against the untenable assumption of two contrasting realms of the macroscopic and microscopic, falsely thought by many to be either independent of each other or needing somehow to be related to each other.[4] Perhaps I should add that "history" can enter in at any level of the matrix: say the history of a nation's economy or the history of an organization. In the conditional matrix, history consists of important changes of structural conditions. Changes of these kinds that are deemed relevant need to be taken into analytic account.

Recollect that in introducing this section on the conditional matrix, emphasis was placed on the matrix and the paths being constructs of the researcher. Whatever, eventually, is the *particular* matrix and set of paths deemed relevant to the phenomena under study, it is the researcher who must make those determinations. Let us now say that more abstractly and more generally. The very natures of the matrix and the paths are opaque until the researcher, with due concern for data, gives them meaning and specificity. Metaphorically speaking, paths come in all shapes and sizes: short, long, thick, thin, loose, tight, startling, commonplace, visible, invisible to the actors. As for the "broader" conditions, the larger circles of the matrix, these can be deceptively clear, rendered all too concrete by the unsuspecting interpreter. To quote Leigh Star:

> Although it's the most taken-for-granted thing in most parts of sociology, [the macroconditions are what] we know the least about. We have this pervading image that we understand "institutional" versus "suborganizational," for example—I don't think we do at all. The conventional labels just don't seem to be working any more—even nation, for instance! (personal communication)

The microlabels and "variables" are equally ambiguous: Not only must "they" be discovered but so must be their specificities. This burden lies squarely on the researcher's shoulders, but the concepts of conditional matrix and conditional paths should be helpful.[5]

PROPERTIES AND TYPES, AND LOCAL CONCEPTS

The theory of action and its associated concepts and subconcepts are directly pertinent to the theory's two principal purposes: to help understand action in general and to guide research. Later, more will be said about these purposes. Useful as the theory may be in those capacities, both the more general understanding and the research endeavors must nevertheless lead to *local* concepts. These are concepts that are specific to the phenomenon being examined. The burden is on anyone who uses the theory of action and its trajectory-related concepts to generate those local concepts. So I shall next discuss properties and types of trajectories in relation to those concepts. My argument here is that a combination of the type of trajectory *and* phenomena or "areas" under study will be the main sources for the local concepts that are ultimately generated.

A moment's reflection about the evolving course of a phenomenon tells us that courses are diverse, varying from each other in the combination of characteristics that they possess. Here are a few dimensions along which they may vary: very brief duration—very long duration; expected—unexpected; voluntary action—involuntary action; much control over—little control over; few interactants (including collectivities)—a great many; enjoyably experienced—not at all enjoyably experienced (painful, sad, anguishing). An example of the use of these dimensions is found in our study of dying and its management in hospitals (Glaser and Strauss 1965, 1968). We conceptualized the course of dying as expected—unexpected; certain—uncertain (in time, for instance); hoped for—not hoped for; disruptive—not disruptive of family and/or staff organization; and so on. The specific concepts developed during this research related directly to those properties of the dying courses. The general point is that the specifying of properties and dimensions leads to conceptually "dense" theory (Glaser 1978; Strauss 1987; Strauss and Corbin 1990).

In addition to trajectory types classified by combinations of their properties, it is useful to distinguish types according to the kind of interactant involved: (1) collectivities, (2) aggregates of individuals, or (3) a single person whose trajectory is central to our interest. Let us look at the individual case first. Examples of this are sometimes called "life histories," because a biographical narrative constitutes the data. Probably the most classical instance of a life history is the very long narrative of a single Polish peasant included in the Thomas and Znaniecki monograph (1918–1920). After many years of being out of fashion, life histories and other case histories or studies have become increasingly popular (Maines 1992).

An especially interesting life history for illustrating my purpose of bringing out the source of local concepts is Gerhard Riemann's *Das Fremdwerden der eigenen Biographie* (1987). The title (*Becoming Strange to One's Own Biography*) and subtitle (*Narrative Interviews with Psychiatric Patients*) signals the subject matter. I will freely translate some of the subheadings to make the two points asserted above: that the type of trajectory (here the evolution of identity) plus the substantive area under study (mental illness) together are likely to yield the local concepts discovered during the research itself.

Here are some of this monograph's conceptual subheadings: "Becoming a stranger to oneself"; "Breakdowns of orientation and reacting to them"; "Experiences of loss in the relationship with one's own biography"; "Experiences of regaining or securing the relationship with one's own biography." These titles clearly reflect conceptualizations of mental illness and individual biography. Similar conceptualizations can be found in Clifford Shaw's life histories of delinquents (1930, 1931, 1936) or the Thomas and Znaniecki (1918–1920) life history of a Polish immigrant. Each has a different substantive content than Riemann's self-narratives about "mentally ill" lives, as defined by families and psychiatrists and consequently often by themselves.

Then there is the trajectory type that I have designated as referring to aggregates, such as the simultaneous migration by individuals to Germany from Turkey. Both the older literature of migration to the United States and the newer literature about migration to or within Europe portray many instances of aggregate action. Again the explanatory concepts in these studies reflect the specifics of the trajectory type and the substantive phenomenon studied, albeit many of these concepts apply both to aggregate and collective migration.

Some of these substantively grounded concepts are easily imagined. For instance, in the older American studies will be found concepts like "cultural conflict," "social disorganization," "personal disorganization," "marginal man," and "strains between first generation and second generation." Recently, when looking at an interview from a study by the late Christa Hoffman-Riem with a Turkish woman who had migrated to Germany at the age of seventeen, I could clearly see aggregate features and their consequences in her narrative. This immigrant rarely refers to any group membership other than her family back home, except for temporary groups of women living and working at the same factory. Most of the concepts that I formed when reading the narrative pertained to the woman's individual experiences, some doubtless shared by other Turkish women in like circumstances. For instance, concepts of body failure seemed appropriate to some of her experiences, because the endless working hours of hard labor resulted in her failing energy and frequent and long bouts of illness. When coding such a narrative, one would also take note of her perpetual confusion in encountering the maze of governmental rules and regulations, beginning with her attempts to leave Turkey and including struggling with conditions stemming from ignorance or only partial knowledge of German regulations and laws. Throughout the narrative various in vivo concepts are scattered that relate to her conceptions about the impersonality of the Germans, to her sense of intense isolation, but nevertheless also to her motivations for staying in Germany as she becomes increasingly estranged from Turkey and her previously Turkish identity.

A third type of trajectory takes place within organizations. In *Time for Dying*, we showed how local concepts reflect the flow of organizational events that pertained especially to the management of dying. A variant type of organizational trajectory refers to an organization as such and attempts within it to shape interaction with respect to its evolving history. An instance might be when an organization is suffering a decline and eventually passes out of existence or gets absorbed by another organization: the question here being how various interactants attempt to shape this organizational history.

So—and this is a central point—the principal function of the interactionist theory of action is not at all to supply or directly develop concepts that will constitute the evolving substantive theory about the particular phenomenon under study. Rather, what the theory is capable of doing is so thoroughly to inform sociological perspectives that a researcher automatically thinks interactionally, temporally, processually, and structurally, as well as in the relatively complex ways ensured by the sociological assumptions built into this theory of action.

It is not that thinking in this way requires you to keep looking over your shoulder, so to speak, at the superego assumptions behind the theory of action: Did I get this in? What have I forgotten? To use the framework in this way would be unreal, unworkable, and deadly for research creativity.

Once absorbed as a perspective, this interactionist theory of action will function relatively silently to order your explanations of interactions taking place around the phenomenon under study. (That is how it has been used when thinking about the materials to be discussed in the content chapters of the book.) One of the striking paradoxes of this theory of action is that just because it has been expressed explicitly and systematically, in these pages, it can function implicitly during the course of research itself, rendering systematic the researcher's ordering of explanations.

A NOTE ON TYPES OF EXPERIENCES

An easily overlooked point is the potentially great range of types of experiencing undergone by the diverse interactants who on the face of it are all facing the same emergent conditions of their trajectories. However, the given phenomenon and the actions taken to shape its evolving will combine. The result may be an enormous range of experiences, including extreme suffering and unforgettable exhilaration. In Dewey's concise phrasing, "Whether the necessary undergoing phase is by itself pleasurable or painful is a matter of particular conditions" (1935, p. 41). A course of illness can cause palpable mental suffering to both patient and staff; the same course can bring excitement and feelings of success and pride to staff during other moments and phases. With an aggregate phenomenon like individualistic migration, some persons can suffer greatly from the associated experiences while others are greatly challenged; and it is likely that many immigrants will have both kinds of experience at different moments or periods of their migrant life.

Apropos of the general point about whether pain and suffering or enjoyment and gratification of one important dimension are experienced, this depends largely on both the initial trajectory properties and the events that occur during its unfolding. An automobile accident that makes a paraplegic of a young man sociologically speaking throws him into an unending disablement/illness trajectory—into attempts to shape life under these permanent new bodily circumstances. Suffering is no stranger to such a situation. However, if the paraplegic can manage sooner or later to gain what is defined as sufficient control over his circumstances, then he may feel challenged and develop self-pride in his new achievements. I am reminded here of one paraplegic who in some sense perceives himself as cooking dinner: He plans the menu, makes out the shopping list for his wife, and from his chair in the kitchen directs her movements as she prepares the evening's meal (Corbin and Strauss 1988).

Apropos of suffering, the type of long-term biographical experience touched on just above also has been well studied as a trajectory by Fritz Schuetze (1983; see also Riemann and Schuetze 1991). Here is a simplified version of what transpires in this type of overall suffering. Persons, or even a cohort or generation, can become caught up in diverse contingencies difficult to control or even manage satisfactorily. Their responses to contingencies have unforeseen consequences, which in turn present such an array of problems that over time their biographies become increasingly marked by almost impossible difficulties. As Riemann and Schuetze express it, "One feels that one is driven, that one can only react to 'outer forces' that one does not understand any more" (1991, p. 337; see also Schuetze 1992.)

In this downward cycle, the entrapped actor, or actors if the experience is collective, seeks reasons for these deep problems and the accompanying dilemmas of existence, but those reasons prove insufficient for controlling the next steps of the biographical drama. Characteristically, there develops a sense of deep alienation from self, periods of great mental anguish or suffering, considerable instability of identity, and changed relationships with the world. Again, to use the immigrant example, even when a person chooses to immigrate, he or she may be caught up in the downward propulsion of unmanageable contingencies.

Suffering, however, although perhaps not of this duration or finality, is no stranger to courses of action with accompanying experiences that are "upward" (as with upward mobility) or "horizontal" (maintaining social position). For instance, the effort of individuals to move upward in wealth and status, as many American novels reflect, can be full of stress, anxiety, inner conflict. The suffering is experienced not only by the principal actor but by his or her family. The same can be said for persons who are struggling to maintain their positions, say in the middle class during the present recession, when many are actually or potentially unemployed.

As touched on above, trajectories that involve suffering may be collective also. For instance, members of an entire generation can have a set of anguishing experiences in response to being caught up in a series of contingencies such as attend a war (Schuetze 1992), an economic depression, or the collapse of a nation. The concept of trajectory and the theory of action it represents are useful for illuminating these kinds of collective courses of interaction, except here the local concepts pertain specifically to internal and external *biographical* processes.

THE USEFULNESS OF A THEORY OF ACTION

Here in summary form, referring both to the contents of this chapter and the previous one on assumptions, is how this interactionist theory of action can function—whether you are interested directly in using it to guide research or in a more general sense to understand the nature of human action:

- It is worth repeating, first, that all phenomena and interactions with respect to them have temporal aspects. Second, the courses phenomena take can often be analytically broken down into stages, phases, or other segments of time for more detailed analysis. And third, despite structural constraints, the interactants are actively attempting throughout these phases to shape and manage the courses through their interactions.
- To remind you also that in any situation involving attempts to shape and manage phenomena there are multiple actors, (a) giving their own meanings to a phenomenon, (b) having their own images of the course it will take, and, (c) ideas on how the course should be handled. Taken together, the meanings, images, and ideas symbolize the stances that actors bring with them to any situation.
- To suggest gathering data about and from as many of the actors as possible in order to (a) discover their various stances, (b) determine the interactional and action processes by which the stances are or are not brought into alignment, and (c) determine also their subsequent impact on action.
- To realize also how the working out of stances interactionally involves a process of self as well as other interaction. The interaction also involves bodies as well as minds and selves.
- To place interaction at the center of any study of a phenomenon and lead to discovering what actors are doing alone and together when attempting to shape and manage the course of a phenomenon.
- To capture not only the more rational aspects of interaction but the symbolic—whether the latter is relatively straightforward or com-

plex, is recognized by the interactants or not (or suspected), is a characteristic of individual or collective action, and is inclusive of the symbolic universe in which the interaction is embedded (see Chapter 6).

- To gain an analytic understanding of both the simple and complex forms of representation and their relationships to interaction (see Chapter 7).
- To think of interaction in both its novel and routine forms: meaning not only how it is usually handled, and the complicated interplay of its forms, but also the relation of each to problematic situations (see Chapter 8 specifically).
- To acknowledge that interaction takes place within a wide range of micro- and macroconditions. These conditions change over time and are handled in various ways by actors.
- To think processually by recognizing that interaction changes in response to changes in conditions.
- To determine the consequences of interaction and how some of those then become an important part of the conditions influencing the next situations or phase of interaction. (This was discussed earlier as "reciprocal impact.")

As can be seen from these points, the theory of action and its associated trajectory concepts, when taken as an analytical perspective or directing framework, give a set of general directives for knowing what questions to ask, where to go and to whom for answers, and how to interpret and organize diverse data. In conjunction with intense scrutiny of data and the generation of local concepts, they provide important elements that contribute to developing a rich, complex, and dense analysis of data.

In the next chapters, which constitute the illustrative aspects of this book, you will see how the theory's directives function to guide empirical research into and reflection about the interactions and their associated and very diverse phenomena. I have chosen to write about certain phenomena because they are of particular importance to further developing this interactionist theory of action, and because they are of special interest to me. For the most part, I have not written about them before or at least the specific aspects addressed here.

NOTES

1. See, however, the writings of another interactionist, Carl Couch, who similarly evaluates action as central. His approach to action is different, but moves in the same directions as mine (cf. Couch 1992).

2. See also Znaniecki ([1919] 1983, pp. 154–69) for a brilliant, and I think definitive, critique, of means-ends conceptions in terms of the relations of past and future actions, and old and new objects created by actions.

3. An instance is the fatefully failed project, during World War II, of the Allies to cross into Germany via the Arnheim bridge, vividly described by Cornelius Ryan (1974) in a book aptly titled "A Bridge Too Far." In the book, we follow the biographical courses and fates of a multitude of key and subsidiary participants in this massive collective trajectory.

4. For a clear contemporary critique of this dichotomy and the resultant popular positions, see Maines (1982). The previous implicit critique is perfectly visible in the earlier Pragmatists, including Znaniecki's *Cultural Reality* ([1919] 1983).

5. After reading about the conditional matrix and conditional paths, Leonard Schatzman wrote the following, which seems accurate, felicitously phrased, and consonant with the views expressed below:

The time-honored method is to relegate, inevitably, such "distant" conditions to mere "background" and "context," leaving their connections to action implicit/taken for granted. Or, as with the marxist theorists/"researchers" bring *selected* distant conditions directly into the hearth and workplace; also *directly* into interactional consciousness. The upshot of it has to do with perspective which assigns *proximity* of conditions to situation for action. Have not feminists done the same by bringing general and historic attributes of gender right into the bedroom and kitchen? So, it also raises the question of who and how (with what perspective) it is decided that some "minor" contextual component is "really" ("deemed relevant") a major condition [chosen] for action. The answer gets at the heart and problem of theory construction, of epistemology itself.It certainly does! And the answer highlights the nature of the theory of action behind the decision is "'really' a major condition [chosen] for action."

PART II

PART II

A PRELIMINARY NOTE AND ANALYSIS

Regard the next pages as a brief illustration of the complex analytic possibilities for research of an interactionist theory of action. The pages will also serve as a transition to the remaining chapters—in a sense also an introduction to their respective topics. In this preliminary note, I will analyze a case study that appeared in the *Wretched of the Earth* (1968), written by the Algerian psychiatrist, Franz Fanon. This once famous and still powerfully effective book was published during the anguishing struggle by the Algerians for liberation from French colonialism.[1]

Here is Fanon's case:

"We had been asked to give expert medical advice in a legal matter. Two young Algerians thirteen and fourteen years old, pupils in a primary school, were accused of having killed one of their European schoolmates. They admitted having done it. The crime was reconstructed, and photos were added to the record. Here one of the children could be seen holding the victim while the other struck at him with a knife. The little defendants did not go back on their declarations. We had long conversations with them. We here reproduce the most characteristic of their remarks:

a) The boy thirteen years old:
"We weren't a bit cross with him. Every Thursday we used to go and play with catapults together, on the hill above the village. He was a good friend of ours. He usn't to go to school any more because he wanted to be a mason like his father. One day we decided to kill him, because the Europeans want to kill all the Arabs. We can't kill big people. But we could kill ones like him, because he was the same age as us. We didn't know how to kill him. We wanted to throw him into a ditch, but he'd only have been hurt. So we got the knife at home and we killed him."

"But why did you pick on him?"
"Because he used to play with us. Another boy wouldn't have gone up the hill with us."

"And yet you were pals?"
"Well then, why do they want to kill us? His father is in the militia and he said we ought to have our throats cut."

"But he didn't say anything to you?"
"Him? No."

"Do you know he is dead now?"
"Yes."

"What does being dead mean?"

"When it's all finished, you go to heaven."
"Was it you that killed him?"
"Yes."
"Does having killed somebody worry you?"
"No, since they want to kill us, so . . ."
"Do you mind being in prison?"
"No."

b) The boy fourteen years old:

This young defendant was in marked contrast with his schoolfellow. He was already almost a man, and an adult in his muscular control, his appearance, and the content of his replies. He did not deny having killed either. Why had he killed? He did not reply to the question but asked me had I ever seen a European in prison. Had there ever been a European arrested and sent to prison after the murder of an Algerian? I replied that in fact I had never seen any Europeans in prison.

"And yet there are Algerians killed every day, aren't there?"
"Yes."
"So why are only Algerians found in the prisons? Can you explain that to me?"
"No. But tell me why you killed this boy who was your friend?"
"I'll tell you why. You've heard tell of the Rivet business?"
"Yes."
"Two of my family were killed then. At home, they said that the French had sworn to kill us all, one after the other. And did they arrest a single Frenchman for all those Algerians who were killed?"
"I don't know."
"Well, nobody at all was arrested. I wanted to take to the mountains, but I was too young. So X— and I said we'd kill a European."
"Why?"
"In your opinion, what should we have done?"
"I don't know. But you are a child and what is happening concerns grown-up people."
"But they kill children too . . ."
"That is no reason for killing your friend."
"Well, kill him I did. Now you can do what you like."
"Had your friend done anything to harm you?"
"Not a thing."
"Well?"
"Well, there you are . . ." (pp. 270–72)

Engestroem notes that "It is not easy to deal with a case like this analytically. One experiences a mixture of moral condemnation, anxiety and pity" (1984, p. 263). He remarks that "Fanon himself states that the causes behind disorders like this [case] are 'the bloodthirsty and pitiless atmosphere, the generalization of inhuman practices and the firm impression that people have been caught up in a veritable Apocalypse'" (p. 263, citing Fanon 1968, p. 202).

You may not agree with Engestroem's characterization of readers' reactions, but probably you could not have read it without some degree of emotional upset. The killing by children is bad enough; killing a friend is worse—and deceptively, and killing as a reflection of the killing by adults! How then to analyze this emotionally disturbing event?

In Fritz Schuetze's terminology (1992), perhaps we could begin by saying that the Algerians and the French are caught up in a *collective trajectory* (a "veritable Apocalypse"). The boys' shared course of action is a small part of that larger trajectory, having its own trajectorylike structure: with trajectory projections (revenge through killing), a trajectory scheme (a plan for the killing), parallel biographical concepts, and so on. Analysis can proceed within this general frame of conceptualization, but also in terms specific to the action sequence itself.

The intention of my brief analysis is less to generate and relate explanatory concepts—as ordinarily would be done when analyzing data—than to adumbrate important phenomena discussed in later chapters. These include body, thought processes, symbolism, social world, arenas, representation, and work: All are important features of the tragic action taken by these Algerian boys. The perspective from which I have analyzed the action might be summarized by the phrase: "representing our respective people—Algerian and French, oppressed and oppressor."

The younger child remarks, "We weren't a bit cross with him [the French friend]" and the older one says "Not a thing" when asked whether his friend had done anything to harm him. These are key phrases to understanding what the killing means to the boys. So we might hypothesize that they have either killed a friend despite his being a friend, or that his being their friend is irrelevant to their action. Each boy makes quite clear that the friendship is entirely secondary, even irrelevant, to another pressing consideration; namely, that he is a European who stood in a particular relationship to them during their action. He represented the oppressing European adults, who in turn were oppressing and killing Algerians.

The symbolism that the boys carry into their course of action is just that. The Europeans are killing "us." Hence, I will interpret their action as a carrying out, symbolically, of an act that is reciprocally equivalent to the actions of European adults, and also straightforwardly equivalent to what their male kin are doing to the European adults. (I will say more about this below.) This symbolism is carried forward in time, since after the killing both boys confess to no remorse or guilt but presumably would have admitted only to pride—if they had been interviewed more extensively—in having carried out their mission. Indeed, we can sense this fairly clearly in at least the older boy's remarks.

The original symbolism carried into the boys' course of action is, technically speaking, a contextual condition; but there are others. They tell us what those were, indirectly or directly. The plan for, or projected aim of, killing is a contextual condition that is internal to the course of action itself. Other contextual conditions bearing rather immediately on the initiation and projection of the shared action are (1) the boys' reasoning that as children they are too weak to kill an adult; (2) nevertheless they are able to kill a child; and (3) the most feasible target is their friend. Another contextual condition is the older child's not being able to go to the mountains (presumably as an adult rebel fighter); this allowed him to be present for the shared action—one that surely would not have taken place without his participation and quite possibly initiation.

Then there are intervening and generally broader conditions that bear, though less directly, on the course of action. The children tell the interviewer indirectly what those conditions are. Their parents and other kin are constantly talking about the French killing them, and presumably about their own retaliation. The boys live in this milieu of intense tension and embattlement that also includes passionate and aggressive discussions of what to do, what might be done, and what was done. This all reflects the broader condition of the historical moment in Algerian-French relationships, both internally to the country and externally in terms of the French colonial system in both its historical and contemporary forms. (Note that this form of colonialism allowed French and Algerian children to play together, at least when they were of the same gender, until at least the mid-teens.) There may be further intervening conditions that affected the boys' actions—such as the Algerian family structure or the town or city in which they lived, but in the case description there are no direct clues bearing on those conditions. Possibly relevant also are the looseness of most teenage friendships, for if the boys had been ten years older they might have established such intimate bonds with their friend as to preclude their killing him as a symbol of their protest against colonial oppression. My analysis here is too brief to do justice to the complexity of conditional influences bearing on the boys' course of action, but it should remind you of the discussion in the previous chapter bearing on the conditional matrix.

Let us return now to the course of action itself. Not enough information is given in the case description so that phases of action can be clearly distinguished. What can be assumed, however, from the children's interviews is that they planned the killing: they would go to the usual place [space], at the usual playtime, and prepare or actually play as usual [routine]. Indeed they reasoned that going to this space to play was the only way they could get someone (their friend) into a killable position.

We can probably also assume that as part of their planning they had individual and collective imageries of their action-to-be, including what mode of killing would or would not be successful [technology]. The photo of the reconstructed killing makes evident that the boys had decided who was to hold their friend (the stronger boy) and who was to wield the knife (division of labor—a work process). They also had initially to discuss whom to kill; or at least one of the boys had to imagine that it was possible to kill their friend and then persuade the other. (The case description is silent on the mechanics of the decision.) They may possibly have argued with each other about how to kill their friend, but at least we know they chose in terms of an everyday technology—true they had never before used a knife for killing but were familiar with knives; they possibly had seen them used in movies in murders, and had probably seen them used to kill chickens or other animals. In this course of action, an essential strategy was to keep the secret of their intentions from their victim: "closed awareness context" in technical terminology (Glaser and Strauss 1964).

All of these considerations, whether speculative on my part or reflected in the case description, are adumbrations of phenomena discussed in later pages, or touched on in the preceding chapter as with the instance of orders (technological, sentimental, informational, and work). To these considerations can be added that any argumentation between the boys about their private action reflects the wider public arena. Also, please note that a body process figures prominently in their action: Killing is a form of body abuse carried out in the service of identity—in this instance, not to destroy their friend's identity but to injure the collective identity of the Europeans and to enhance that of the Algerians, for whom they are acting as representing agents.

My analysis closes with just one more set of points: These concern the consequences of the killing. Fanon does not tell us how the murder and the identity of the boys was discovered. If it had remained a secret, we need only have considered consequences for the perpetrators and for the victim's family, who would not have known the circumstances leading to the boy's death. Because the killers' culpability was discovered, analysis of this case faces questions about consequences because of the gap in pertinent data on these in Fanon's report. (As a psychiatrist, he was concerned only with clinical issues, and also in this book with political issues arising out of colonialism.) Discussion of the killing probably was followed by a range of questions pertaining to consequences, with which an analyst—especially one concerned with the phenomenon of representation—might also be concerned. What were the consequences not only for the boy but for their families, the wider world of Algerian natives, the

French settler community, the relationships of Algerians and French set-
tlers and the colonial government, and quite possibly for the wider
French public and the French government?

So the kind of analysis presented here raises a number of additional
questions, but also suggests what future interviews (about this or similar
cases) might additionally focus upon. Generally speaking, in a substantive study (whether of children's "crimes," "colonial civil wars," or anything else) analysis of a single case would be used only as an initial step
in the total investigation. However, this is how I would, using the framework addressed in the foregoing chapters, go about the analysis of the
initial data.

In the remaining chapters, I will take up a series of topics including
those mentioned earlier. Essentially essays, the chapters are intended to
suggest the usefulness of this interactionist theory of action for conceptualizing important phenomena *and* to provide illustrations of it "at
work." Almost all of the materials used in these chapters are unpublished, though occasionally I have quoted or cited published pages where
they were especially relevant.

NOTES

1.   One reason I have used this particular material is that the it has also been
analyzed by Engestroem (1984), using a "cultural-historical theory of activity"
that derives principally from the innovative research and writings of two Soviet
psychologists, Vygotsky (1978) and Luria (1978). This theory of activity is being
developed further by contemporary researchers, especially in the fields of education and psychology. There seems to be much overlap between this theory of
activity and the interactionist theory of action, and both have their grounding
directly in research. I am not paralleling Engestroem's analysis to compete with
it, but am analyzing Fanon's case because it interested me so much when reading
it in Engestroem's book. However, some readers may wish to read both analyses
for their similarities and differences. One difference is that his analysis is organized largely around "the transformation of play through the intrusion of genocide."

Chapter 3

Work and the Intersection of Forms of Action

Work as interaction is the central theme of sociological and social psychological study of work.

—Everett Hughes, *The Sociological Eye*

There is something about constraints that distinguishes work. . . . The work part comes in when you have to operate under constraints, apply effort. . . . Something you have to make yourself do, even if you love it.

—Leigh Star, personal communication

[S]o how could work not be charming that presented itself as daily beauty?

—Henry James, *The Turn of the Screw*

The linguistic and symbolic nature of activity ensures that the work done by humans is radically different than that of other species, no matter how marvelously organized this is. Human work is such a pivotal activity that the discipline of economics could not exist without a focus on it; as for sociology, it has its roots in early but still well cited founding fathers, Durkheim, Weber and Marx. Contemporary sociologists produce a steady stream of research about aspects of work that are of theoretical and practical interest.

Work is only one of a host of forms of action, but such a significant one that a theory of action must address it directly *as interaction*. It should also, I reason, address a set of questions pertaining to work as only one of many forms of action: How does work intersect with those other forms? And what difference does it make if students of work would look more systematically and in theoretical terms at the intersections? Those issues will be explored in this chapter. In the earlier sections, the focus will be on work as a form of action; in later sections, the two intersectional questions are our center of attention.

Once again I will begin by touching base with the Pragmatist tradition, in this instance with Mead's discussion of cooperative interaction (1934 especially). Recollect the cluster of concepts that he coined to analyze this universal human activity. These include the verbal and nonverbal conversation of gestures, taking the role of the other, language, significant symbols and meaning, the generalized other, and the interplay of the I and the Me. Mead places the organization of cooperative acts firmly in group settings and in the larger society. He speaks of "the various larger phases of the general social process which constitute the group's life and of which . . . projects are specific manifestations" (1934, p. 155). Mead's concepts constitute tools with which we can generate a general understanding of the mechanics of cooperative interaction and also reference the broader contexts that affect interaction.

A sociologist thinking substantively rather than in Mead's more abstract language might note that cooperative activity characterizes every form of interaction, at least when it involves two or more interactants. This is so whether, say, it be ritual, ceremony, lovemaking, dancing, negotiating, playing sports or games, or engaging in social movements or casual conversation. Work is, of course, among the most prominent of these. (Please note also that, though in this chapter I shall mostly refer to "action," this often translates into "interaction.")

Now, a brief definition of work is needed. The *Random House Dictionary of the English Language* has supplied a conventional one, as quoted below, albeit the lexicographer seems to have assumed rather than stated that work can be a cooperative affair as well as an individual one:

Work: 1. exertion of effort directed to produce or accomplish something. 2. . . . something to be made or done, a task or undertaking. (Stein and Urdang 1981, p. 1644) [To "exertion of effort," one might wish to emphasize the output of energy involved in work even to the extent of exhaustion; also the time that work consumes, whether a great amount or relatively little for "something to be made or done."]

WORK AS RATIONAL AND ITS RATIONALIZATION

Very frequently when social scientists write about work, the organization of work, and work processes, they focus on their rational aspects: planning, goals, procedures and other means to reach goals, and so forth. Admittedly work is not always fully rational; therefore much of the literature is devoted, explicitly or implicitly, to improving either its rationalization/efficiency (through further rationalizing of its procedures or context) or its equity (again through rational changes to make a more equitable distribution of tasks and rewards).

Elihu Gerson (1977) has suggested the following as elements of the rationalization of work: (1) clear, unambiguous, mutually compatible goals; (2) predictable inputs; (3) component tasks that are articulated in an unambiguous manner; and (4) "in every situation, the conduct of the activity is unambiguously evaluated." He argues that there are four basic classes of inherently nonrationalizable tasks: (1) policy tasks in which there are multiple, vague, or conflicting goals; (2) engineering tasks in which the inputs are inherently unpredictable; (3) managerial tasks in which the articulation of component activities is ambiguous; and (4) evaluative tasks in which the relationship between means and ends is not perfectly clear—hence outcomes cannot be evaluated accurately. If so, that covers a very great amount of the work done daily in any organization—or nation.

In fact, there are a number of major difficulties of conceiving all work within a rationalistic framework. These are detailed in the following, where the authors were writing about medical and nursing work in hospitals:

Alas a number of conditions affecting medical production mitigate against its rationalization [and] the *sources* of these conditions are even more striking evidence of the magnitude of hazards besetting the "good coordination" of medical work.

First, let us begin with [the courses of illness] themselves, for they constitute a prime source of potential disruption. An illness . . . however simple in appearance, however experienced the health personnel in handling it, can prove unpredictable. . . .

A second source . . . is part [illness course] and part organizational in nature. . . . It is immensely difficult . . . to standardize [a ward and its work] by disease and [medical] condition: realistically, only very specialized wards can [do this]. . . . So . . . a host of potentially disruptive conditions will threaten the articulation of work for each [patient's illness].

A third source is related to the second. There is actual or potential competition among patients for available resources, notably the staff's time, attention and skills. . . .

The patients themselves constitute a source of potentially disruptive conditions. . . . The degree of disruption and the kind will depend on the contingent aspects of how, when, and where the patient entered the [staff's self-circumscribed] division of labor. The entrance of the patient is what makes medical work *fundamentally* nonrationalizable.

A fifth source is medical technology, which harbors a host of conditions that can spawn contingencies affecting the articulation of the . . . work. . . .

A sixth and very potent source of disruptive conditions is the hospital's organization. . . .

A seventh source is the interaction of various types of work . . . for some of this interaction will threaten effective articulation. . . .

An eighth source . . . is the thorny problem of how to evaluate work performed. . . . [E]valuative dissensus leads in more or less degree to the disarticulation of the . . . work.

Finally over the course of the [illness] there may be . . . an explicit or implicit reconstruction of the patient's self. Thus new "outside" commitments, biographical developments, and the like are very likely to intrude upon the staff's . . . work. (Strauss et al. 1985, pp. 153–55)

This flawed approach to work as rational action meets up with another difficulty insofar as workers may encounter contingencies among whose sources are the workers themselves. Unforeseen consequences of their work may affect them adversely, or bring about changes of their attitudes toward working conditions or toward the work itself. Inevitably in some kinds of work, the relationships among workers evolve. (Perhaps the mass production line is an exception, though not totally.) This evolution results in still other contingencies that affect the maintaining or improving of rationality, efficiency, and quality control. In short, the rational and rationalized aspects of work are obviously important, but are neither all important nor sometimes the most interesting, and certainly not the most profound aspects of work that social scientists need to understand.

Furthermore, specific instances of work activity always take place within some context that influences how the activity is carried out, by whom, for what purposes, when, and with what consequences. This is so whether or not the setting for work is an institution [("the" government, "the" family), an organization (an agency, a business firm), a formal group (a committee), an informal or even temporary group (responsive people after an auto accident)]. Even work by a single individual takes place in some setting with discernible contextual properties. Most work anyhow is not done in an ivory tower, for the tasks of one worker are related to those of others. The collective work is also usually related to other lines of work or other projects. Inevitably the context is subject to change—either through work processes themselves or from external contingencies that bear upon the original contextual conditions.

HISTORY WITHIN THE WORK

History is also crucial to the work in the sense that the contextual conditions *and* the work itself have histories. The histories enter, so to speak, as sedimentation into the context and the work itself. Consider the example of American slavery in the eighteen and nineteenth century: Any slave before the Civil War understood, and any of his or her descendants since will understand, that the labor or work of blacks (African Americans) was and is profoundly and directly affected by the context of slavery and later by discriminatory racial relations in the United States. The immense importance of discrimination is also emphasized by feminists apropos of the work of women, though its specific forms change under different historical conditions.

Exploitation and power relations aside, history is embedded in both obvious and subtle ways in work relations and in work itself. If the work takes place within an organization, the organization has had a history; or if it is a new organization then there is another history or histories to which it is reacting in the form of preceding or contemporary organizations and their rationales. The same is equally true for suborganizational units. For instance, every hospital ward and type of ward has its own history. Components in that history are the technologies and procedures inherited from their innovators elsewhere that are now adapted and developed further at this site of the borrowing organization. Affecting the work too—the hospital is an especially good place to observe the next point—are the histories of the social worlds (Chapter 9) from which the workers come. In the hospitals, one can see the histories of the various professions and their specialties embodied in the attitudes, gestures, activities, and often the bodies of the respective professionals working (more or less) cooperatively on the same wards (cf. Wiener 1979).

Among the most subtle instances of histories, because even less visible usually, are those of scientific technological usage. Typically scientists in one discipline or specialty invent a technical procedure or instrument, for specific purposes. But then a cross-disciplinary diffusion takes place. Another discipline or specialty finds a use for the borrowed item. However, the specific and well known original uses and limitations of the item are "blackboxed"—they are forgotten, ignored, or not realized by the new users. Thus history is rendered invisible, though embodied, buried in current work with these transported objects and activities. [See Star (1989a, 1989b) and Fujimura (1987, 1988), for detailed studies of these points.]

ROUTINES AND CONTINGENCIES

History leads easily into the topic of routine and routines. Those developed by scientists are especially revealing, since they are generally viewed as the antithesis of routine and the embodiment of creativity. A scientist who has borrowed from another discipline an established procedure or instrument is often enabled, through its use, to make routine certain aspects of his or her own work. In other words, the borrowed item as converted into a routine enables work to get done that might otherwise be impossible to accomplish or makes it easier, faster, or more accurate. Repetition will, of course, almost inevitably lead to the routinization of some or most of the work. Life in a new organization until its members build a fund of standard operating procedures is likely to be relatively chaotic. In any organization, if routines break down then the organization and its performance will be affected.

A more subtle point, however, is that routines are always in danger of breaking down in the face of actual situations. No routine can be fully appropriate to every situation for which it was designed. So the past histories of routines carry inherent weaknesses as well as strengths. A parallel point is that by having learned routines as sets of skills the worker has certain trained incapacities when faced with new situations, especially situations that are radically different or new. Also, as discussed earlier (Chapters 1 and 2) every course of action, including those involving work, will over time produce contingencies that are both external to the action and internal to it. These contingencies—representing new and often unexpected conditions—call for adaptation, adjustment, or change of some routines and require new actions. In time, some of the new become habitual, become crystallized as part of the total routine. (For a more elaborate discussion see the section on routines in Chapter 8.)

THE CENTRALITY OF INTERACTION FOR WORK

Consider next Everett Hughes's assertion that for the study of work, the central theme is "work as interaction." If this assertion is taken literally, then work and interaction are basically equivalent; but of course they are not. Yet Hughes's phrase does raise a significant question: What is the role of interaction in the carrying out of work? Hughes never directly addressed that question and only a few of the Chicago interactionists have done so (and few non-Chicagoans), although less abstractly than I will here (cf. Becker 1970; Bucher and Schatzman 1964; Stelling and Bucher 1972; Dalton 1954). One reason for the delay in examining this issue by Chicagoans and their descendants was that the prime focus of this sociological tradition was on understanding occupations and professions, and for the most part they studied patterns of work and work relationships in respect to those social units. Only in the more recent studies have the micromechanics of work been thought of as a special and significant focus in the research (see Becker 1982; Freidson 1976; Clarke 1990a, 1990b; Fagerhaugh, Strauss, Suczek, and Wiener 1987; Fujimura 1987, 1988, Forthcoming; Gasser 1986; Gerson 1983; Gerson and Star 1986; Glaser 1976; Star 1989a, 1989b).

In line with this sociological tradition, and intrigued by this important question, Juliet Corbin and I have addressed it recently, with regard to work in organizations, though it would apply generally to other social units (1993). I will briefly summarize our answer to it here.

Major Concepts

Several interrelated concepts are especially useful in thinking about the question: *articulation, arrangements, the process of working things out,* and *stance.*

Articulation stands for the coordination of lines of work. This is accomplished by means of the interactional process of working out and carrying through of work-related arrangements. Articulation varies in degree and duration depending upon the degree to which arrangements are in place and operative (Strauss 1988).

Arrangements refer to the agreements established among various actors; in organizations these would include those between subunits, such as departments or divisions. What are the arrangements about? They are made with regard to the actions necessary for carrying out the work, as conceived by the participants to it. The arrangements pertain to such questions as what work, by whom, where done, for how long, for what payback, for what purposes, and according to what standards? The arrangements may be concerned also with other issues, such as what resources, technology, and supplies, with what information, in what space, and with what other backup services that may be needed to do the work? An encompassing organization itself also creates and maintains arrangements with other organizations in order to keep the supply of information, services, and resources flowing to itself, then to be distributed within the organization. Only by virtue of this multilayered, complex network of arrangements within and between an organization's subunits can articulation occur. When arrangements eventually break down, so does the articulation.

Even when institutionalized as policies and procedures, arrangements are not necessarily permanent. To begin with, although new arrangements may be worked out in long-standing organizations by experienced persons, it is not possible for them to forecast all of the structural and organizational conditions that will affect the arrangements and the subsequent performance of work. Some conditions surface only after the work has started. Also, it is often found necessary to make adjustments in the arrangements when responding to fluctuations of daily contingencies, such as understaffing due to illness or vacation, a sudden increase in demand for a resource, or a breakdown in technology. Although arrangements may be working well, nevertheless changes of broader structural and organizational conditions inevitably bring about the reworking of arrangements.

Their stability depends upon the structural/organizational conditions present when they are being worked out and then made operative. In response to these conditions, the workers have the ability to manipulate, use to their advantage, avoid, or in other ways manage the conditions. The greater is the ability to control particular conditions that sustain the arrangements, the greater then is some actor's ability to shape the arrangements themselves and to maintain them once they are in place. Broader structural and organizational conditions become significant in the arrangement-making process in relationship to workers' abilities to control such matters as resources (kinds, amounts, distribution, use); division of labor (who does what tasks, when, where, and how); flow of information; standards; and planning (what is to be done, when, where, at what cost).

The third concept, mentioned earlier, is *working things out*. This refers to the interactional process through which arrangements are established, kept going, and revised. This process consists of a series of strategies and counterstrategies taken by participants, in response to what is said or done by others before and after the actual work begins. Strategies include negotiating, making compromises, discussing, educating, convincing, lobbying, manipulating, threatening, and coercing (Strauss 1978).

Stance, a fourth useful concept, denotes the *position* taken by each participant toward both the working-out process and the work itself. The position is taken in relationship to perceived power for gaining control over the broader structural and organizational conditions upon which the arrangements stand. Thus it can influence the arrangements themselves.

An actor's stance is expressed through the interactional strategies used during the working-out process unless, for some covert reason, the stance is deliberately misrepresented. The stance will shift and change during the working-out process in response to stances taken by others. So strategies may be aimed at gaining, sharing in, and regaining power in order to work out the best possible arrangement(s) for oneself (or organization or suborganization). Each actor, of course, wants but does not always have the balance of power in the interaction. Just because a person or organization is in a position of legitimate authority or power does not necessarily mean that this actor can control the arrangement making. Nor is there any guarantee that any actor who enters the interaction with a favorable balance of power will end up with an arrangement that maintains or increases this power.

Concerning power, what enters into the stances are not only the perceptions of power to influence broader conditions but also the history of the workers' past interactions, the meanings of their arrangements to them, their perceptions of how the arrangements should work, their knowledge about the nature of the work and what is necessary to carry it out, and also their personal or organizational values, ideologies, and interactional skills. Each arrangement-making process is built also upon history, including personal histories, and the history of the organization, the interactions within and between departments, the power distribution within the organization, and the past experiences with both the current arrangement and similar ones.

Perhaps the argument to this point should be summarized. The performance of work within any organization, whether the organization is constituted formally or informally, is a coordinated collective act (Blumer 1948). Since different people are doing different types of work, there must be *arrangements* in place about what work is to be done, to what standards, in what space, during what time period, with what resources, by whom, and with what payback, in order for *articulation* to occur. Arrangements are arrived at, kept going, and revised through a *working-out process*, which includes interactional strategies such as negotiation, discussion, educating, lobbying, manipulating, threatening, and coercing. The particular strategy chosen during the course of the working-out process is influenced by the *stances* taken by various actors. Stance represents the position taken by actors toward the work and the working-out process and is comprised of a combination of the perceived ability to influence the structural/organizational conditions and the particular meanings, images, and history of interactions of actors.

Therefore, when we say that work performance requires interaction, we are speaking of interaction in both its broader *and* narrower senses. Interaction refers first of all to the articulated collective act of work performance. Interaction also refers and to the strategies used in working out the arrangements that allow for the articulation of those collective acts within any given structural/organizational context.

Hospitals, for example, like other complex organizations have a variety of people doing various types of work, which must be articulated through arrangements. The work of a nursing staff requires coordinated and cooperative arrangements with physicians and other departments such as pharmacy, engineering, housekeeping, dietary, surgery, central supply, X-ray, and various labs. Without arrangements, the nursing staff could not ensure that treatment plans were available and up-to-date, that medications were on the unit when needed, and that patients were fed and could be operated on, that rooms were kept clean, that sufficient man-power and supplies were on hand, and that equipment was kept in working order. These arrangements are usually worked out within and between departments through a series of interactional strategies that commonly but not always involve negotiation and persuasion. When arrangements break down, as they so often do because of contingencies, the breakdowns can result in problems for articulating the work. The work may be delayed, suffer in quality, and sometimes not get done at all. This makes it difficult to articulate work within and between units/departments and can lead to conflict and the need for further arrange-ment making.

A hospital pharmacy, to give a specific example, was understaffed on a particular evening shift because two pharmacists had suddenly become ill. Also, several medical emergencies had arisen to which the pharmacy needed to give immediate attention. Consequently, a routine intravenous medication ordered by a medical unit arrived too late for administration by the evening shift. Meanwhile the physician was anxious that his pa-tient be medicated, so arrangements to administer the medication had speedily to be made with the night shift nurses by those working on the evening shift. However, this particular medication required constant monitoring of the patient while the drug was infusing. Since even fewer nurses were working at night than during evening hours, the night staff's stance was one of anger and frustration. They had neither the power to bring in more personnel nor a choice in whether or not to administer the medication prescribed through the physician's order. They questioned the evening shift's delay in giving the medication: "Why did evening wait for the med to be delivered? Why didn't someone go to pharmacy and get it?" In turn, the evening shift tried to convince the night shift that the delay was not their fault. In the end, the night shift had to make temporary arrangements to fit this task into their routine activities. How-ever, the next morning the night shift complained bitterly to the head nurse, who tried to identify the cause of the problem and to smooth over the conflict between the shifts. She also had to answer to the physician's protest that the medication had been given tardily.

The Interactional Mechanics of
Arrangement Making

Just as arrangements are routinized through policies and procedures, so are the patterns of work. People working together over time establish such patterns. Sometimes these are so well established that there is no need to work out new arrangements or rework old ones in response to minor organizational or personal contingencies.

For instance, on a medical ward the nurses had long worked together, and so had developed a flexible division of labor patterned in accordance with the number of staff available on any particular day. At the beginning of each morning, they immediately moved into those established patterns without discussion. Yet initially those arrangements had to be worked out, agreed upon, tried out, and then kept going by the staff. Let us look next at the interactional mechanics of how arrangements are originally worked out.

Recollect that each actor, whether person or organizational unit, comes to the arrangement-making situation with a stance. For sustained work to proceed, the various stances must be brought into some degree of alignment. Agreement must be reached about the nature of the work to be done, its meaning, the standards pertaining to it, how it is to be done, with what resources, and so forth. Not that there must be complete consensus; but regardless of whether or not an arrangement is brought about by domination or negotiation, there must be some agreement about what actions are to be taken, when, where, and why. Otherwise no arrangement will be made. To arrive at an arrangement then involves arriving at a common definition of the situation. This means that discrepant understandings (such as who has what power to control structural organizational conditions and a willingness to share or relinquish some of that control; or expectations about what is to be done.) must be discovered, thought about, and ironed out through interactional strategies.

Ordinarily, the first step is that each participant *defines* what is involved in the arrangement, such as what needs to be done, by whom, what resources are needed, what one has to offer, what one expects from others, and who has power to take what action. Defining gives rise to the stance taken, which is then expressed through interactional strategies. The next step is *interpreting* the stance of the other(s) as reflected in the strategies used. Actors respond by continuing with or revising their own stances and associated strategies. The process of defining, interpreting, and acting in response continues until arrangements are reached.

Since any given arrangement may involve many different issues (who, where, when, how), and because participants may take different positions toward each issue, the working-out process can be long and complex. During the process, the balance of power may shift back and forth. Broader structural and organizational conditions enter by influencing actors' perceptions of their power to control what they have to offer or work with in the working-out process.

For example, because of economic retrenchment in the hospital, one hard-pressed head nurse could only offer compensatory time off to her staff rather than time-and-a-half salary as compensation for working an extra shift when the unit was short of staff. Without the power to offer compensatory money, she had difficulty in recruiting employees to work then. Consequently, she expended much time telephoning possibly relevant people, trying to work things out.

To actors themselves, the working-out process appears to be a series of strategies and counterstrategies aimed at convincing, educating, discussing, negotiating, threatening, extracting, demanding, and/or dominating. By interacting strategically, they are attempting to shape the specifics of a given arrangement, thus to exert control over the work, resources, and working conditions.

Besides the original stances with which participants approach their making of agreements, the interaction itself—unless brief or simple—will generate additional *specific interactional positions.* These pertain to aspects of—or issues associated with—the arrangement that is being worked out.

Another brief example can illustrate this initial working-out process. On one of the surgical wards, the staff's work was highly articulated. Since surgeons are busiest during the morning hours, the head nurse had arranged beforehand with the surgical team for a set of standard orders to guide the nurses' work. Thereby they could complete all of the routine nursing work in the quiet morning hours—and be ready for the early afternoon hours when the newly operated on patients would be returning from the recovery room and surgeons would be making their rounds.

However, there had recently been changes in the hospital's admission policies. These were in response to legislated changes from Washington that free care of veterans be limited to service-connected disabilities or problems. Hence, suddenly fewer surgical but more medical patients were being admitted to the hospital. To handle the overflow of medical patients, the admissions staff routed them to the surgical ward. Unfortunately, the internists tended to begin their rounds on the medical floors, thus arriving at the surgical floors about the time that the surgical patients were coming from the recovery room. This convergence threw the nurses on the receiving unit into turmoil. There were new medical orders to deal with, new surgical patients to monitor, and changing staff shifts although these were staffed with fewer evening nurses. As a consequence, medication errors were being made, work was not getting done, and the safety of the new surgical patients was compromised. The nurses as well as the physicians then began to complain.

Faced with this problem, the head nurse approached the head of the medical team to negotiate a change in policy. She was willing to accept the overflow of medical patients, if the physicians would leave a set of standing orders such as those left routinely by the surgical team. In this way, they could do much of the nursing work in the morning, when the unit was quiet. They would only have to make minor adjustments in the care given in the afternoons when the internists made their rounds. For the medical physicians this was a new kind of arrangement; they were unsure of what this would mean in terms of patient care or what problems it might create for themselves. So they were reluctant to agree to this arrangement.

The head nurse had to convince them that this arrangement would be advantageous for everyone. The unit would continue to receive medical patients, their care would be easier to articulate with the care required by surgical patients, the quality of care would improve for both types of patient, and the physicians would not have to hurry their rounds on the medical units in order to see their other patients who were housed on the surgical floor. After much discussion with the physicians about what their standing orders would entail, an arrangement was made that satisfied the surgical nurses. Some problems still remained because the lines of medical and surgical work were so different, yet overall the work on this ward proceeded more smoothly, with less error, and with less interpersonal conflict.

This working out of arrangements is a repeated process since *re*working will occur. Sometimes, however, the reworking fails and with discernible negative consequences for carrying out work. In addition, what makes the working and reworking of arrangements within organizations so complicated is that more than two parties may be involved, and these may be groups or organizations (and suborganizations) of various size and complexity. This requires networks of arrangements about what work, when, where, to what standards, and so on, will be necessary.

That mode of thinking about interaction in relation to work makes quite clear that any rules, regulations, or agreements covering aspects of work are constraining but not fully determining of the work itself. Some types of work situations (mass production, for instance) approach the limits of tight restraint; others set sharp limits on changes workers can make in the work (slavery, concentration camps); but none can be totally determining, and much contemporary work is assuredly shapeable and shaped by workers, at least to some degree.

WORK IN RELATION TO OTHER FORMS OF ACTION

In this and the next section, I argue that work and other forms of action are not sharply separated, one from the other; but that if we conceive of them as complexly related, fused or combined, our analysis of each form will become more powerful.

Several years ago, my co-authors and I (Strauss et al. 1985), who had been studying work in hospitals, wrote extensively about several types of

work observed there, including safety, comfort, "sentimental," and technological work. This led us at the close of the book to broaden the concept
of work well beyond its traditional boundaries. I will quote from those
paragraphs because they will set the scene for my comments in the pages
below. The title of the section from which the quotation is taken is "The
Sociology of Work—But What Work?" You will see that the quotation
(Strauss et al. 1985, pp. 289-90) does not equate work with every form of
action; rather it points toward the overlapping or combination of all these
forms.

> Most work goes on within or in connection with organizations. And a great
> proportion of work is done by people who have various occupational or
> professional titles. So it is not surprising that sociologists and other social
> scientists who write about work do not separate their analyses or commen-
> taries or critiques of work from considerations of work-place and occupa-
> tions/professions. Indeed, most writings that comprise the "sociology of
> work" turn out, on scanning, really to be about occupations or professions
> and the organizations worked in. . . . Not incidentally . . . there are descrip-
> tions and analyses of work done by members of professions, occupations,
> and by organizational members, but intense focus on the work itself—its
> task sequences, its organization, its many variants and their conditions and
> consequences, its articulation, its evaluative processes—is far less usual. . . .
> The literature of the "sociology of medicine" is quite representative of
> emphases in the more encompassing field which, in fact, is traditionally
> called—all in one breath—"the sociology of work and occupations," a link-
> age exemplified by the journal of that name.
>   Those observations are not so startling. . . . A more unconventional ob-
> servation is that work which is not linked with work places or which is not
> paid work has generally not been regarded as work, as Freidson . . . and
> various women reformers and scholars have remarked, by official agencies
> such as the U. S. Census Bureau, by the general public, or even by social
> scientists. We shall carry the line of argument still further. . . . We suggest
> that studies of work, done from whatever disciplinary perspective, should
> include *any enterprise*, even when those engaged in the enterprise do not
> think of it as involving work. We have in mind not only enterprises like
> some touched on [here] (dying with grace, living as decently as possible
> despite an intrusive illness), but the thousand and one lines of action that
> anyone can quickly imagine, if one thinks of lines of action as lines of *work*:
> escape from a prisoner-of-war camp, a political campaign, a fund-raising
> campaign by unpaid volunteers, or further out on the margins of what
> seems at first blush nonwork; going through therapy, keeping a marriage
> going, raising a child properly, making a quilt or doing a puzzle, learning
> to ski or skate.
>   Any or all of those activities may be fun (one's paid work can be fun, too),
> but they also involve some, even tremendous, amounts of work. Each can
> usefully be conceived of as a [course of action], with its arc of work and

implicated tasks. . . . A genuine sociology of work can be germane to many activities not now studied by students of work.

These suggestions for extending the concept of work struck one reader as representing too broad a set of claims for the concept; it would not be useful thus conceived (Davis 1986). In his review, he questioned whether we were not making work coterminous with all of action. We were *not* then nor will I do so here. Strictly speaking, work as defined in my dictionary, as previously noted, does leave open for social scientists the question of whether it is useful to name some actions as work when it does not occur to the actors themselves that what they are doing is work. Without giving an answer to that—which I sense might foreclose on understanding the interplay of work and other forms of action—let us at least be aware that situationally there may be a difference of opinion between the researcher and the actor, and to note when and why this occurs.

Obviously, work is only one of many forms of action. Indeed, as a friend of mine says, "Work is certainly a very important part of life but if it were the only thing then I'd check out of life tomorrow!" Nonetheless, as I replied to her, work should not be so narrowly construed as to simply raise images of hard labor, routine acts, or intensely pursued enterprises, and should certainly not always be conceived of in sharp opposition to or even inevitably separate from other forms of action.

Besides work, other forms that come readily to mind might include play, games, casual conversation, "expressive" action, very "emotional" action, fantasizing whether by individuals or collectivities, passing rumors, following fads, and forms of "collective behavior" like mass panic, crowd behavior, or nationalistic hysteria, and symbolic actions such as the sacrificial and the devotional. None of those actions are equivalent to work. Nevertheless, in many instances aspects of work may be associated with them. They may sometimes even depend on work for their initiation, continuance, or completion.

Yet, frequently work and nonwork activities are viewed even by social scientists as dichotomous, the activities being reified, as in work and play, work and expressive action, rational or impersonal work and irrational or emotional action. It is *not at all* necessary to claim the primacy of work in order to realize that these dichotomies and their inherent antinomies can block a deeper understanding of the relationships between work and other forms of action.

Consider the recreational activity called "going on a picnic." The very phrase conjures up—at least for many women, who are usually in charge of preparations for this "fun" expedition—planning the menu, shopping for food and other supplies, cooking or at least cleaning and packing the food, and so on until the end of the picnic when these now very tired workers are often relieved that their ordeal is over. Yet I am not asserting that picnics can't be fun for everyone involved nor that the women think that they are "working," or even that picnics can't involve a bare minimum of actual work. From a sociological perspective, aspects of the picnic do follow the dictionary definition of work, and sometimes the participants see some of the event in terms of that definition too.

Many recreational activities may involve work, as in planning, making preparations, getting to the site, parking the car, getting home. The skier or the concertgoer may not regard these activities as involving work, but if the trip to the ski slope is found arduous after a tiring week at the office then the drive there is likely to seem very much like work. Indeed, imagining it beforehand may lead the skier to decide not to put out the requisite energy on a particular weekend.

Aspects of work may be so much part of play that they are implicit; for example, only when a player becomes temporarily somewhat disabled (as with a sprained hand or foot) does he or she realize the work involved in, say, putting on a swimming suit or walking to the theater. You might argue, of course, that this "work" is not implicit but only should be termed as such if a person becomes disabled and therefore perceives it as such. Perhaps that is a more accurate way to express the matter, but the line between work and play is nevertheless a delicate and somewhat blurred one, is it not? I draw the conclusion that to think of work as implicit in such instances might be analytically very useful.

Another point about play: Many kinds cannot be engaged in until appropriate skills are learned, and this may take many hours of strenuous work. Team sports are an instance. These also may involve both explicit and implicit work. Explicit work in tennis matches is done by the umpires, ball chasers, and often sports commentators and TV crews. Also, the players may get paid for their work or for winning, even if they actually revel in the playing itself. As for implicit work, consider the common phrase "working hard" used, say, when we are playing tennis even though we are very much enjoying ourselves. We may not actually think of this as "really" work, as compared, say, to practicing strokes, but the phrase is analytically revealing.

As this last example suggests, it is important to understand that there can be subtle and significant fusions of working and playing, and the players may well understand this. When I play the piano, I can feel myself "at work" particularly while playing the more difficult passages, although savoring both the sounds that are resulting from the movements of my fingers and the hard-earned accomplishment of overcoming the barriers to making those sounds. Whenever my playing seems effortless I am far less conscious of the work that is involved than when playing those difficult passages. However, sometimes I may enjoy the experience of playing without appreciable effort primarily because I have overcome the challenges of playing them unexpectedly well. On some evenings when after an hour or two of playing and I am "really warmed up," then I am scarcely aware even of playing, let alone of working. Rather I experience a buoyant feeling that is closer to floating effortlessly in a cloud of gorgeous sound and am intensely "in" the bodily motion itself. This bewitchment is closer to "having an experience" rather than merely playing and enjoying. Yet, as the evening wears on and I begin to tire then the subterranean work emerges, to the point where the "fun" of playing lessens sufficiently so that I stop.

This characteristic interplay of playing and working is just as true of expressive behavior and work. The point should be clear enough, so will not be dwelt on further. I only remind you that, *conversely*, a great deal of work—even paid work—can be fun, playful, accompanied by fantasy, expressiveness, strong esthetic feeling, and withal highly symbolic.

BIOGRAPHICAL WORK AND ITS INTERSECTIONS

So work is unendingly variegated, by itself and in conjunction with other forms of action. Among the interesting types of work, and certainly among the most significant for social scientists, is "biographical work" (Corbin and Strauss 1988). This type of work can be carried out by collectivities and their members, not only by persons. I will explore below some aspects of this genre of work.

In this exploration, case illustrations will be presented to highlight several points: (1) the linkage between individual and collective biographical work; (2) the complexity and variation of biographical work and its relationships with other forms of action; (3) the symbolic character of all these forms of action (more will be said about action in Chapter 6). I shall conclude this section by suggesting that sociologists of work could usefully in their studies (1) extend the range of types of work well beyond the currently popular ones; (2) look for and examine *types* of relationship between biographical work and other forms of action; (3) consider more theoretically—and not just substantively—that work always occurs in contexts, including the historical; (4) include in the conceptualization various levels of process (such as organizational and personal biographical processes), which in effect constitute clusters of action-over-time.

Biographical Ideational Processes

Let us begin with the Pragmatists if only to highlight again the connecting flow of concepts and theoretical problems between this philosophic movement and Chicago interactionism. Mead (following Dewey's line of problem-solving) occasionally used the term *ideational processes*:

> Now it is by these *ideational processes* that we get hold of the conditions of future conduct as these are formed in the organized responses which we have formed, and so construct our own past in anticipation of that future. The individual who can thus get hold of them can further organize them through the selection of the stimulations which call them out and can thus build his plan of action. (1932, p. 76, italics added)

What Mead is pointing to can easily be converted into the idea of biography: that is, a life course; life stretching over a number of years and life evolving around a continual stream of experiences that result in a unique though socially constituted identity. Both Mead's sentences about ideational processes and the idea of biography, as a continual stream of experiences, can be applied not only to persons but to nations, organizations, families, and other collectivities.

It is only a short step from conceiving biography to an understanding that the kinds of thought processes and self-references embodied in Mead's interactional processes imply an actor "working on" those biographical experiences. This commonly used term can be translated substantively into descriptive language such as "thought over," "struggled with," "fought out with himself," and "finally got a new slant on himself." Such descriptive phrases sometimes unquestionably imply self-interactive work as well as work with others (family members, therapists, support groups, consultants). Some of it is likely to involve personal and/or collective indecision, anguish, and suffering (Riemann 1987; Riemann and Schuetze 1991; Schuetze 1981).

Biographical Processes in Comebacks from Illness

Biographical work is carried out in the service of an actor's biography, including its review, maintenance, repair, and alteration. This work must be done by the actors themselves although, as just noted, possibly also with others' participation. The onset of a severe long-term illness, whether disabling or life threatening, is likely to require thereafter a fair amount of biographical work, primarily by the ill but often also by kin and friends. Life-styles may of necessity become profoundly altered (but to what?), images of dying combatted (but how?), and so on. After personal disasters like a stroke or a heart attack, the ill must find their way either back to approximately their previous lives or reconstruct them considerably and even drastically. These reconstructive "comebacks" may take many months or years of biographical work (Corbin and Strauss 1988, pp. 68–88; 1991). As expressed earlier, this work:

> involves four separate but overlapping *biographical processes*. Though ana-
> lytically distinct, each process occurs simultaneously and feeds directly into
> the others. The processes are (1) *contextualizing* (incorporating the [course of
> illness] into biography, (2) *coming to terms* (arriving at some degree of un-
> derstanding and acceptance of the biographical consequences of actual or
> potential failed performances), (3) *reconstituting identity* (reintegrating iden-
> tity into a new conceptualization of wholeness around the limitations in
> performance), and (4) *recasting biography* (giving new directions to biogra-
> phy). Each of these processes evolves over time. . . . [I]t is important to
> recognize analytically that [each of these processes] rests inevitably on the
> *biographical work* entailed in it. (Corbin and Strauss 1988, pp. 68–69)

As might be imagined, this strenuous self-to-self and self-to-others work is not solely biographical. It is thoroughly infused with other types of actions. It also intersects, thus affecting and being affected by, other kinds of *non*biographical work. Also, if the ill person is a spouse and a parent with children still at home, then the family will share in the biographical turmoil and alteration of identity. Each family member will be having a series of biographical experiences that together may alter both the personal identities and the collective familial one.

No Biography without Biographical Work

We need not look only at illness and other personal disasters to find biographical work being done. The actual contradictions and dissonances of experience that mark even relatively serene life courses require some "inner" work to yield a sense of seamless continuity of identity. In the following passage, nothing is said about "work" but its presence can be sensed clearly throughout the description:

> The persistence of identity is quite another thing than its imagined persis-
> tence. . . . Through the years, much that a person recognizes as belonging
> characteristically to himself—as for instance an intense liking for foods
> characteristic of his ethnic group—obscures recognition of other, seemingly
> less important, shifts in taste and conduct. Awareness of significant change
> is a symbolic matter. A change must be deemed important before it and
> kindred changes can be perceived as vitally important. Everyone's behavior
> changes in some regard but not in all; and which changes are worth taking
> into special account and which are trifling, peripheral, irrelevant, and even
> believed spurious does not depend merely upon the appearance or disap-
> pearance of actual behavior.

Each person's account of his life, as he writes or thinks about it, is a symbolic ordering of events. The sense that you make of your own life rests upon what concepts, what interpretations, you bring to bear upon the multitudinous and disorderly crowd of past acts. If your interpretations are convincing to yourself, if you trust your terminology, then there is some kind of continuous meaning assigned to your life as-a-whole. Different motives may be seen to have driven you at different periods, but the overriding purpose of your life may yet seem to retain certain unity and coherence. . . .

Such terminological assessment is crucial to feelings of continuity or discontinuity. If past acts appear to fit together more or less within some scheme, adding up to and leading up to the current self, then "they were me, belong to me, even though I have somewhat changed." It is as if you were to tell the story of your life, epoch by epoch, making sense of each in terms of the end product. The subjective feeling of continuity turns not merely upon the number or degree of behavioral changes, but upon the framework of terms within which otherwise discordant events can be reconciled and related (Strauss [1959] 1969, pp. 144–46).

Much of this self-interaction, this flow of thought processes, I would interpret as work carried out in the service of personal biography. Done in a psychotherapist's office, it may definitely feel like work! Or if there is great struggle involved, fateful decisions to be made about oneself and one's life, then again the person may come close to defining this inner turmoil as work. But perhaps not—whatever a psychotherapist or a social scientist would say. If in fact there are those differences of definition, then I would argue that they are significant for better understanding of the turmoil itself. Again, all of this characterization of work and personal identity applies to collectivities under both ordinary and extraordinarily critical conditions.

Collective Interaction in a Collective Enterprise

After World War II a number of American movies appeared with the theme of how captured soldiers escaped from German prisoner of war camps. The details should be familiar: the vision of escape, the making of a plan with all of its minutia, the gathering and hiding of implements and other supplies, the organizing of a division of labor by specialization and personal skills, the coordinating of the project by a trusted leader. It is instructive to supplement this picture of organized, rational action with what gives the movie versions their human qualities: mostly the collective interaction, whether this be in scenes involving all or most of the prisoners, or just two of them, or when a single prisoner is chosen to represent the group before the prison commander or even spontaneously confronts a prison guard. This collective interaction gives a dense and believable texture to the bare and otherwise perhaps boring plot line, Will the escape be successful or not? (Think of the textures of *The Great Escape* and *Bridge on the River Kwai*.) The collective interaction again involves the enactment of various kinds of action, not just the work entailed in the escape. All of the action is bound together in intricate interplay, albeit it is certainly possible to analyze the work as such or alternatively focus on play, expressive action, or the "collective behavior" (panic, crowd) aspects of the total interaction. Any such focus, however, becomes enriched by consideration of its *intersections* of the action forms. Indeed the focus is correspondingly impoverished when intersections are analytically ignored.

Converting Civilians into Soldiers

The next case may not be entirely accurate in detail but should be accurate enough to sustain my points. Descriptively, I have in mind the training of American civilians who volunteer, presumably with a high degree of enthusiasm and with some prior imagery, for the high-status Marine Corps. The theoretical points especially to be touched upon are the relationships among organizational processes of the Marine Corps and the personal biographical processes of the inductees; also the combination of types of work and other types of action, including collective interaction.

You can easily imagine some of the organizational processes. (By the participants themselves, these are seen as organizational action, often defined specifically as strategies.) Recruitment, which is highly selective, is one process. Training is another. This is quite a complex process involving many traditional procedures for "hardening" the men physically, exposing them to simulated battle situations for developing their understanding of the why, what, and when of soldier actions, testing them psychologically as well as physically, and so on. Among the many other organizational processes, a particularly important one is the obtaining, maintaining, and distributing of various types of supplies.

Organizational processes are expressed in rules, regulations, procedures, decision-making, and the strategies of its officers. Organizations as such also possess biographies—expressed by traditions, legends, stories of valor, ceremonies, and rituals that support the constructed history of the Corps. This organization is constructed so as to maintain all of these as well as to convert new events into its ongoing symbolic history.

Organizational processes strongly affect but do not deterministically produce the biographies of the novitiate marines. Among the biographical processes in which all or most inductees are caught up are undoubtedly the following items. Surviving the ordeals faced: whether deliberately produced by the organization or incidental to it because of the inductees' differential physiques and psyches—surviving both physically and mentally. Managing to stay afloat: being successful enough not to be rejected from the corps because one's level of competence is judged inadequate. Being competitive: "holding your own"—as the inductee himself sees his performances—against the competition of peers' learning and accomplishments of a potentially skillful "fighting Marine." Controlling himself in different realms of action: as new and disturbing and frightening situations are met, also unfamiliar and unexpected behavior of others (and his own); for there is a yawning gulf between the recruit's army and his previous civilian life. The gulf cannot simply be described, as it often is in novels and depicted in movies, as a conflict between the relative personal autonomy of the civilian and the relative restriction of the inductee.

But organizational processes and personal biographical ones are not all there is, for a great many other forms of action—among them expressive, playful, interpersonal—fill the lives of the men. Not only do these fill the emptier nonwork hours, but permeate and are permeated by the hours of work. This overall collective interaction is paralleled by the overlapping of different types of work; each can be found in combination with nonwork activities.

Nazi Concentration Camps and Survivors' Biographies

One need not read much of the torrential flow of writings about the concentration camps of World War II to understand something of their excruciatingly crushing consequences for the survivors. Given my purposes, a few paragraphs about highly selective items in the total mosaic should suffice for this brief case history.

The concentration camps were only part of the Nazi design for ridding the world or at least Europe of the Jews, the Gypsies, and other undesirables; but they were developed also for exploiting expendable and almost cost-free labor. "Recruitment" of this work force was by fiat or capture, and those who failed the crucial test at any point of their imprisonment were killed. The principal organizational process affecting the prisoners' identities and fates was a grinding down, or wearing down, of them, elaborated in a variety of ways that came to light after the war. This deliberate wearing down of prisoners was directed at their bodies, minds, spirit, and morals. All of this entailed organizing and articulating the prisoners' labor—the accounts of camp activity are replete with repulsive detail about this.

The counterimage of this organizational process is mirrored in the biographical processes of the victims. The most basic biographical process, with respect to the camp survivors at least, was purely physical bodily survival. Life came down essentially to just that brute fact. Cold and hunger had to be endured at least to the point of not actually dying. Virtually all actions and thoughts were bent toward this end of just staying physically alive. As part of this, the prisoners developed a host of canny tactics or ways of enduring, including fearful monitoring, if they had any remaining energy, of their own bodies for cues indicating they would be assessed by camp personnel as ready for shipment to the ovens. Abstractly speaking, survival depended on ability to control the camps' destructive conditions sufficiently so as to stay alive, if only barely so.

A second biographical process was willing oneself to survive, or at least this was an essential condition for surviving under such ruthlessness that was so inimical to survival. An important corollary process was also the controlling of the self and its desires, and of behaviors that reflected the self. All of this was basic for survival. For instance, a presentation of self deemed inappropriate by the guards could lead to severe punishment or death. Behavioral control had to be maximal even when, because of extreme exhaustion, prisoners could scarcely be attentive to anything around themselves, let alone to possible slips in their behavior.

These biographical processes were paralleled by those of the Kapo, inmates who became camp guards, most of whom were treated only sufficiently better to increase their chances of survival as long as they remained in favor. Their existence should alert us to aggregate interaction wherein people are betrayed and betraying, using others as a means to survival rather than interaction as humans. However, survivors' writings sometimes reflect their persistent shame, guilt, self-accusation, and self-directed rage at their own behavior during the camp days.

Yet there are significant moments and moving episodes of collective action: concerted actions, forms of concern and heroism, giving care to the sick, and sharing or giving scraps of clothing—enough sometimes to save the recipient's life. Occasionally someone potentially or actually sacrificed his or her life for another person, as in sharing food. Yet the survivors' accounts seem to reflect far less collective than aggregate action, each person struggling to survive. We must not overlook, however, the more subtle collective interactive forms like storytelling, joking, and sessions of exchanged memories.

In the last book he published (1988) in his lifetime, Primo Levi takes sharply to task the faulty memories of many survivors who reduce the months after release from the camps to a kind of honeymoon period of relief, when in fact depression was rampant among them. Many other personal consequences have been written about, but I am interested here more in the consequences for the collective historical biographies of Germany and Israel. The actions by each government and of public opinion in those countries reflect their past histories: Germany and Germans still struggling with what the camps signify about their nation and their culture, and Israel—which was born from the holocaust—still debating the deeper meanings of it—and so of being Jewish as well as Israeli. Aside from these unceasing debates there is, as we would expect, continuing reconstruction of the past, and continuing collective forgetting and remembering. Incidents such as occurred around Reagan's visit to the Bitburg cemetery indicate that the past, of which the concentration camps are a salient feature, is still vibrantly alive for nations and their citizens, and also for those living in other nations, whether or not they were actually alive during World War II and so with personal memories even if the memories derived only from the media of that era.

The last paragraphs of this case narrative might seem to have left the track of focusing on work and other forms of action. Not at all! To reconstruct the past is also to work; so is the selective remembering, whether it is interior self-interaction or overtly expressed as collective interaction. The more overt collective forms perhaps reflect the calculated work of manipulating symbols, but other overt instances may be innocent of this.

Building a Collective Past

The concentration camps embodied coercion at its most brutal extreme. Other phenomena are equally suggestive for showing cooperation displayed in the interplay of work and other forms of action. One instance is the building of a collective past where it never existed, and where skeptics will insist that this past is entirely fictional. This too can be fabricated, but much of the construction is honestly done. Familiar examples of fashioning a collective past are those of newly born nations that work with self-conscious effort to develop a full armamentarium of institutional and symbolic means to find a (mythical) past, such as by developing legendary heroes, creating memorable iconic national events, and cutting the innocently neutral flow of time into historic periods to accord with the drive toward national unity. Even the seemingly very rational scientific disciplines share in this symbolic biographical work (Fujimura and Chou Forthcoming).

Reconstructing Collective Identity

My final brief note about cooperative action touches on a type of national drama that involves more poignancy and much more conflict: This is when a nation suffers a blow to its collective identity. For instance, there is the case of French citizens reliving the military, political, and moral weakness of France and themselves displayed immediately in the years after their capitulation to the German invasion of World War II. Shame and guilt have haunted many of the French for some decades since, and still do. That war evokes in them images of the complete and amazingly swift collapse of the French armed forces, the collaboration of the Petain government and many citizens with the conquerors, informing and other forms of betrayal by neighbors or coworkers, and many haunting or still outrageous sets of images and memories. Though counterbalanced by more comforting images of incidents concerning civic disobedience and armed resistance, from time to time the national shame surfaces when stimulated by an event such as discovery or capture of an important ex-collaborator, or by the filming of a documentary film consisting of interviews with French men and women recounting their experiences during that era.

In the recurrent debates, and also in the frequent periods of monumental silence over these issues of collective and individual identity—as in the United States over the meanings of the Vietnam War—we see again the collective forgetting of events, the reconstructing of events, and the blaming of self and others. Symbolic and actual work is patently involved in such processes, and as the forms of action intersect in complex and not always clearly visible ways.

Reprise

I mentioned four suggestions at the outset of this section of the chapter that the case illustrations would bear upon. The first suggestion was that sociologists of work could usefully extend the range of types of work beyond the usual ones. The second, which bears a bit of discussion here, is that they might look for and examine *types* of relationship between biographical work and other forms of action. What I have in mind is that their relationships are varied. Sometimes the relationship is marked by conflict, as in the concentration camps. Sometimes the two are quite fused (building a collective identity or, as touched on previously, intense playing of the piano). At other times, as we all know, the interactional forms can be done together or alternately in fairly quick succession, like thinking about a personal problem while yet enjoying pleasant Baroque music. There must be many more such relationships. To name them is, however, not to yet to study and analyze them. A third suggestion was to consider that work always occurs in contexts including the historical. The last suggestion is that our conceptualization should include various levels of process, such as the organizational and the personal. The cases certainly illustrated each of those points. Hopefully they also highlighted the ones promised earlier: the linkage between individual and collective biographical work; the complexity and variation of biographical work and its relationship with other forms of action; and the symbolic character of all these forms of action.

Chapter 4

Body, Body Processes, and Interaction[1]

[N]ew glasses invented by the Retina Institute in Boston have lengthened my reading time, improved my ability to distinguish letters instead of "guess" reading. . . . I now have about three hours a day of reading time. . . .

In the classroom there is no problem. It takes students about a week to get used to this nut with her nose in the book—a student recently suggested I am the only teacher in the school who knows what paper smells like.

But in the "real" world are real problems. The supermarket: there I am trying to decipher the blood-blurred price on a raw rump roast when the store manager approaches: "Lady," he says "don't eat the meat here. Take it home and cook it first." . . .

And then there's the business of distinguishing between the ladies' and the mens' rooms.

—N. Woronov, "A See-By-Logic-Life"

[M]y body is a thing among things; it is caught in the fabric of the world, and its cohesion is that of a thing. But because it moves itself and sees, it holds things in a circle around itself. Things are an annex or prolongation of itself; they are incrusted into its flesh, they are part of its full definition; the world is made of the same stuff as the body.

—M. Merleau-Ponty, *The Primacy of Perception*

Concerning bodies, and their biological connotations, there are ghosts that haunt the social sciences. One kind, let us call (Oscar Wilde's) Canterbury ghost, whose fate is not to scare but amuse us or at whose antics we scoff. These ghosts are represented in the scarcely credible claims made for extreme biological determinism, or in popular but uninformed assumptions about instincts and other relatively harmless biological beliefs. Alas, another kind of ghost we must take seriously because it strikes

to the heart of our disciplinary perspectives, and implies moral and political consequences that at best are dubious and at worst are dogmati-
cally asserted and yet give justification to action. Genetically based claims
about race, gender, social class, crime, and differences among ethnic populations are among those haunting spirits (cf. Duster 1990). If not ever
present, they appear often enough and with sufficient ferocity to be taken
with the utmost seriousness.

Indeed it is part of the social science heritage that its practitioners have
largely freed themselves from the assumptions that lie behind any form
or degree of biological determinism. Although the social sciences now
have sufficient credibility and although most practitioners scarcely think
about biology as in any way relevant to their research, the gender-biased
assumptions are far from banished from social scientists' writing, as the
feminist movement reminds us. That movement has also focused attention on the social, political, and economic aspects of the body, as have
contemporary publications in the sociology of emotions, medical sociology, sociological and psychological phenomenology, and certain aspects
of social anthropology. The body as a phenomenon is rapidly coming
back into focus as worthy of social scientists' attention. (See the brief
discussion and quotations bearing on the body in Chapter 2.)

My interest in writing about "the" body (really, aspects of the body and
body processes) here is only in relation to elaborating a theory of action.
So this chapter addresses the major question: How can the relationships
between body and interaction be effectively conceptualized? Although
the answer was touched on in the previous chapters, it should be obvious
that body-interaction relationships are enormously complicated. Unless
these relationships are clearly delineated, then their conceptualization
will be confused and confusing, and lead to ineffective substantive studies and theoretical interpretations. Adumbrating the discussion below, I
will assert first that what is required is a set of related concepts—a conceptual framework—that will bring the body into line with characteristically human activities: how they are carried out, managed, and the
contexts in which they take place and that affect these activities. *Action/
interaction is where our focus should be.* The challenge is to relate body to
this focus.

BODY AS A NECESSARY CONDITION FOR ACTION

In a general sense "the" body is a necessary condition for all of our
actions and interactions. It is the medium through which each person
takes in and gives out knowledge about the world, objects, self, others,

and even about his or her own body (Merleau-Ponty 1962). In considerable part, this is an unconscious process (Whitehead 1923). It takes place through both sensory contact with the environment and perception through the body. But of course, "communication occurs [also] through the body. Communication entails cooperative activity with others and is the basis of shared significant symbols (Mead 1934), giving meaning to what one feels, sees hears, smells and touches" (Corbin and Strauss 1988, pp. 53–54).

In still another general sense the body is necessary to interaction because without its physiological processes there is literally no life. Indeed this very feature lends to life something of its mysteriousness, exemplified by what is often felt as a sharp divide between life and death. One minute a person is alive, the next totally gone! Indeed, even the body may be totally gone, as when life *and* body vanish in an explosion. Ordinarily the body's physiological processes may continue for quite a while after the person's "life" is finished, unless the bodily remains are cremated. Nevertheless we define socially, and legally as well, that someone is dead when a certain defined threshold of mental functioning has been crossed. The dead can act, in a certain sense (through their wills for instance) after they have physically perished, but strictly speaking any action requires a live body.

Both the limits and the possibilities for action are tied to the species-derived nature of our bodies. By nature, we cannot fly in the air like birds, but we have defeated that limitation with clever inventions. Yet, though we can reach the moon now and live there for a few hours, we still cannot keep anyone alive on the sun or on Jupiter. No doubt someone is currently dreaming that eventually even this will be possible. Following through on the dreams of yesteryear, such as that we might reach the moon or break a track record, nevertheless we are still tied to the nature of our bodies: in the former case, tied to the body's safe transmission through space and keeping it alive through the whole adventure; in the latter case, discovering just the right combination of techniques, training, shaping of body, and selection of runners who have bodies with potentials for breaking track records.

Having asserted all of that, it is crucial to add that the position taken is very far from biological determinism. Human life is far too complicated to settle for its physiology as a sufficient condition for much of its action and interaction. The social scientist's skepticism of genetic imperialism—a view that seems continuous over the decades—need only be mitigated by openness to what *might* be contributed by biological processes in conjunction with social ones. So let it be understood that in this book, when "body" or "the body" is referred to, what is being discussed is either aspects of body or, more broadly yet, body processes.

BODY AS AGENT

Since every action or interaction requires a body in action, this can be characterized as *agential*, the body, or some of its aspects, being employed as an instrument or means to the interaction. Some sort of body movement, whether subtle or gross, trained or native, planned or impulsively reactive, is involved. As those dichotomous adjectives suggest, sometimes bodily involvement is taken into account or noted by the acting person, but sometimes not. Certainly the bodily involvement does not constitute *all* of the interaction, but its agency is a constituent aspect of the interaction. When an important part of the body is badly injured or permanently impaired, then the body as a partly limited agent becomes particularly evident, at least to the actor if not to others. The newly disabled are all too aware of their dependence on their bodies for actions that are now rendered difficult or impossible.

So no action without some agential bodily involvement; but do not read that assertion as *explaining* the action. As Martha Graham's eloquent statement about her dance and dancers reflects, collective acts require bodies but they also require "culture," in the anthropological sense, and traditions and sometimes ritual and other sociological-anthropological-type agency. Our acts are infused with collective pasts being carried out in the present and quite often just as representative (see Chapter 7) of others and their organizations as of us as "individuals."

BODY AS OBJECT

Paradoxically also, body-as-agent can be part of action toward or with respect to one's own body. However, the body cannot directly be an object to itself. It is an object only to some actor. This can be another individual, groups of individuals, or representatives of organizations who act toward that body in some fashion: admiring it, servicing it, protecting it, hitting it, abusing it, or destroying it. But as Mead (1934, pp. 368–78) cogently argued, the body can also be an object to the person whose body it is, but only insofar as a self is involved. That is true whether your body is an object to yourself or to another person. An actor with a self is involved in either case. As an object, the body can be viewed as other persons (with selves) see it, as well as reflected upon in its parts and as a whole, in terms of its appearance and ability to perform. Like others, you can act toward your body (that is, command yourself to act toward it or some aspect of it): hitting it, adorning it, even destroying it through suicide.

Mead argued also that since very young infants have no selves yet but must interact with others in order for selves to evolve, understandably he would also assert (1934, pp. 368–69) that an astute observer could see infants reacting to their body parts much as animals do to theirs. However, they could not yet have a conception of a body qua object nor of parts in relation to the whole. Whether or not one accepts this Meadian argument, it is important to understand that every individual or group of individuals has a differentiated world insofar as a great many objects are discriminated in relation to oneself and these objects have meanings and are acted toward. Among these objects are the body, certain of its parts, and possibly some of its physiological systems.

Assuredly, the body must be a special kind of object among all the other objects, just because it must represent the self in a special sense. By that, I do not mean that one's body is loved, highly regarded, esteemed more than one's reputation, status, honor, or one's children. I mean only to emphasize the special character of a body with regard to which one necessarily acts quite consciously, either much of the time or at certain critical junctures in life. In this sense, acting toward your body "unconsciously," like scratching an itch when your attention is elsewhere, is not at all to act toward it with respect to the self. Only when we become aware of the scratching and tell ourselves to stop or how good the scratching feels does the body move into the realm of the self.

Saying this implies that one's body qua object is something that moves in and out of focus for oneself, just as a matter of fact it does in someone else's focus. Awareness of body can vary in degree, intensity, duration, salience to the self, kind or amount of action precipitated, and so on. It is important to see that some sort of mental process is involved in this awareness of body, including mental activity with regard to the body as object—admiring it, being ashamed of it or self-criticizing of it, and so on. Again, this is true whether the body is your own or someone else's.

SELF—AS SUBJECT, AS OBJECT—AND BODY

For Mead, the self was essentially an interplay between self as subject and self as object. That is, the self is a *process*, not a thing or substance (1934, p. 186). We can adapt his position usefully with regard to our own discussion of body. First, let us be clear that, in common parlance, one can think about, as well as act toward, one's self. We scold ourselves, we are ashamed of ourselves, we command ourselves to do something, we are guilty about some of our acts. To ourselves, we also relate "things, persons, and their meanings" (Mead 1938, p. 445). There is a dynamic relationship between the acting self (subject) and the viewed self (object), as the individual shuttles back and forth between the active and passive phases of the self.

To this can be added that a deformed body or a deficient bodily performance becomes very much a part of the self qua object that is acted toward by the acting self. Hence, we may react to the deformed body or the deficient bodily performance, deciding to do something to improve the other less than perfect aspects of the body. With the permanently deformed, there can be a chronic sense of stigmatization (Goffman 1963). But this is not at all inevitable since some of them, given other circumstances, may overcome or avoid that negative self-reaction. As one dwarf pointedly said: "We are a contradiction in packaging, for encased in our small bodies are not small minds, not small needs and desires, not small goals and pleasures, and not small appetites for a full and enriching life" (Julia Rotta, quoted in Ablon 1984, p. vii).

The dynamic polarity of self as subject-object can be brought out also by considering the concept of "self-conception" often used by social psychologists. One can have attitudes toward oneself, it is said, or have images of oneself: that is, have conceptions of self. But it is impossible to imagine oneself (including one's body or aspects of it) or to take an attitude toward oneself without an agential self bringing under regard the self as object. Furthermore, after this is done, the person is likely either to continue self-reflecting about the object-self or to take overt action with regard to it. In the latter instance, the action then doubles back, precipitating further self-regard and a further judgment passed on the self that has now acted. It follows that the object-self thus involved may include the person's body, just as any action toward this object-self (overt or covert) must involve an acting body. Analytically, the self-conception refers to the overall organization of various aspects of "the" self, which is necessarily inclusive of stances and actions toward aspects of "the" body.

MENTAL ACTIVITY AND THE BODY

When people speak of the mind, here too they may speak of "it" in an active sense, as when they say respectively "I put my mind to the problem and solved it," or they may speak of it as an object: "I thought about my mind and decided it was a good one." In either mode of referring to the mind, one does not really refer to a noun but to a verb, that is, to mental activity or, as commonly said, "thinking." (See Chapter 5 on thought processes.)

In humans, these mental actions are highly trained even when an action is a simple one. Of course, people are not always self-aware of or self-conscious about themselves when thinking. Again, note that we are able to perform mental operations concerning our mental activities ("stop daydreaming and get to work!") but also concerning our bodies ("I'd better walk faster," "I think I will stop drinking so much, but now how will I go about doing that?"). Self-reflection about our thought processes and our bodies in a more extended and significant sense is part of everyone's life. To say this another way: Mental activity involves symbolizing, including symbolizing about aspects of the body. (See Chapter 6 on symbolization.)

To make an analytic distinction between mind and body does not imply that mental activity is different than bodily activity, except that generally it is internal and therefore unobservable, although there may be external signs that this action is going on or has already occurred. Moreover, mental activity may be quite as exhausting as many forms of more obviously bodily activity (exercise, movement, "labor"). Everyone who has tried for an hour or two to follow conversation spoken in a foreign language in which he or she is not very skilled will remember how mentally and often physically exhausting this experience was. In fact, in every action and interaction, except those which are purely and physically impulsive, body and mental activities are part of the interaction. Looking at the Golden Gate Bridge, we are perfectly aware that both intelligence and bodily actions went into its construction. Listening to a Beethoven symphony, we also understand that not only musical intelligence but the hard work of writing down the composition was required. ("All those notes, just think of the labor to get them down!") In the case of the composition, the body's contribution to the product is likely to seem of far less importance, and is scarcely at the forefront of our attention. The point is that either mind or body may be salient when we consider the product of a given activity. Strictly speaking, however, both are involved, and it is *only* an analytic artifact that distinguishes between them.

INTENTIONAL AND UNINTENTIONAL ACTION
IN RELATION TO BODY

Among the most important actions toward or with respect to the body are the actor's commands to the body: Now jump, but quickly, or Hold still, don't move! Perhaps it is more accurate although more cumbersome to say that one commands oneself to send commands to the body; quite as someone commands others to do something with their bodies, like,

"Present arms!" In whatever way this might be phrased, it is clear that this means some kind of intentional rather than unintentional action. Of course, every deliberate action does not necessarily involve fully conscious commanding of the body, for when you decide to walk to the store this does not usually involve an explicit command to the body, as compared with a high jumper who is telling himself to time his running quite precisely, and to get his body into a well-tested position as he "takes off." On the other hand, unintentional action has a spontaneous or impulsive character, like reacting to an insect by brushing it away while one's mind is focused on something else. Reacting in panic is another instance of impulsive action, whereas stopping oneself from panicking involves a self-command. As these examples illustrate, as soon as self-interaction is involved, made part of an action, then it becomes possible to change, correct, or in some other way attempt to control the body's action even after it is underway. In fact, if you catch a spontaneous reaction before it actually moves into overt or visible behavior, then you can sometimes stifle it or change its character.

There are limits to what one can command the body to do, limits set by the physical body itself or by lack of its training. Thus, I cannot run through a brick wall even if I were to be given a million dollars for accomplishing that feat; nor can I swim across a swimming pool to save you from drowning if I have never learned to swim. Once, however, I have learned to swim or, say, learned to dance as the Balinese do, then I can will myself to save you or to entertain you with my exotic dancing skills. There are also limits to commanding the body to act when my self throws up a barrier: I can't save you because my courage fails me; or I can't compel myself to eat a strange or repulsive looking food provided by my Moroccan host, because my fastidiousness prevents me even though I'd like to please him, and so I find some good excuse not to eat it.

Moreover, there are limits to getting the body to act by sending it commands because there is some bodily or mental impairment. A friend of mine once had an infection of the brain that for some months rendered impossible his ability to shut his retina one iota. As he said, "I discovered the limits of my will." If the impairment is permanent, as with the aftermath of some stroke episodes, then loss of some intentional behavior is also permanent. The same is true also of experiential impairments of self, as with the development of various phobias, when the victims literally cannot force their bodies to climb heights or enter certain confined spaces.

One of the more striking features of action is that much of it can be automatic. By this, I mean that actions are performed without much awareness of them, such as driving a car. Some of the time you are likely to drive along, automatically making skilled movements without commanding yourself to do this, indeed without much noticing what you are doing because either you are thinking about something else than the driving itself or you are paying attention to the scenery or to what is being played on the radio. In effect, built into your body is so much skill that it can act without an active guiding self. Most body movements are like this. They become noticed when the movement somehow becomes problematic, as when someone has sprained a wrist and so is driving with utmost care. More usually, as with driving or walking, you decide to drive or walk somewhere, so set yourself into action, and then go into a kind of automatic gear until perhaps something untoward occurs (a dog crosses the road, or a car swerves in front of you). Then the active self takes over.

Said another way, during the skilled automatic action, the body is an unnoted but completely necessary agent. Yet as an object, it is temporarily out of the field of consciousness. Our lives are full of such examples. Thus, if I say to you, "What's your elbow doing right now?" then the elbow immediately springs to your attention, and in consequence you may decide it aches from leaning on the table and so move it to a more comfortable position. In other words, if your attention is elsewhere, if you are engrossed in some other object, then *this* particular object is not in focus. Therefore you will not be directing commands at it. This is true even when a body part, say a broken limb that aches, is temporarily out of attention because something else—a person, an event—has usurped its engrossing status.

Engrossment is an important body phenomenon; the body can very much be in engrossed focus. We all recognize this even if we are not involved with sports, where focused attention is on body or body movement (the athlete's, the coach's and often spectator's too). Engrossment of course carries potentialities for issuing commands to self, and to body. So this phenomenon of intense attention is much like a searchlight playing over a field: Any object can be in or out of focus at the moment, whether the object be self, mind, event, person, or body (or body part or body movement).

I will make three additional points before leaving the topic of intentional and unintentional action. Since interactions are not necessarily over quickly but may take considerable time to complete, it follows that some are composites of the intentional *and* the unintentional. This was implied previously in the example of driving a car. During some moments or even minutes the driving was out of focus and rather automatic, while at other times it was very much in focus and subject to careful commanding. Some actions are almost completely purposeful all through their courses, as when someone is engaged in intently practicing at the piano, paying careful attention to every relevant arm and finger movement—every movement being evaluated along one or more dimensions: speed, easy weight, and musicality. On the other hand, when a professor leaves her house and walks to the nearby campus, thinking perhaps about her first lecture, then virtually all her walking along familiar streets is likely to be out of attention, and sometimes there is surprise when she looks up and finds the familiar building right there "so soon." For the most part, longer actions are likely to involve some shuttling back and forth between their automatic and attentive aspects. Anything problematic about the action is very likely to bring the actor back to his or her action.

The second point about intentional and unintentional action pertains to the infinite variety of objects that human beings have the capacity for possessing. In Pragmatist terms, the world out there is full of potentialities: There are as many objects to be discovered, created, and given meaning to as there are potential actions by us to make them objects. Mead also used the striking example of the ox, to whom grass is an edible object whereas to humans it is not. On the other hand, things that were not even conceived of by our parents, or are thought inedible today by the culinary unsophisticated, are now bought in health food stores by people "in the know" who may eat them with gusto and even regard these foods as especially nourishing.

The body as an object also has an enormous potential to be split into subobjects, as when children first learn about body parts and as medical students learn about body systems and subsystems. As every devotee of skiing or any other sport quickly discovers, the body has numerous muscles that now must be learned about, as well as both proper and improper movements, or suffer the consequences of not learning. Coaching— whether of singing, ballet, football, piano, or wallet snatching—is not only a matter of training the mind but also the body to make fine discriminations. In essence, we are trained to make those discriminations among many bodily objects, just as a trained masseuse makes many bodily distinctions that ordinarily are not made. Besides, when we watch skilled athletes or listen to skilled musicians, if we too are well trained in their particular skilled actions then we can make those discriminations about *their* use of their bodies.

My third point can be phrased very simply. What is willed, and when, where, and why, are usually or frequently perceived as very personal. Yet it should be clear even from the examples given in this section that both the socialized selves of the actors and the interaction with others profoundly affect intentional and unintentional actions. As the experiences of a Robinson Crusoe imply, though he was physically alone nevertheless his self-commands as well as what was in and out of his awareness, his automatic actions, and his moral behavior, all testify to the impossibility of purely personal intentional action.

THE BODY AND TEMPORAL ASPECTS OF INTERACTION

Actions and interactions have temporal properties: duration, frequency, pace, whether scheduled or not, when they occur, and so on. Among the most relevant is the property of duration, since every interaction has some duration even when it is very brief. As noted in the first chapter, this duration is a basic condition that allows the redirection of interaction. In their more complex actions, actors are involved in making reviewals, reassessing, reprioritizing, and redirecting the course of actions and interactions. Among the unanticipated contingencies that will change aspects of planned action and lead possibly to its cessation or redirection are the body as an agent (acting better or worse or at least differently than expected) as well as the body as an object (acted on differently than expected). The body's becoming such a contingency is more than likely to change some aspects of the action of which it is a constituent part. Indeed sometimes the planned action takes into account bodily skills as well as potential failures of bodies during the action. Perhaps more often a reliance on the bodily skills and capacities is implicit, remaining so unless failed action is attributable to bodily causes.

Among the contingencies associated with the duration of acts, especially those of long duration, is the *interplay* of self and body over the course of the action. Over lengthy interaction, both bodies and selves can change—the self as agent as well as object, and the body perhaps as agent as well as object (cf. Charmaz 1991).

It is notable that interactions of varying degrees of complexity will embody, over time, different patterns of interplay among self-interaction and body. In some self-interactions, the interplay between self as object and subject does not involve body as an object. In other interactions, for example, the self directs commands to the body, which consequently acts, with overt action then being assessed and in turn affecting the next self-reflections about the self—with perhaps significant consequences for the body as object or subject, or both. There is here a *temporal interplay between self and body.* The fact that we all have life courses and their associated experiences underscores this conceptualization of temporal interplay.

CONTEXTUAL CONDITIONS FOR BODY IN INTERACTION

There are two immediate contextual conditions that affect action and interaction. One is the specific *body state* of the actor or actors. The other is the *biographical moment* at which the actor is taking action. Body state and biographical moment are components of separate phenomena, each of which entails movement over time. Each phenomenon also involves a temporal course. In the one instance, there is the movement and inevitably change of the body itself. This is the *body's course*. In the other instance, there is movement of the person's biography over time. This is the *biographical course*. These contextual conditions are operative at the beginning of an action and at each phase of the unfolding action. Unless the action is of relatively brief duration, neither body state nor biographical moment is likely to remain the same as at the beginning of the interaction. The relationships between the body and biographical courses are then also varied and important.

Among the other contextual conditions that affect interaction and thus the body *in* interaction are the following. (1) Most interactions are not separate from other actions, but are intertwined. Longer ones, including projects, are composed of smaller interactions or subprojects. So the interaction under study may be affected by another; or in affecting the latter then the former may be affected in turn thereafter. (2) Except for very brief interactions, an actor (or actors) is engaged in more than one, each of which is going on simultaneously or intermittently, and may even interrupt one another. Thus the interactions are cutting across each other, providing conditions for each other. (3) Contingencies that affect one interaction may also therefore affect another linked to the latter. (4) Each that has much duration is also likely to precipitate contingencies internal to its own course. (5) These in turn may affect other interactions that come back as contingencies to affect the original—and possibly again and again, if the interactions are spread out over much time. In addition, there are other conditions that were touched on earlier when discussing the *conditional matrix*, all relevant to the body in relation to interaction.

BODY-MIND METAPHORS

In the Western world, and hallowed by centuries of tradition, people make distinctions between mind and body. However, the ways in which they see the relationships between those two are extremely varied. The body-mind metaphors that convey the imagery of these relationships are likely to be expressed vividly by those who suffer critical illnesses. For instance, when someone after a shattering stroke episode describes the experiential aftermath, then he or she is likely to use a metaphorical imagery to convey the nature of the experiences. Here is one instance: Agnes de Mille, the well-known choreographer, suffered a stroke and so for some days lacked neural feedback on one side of her body. She expressed the experience in this way: "Half of me was imprisoned in the other half." She seemed to be "incarcerated in a carapace of iron. . . . If I tried to move or bend or turn my head, there I was, locked in, trapped." This metaphor of imprisonment of self inside the crippled body also leads her to write, "Inside my mummy of unfeeling insulation, inside my corset, I had to keep alive and intelligent and eager" (1981, pp. 35–36). Yet another more severely and permanently paralyzed woman, ill from multiple sclerosis, writes about being imprisoned in her body. She is saying clearly that her will cannot move her body, even though she has crystal-clear mental processes. She expresses the anguish of having her self profoundly affected by this completely restrictive body: "In this state I cannot avoid the reality that I am my body. I am not consoled by the remark that my illness has only to do with my physical shell: I know, as you cannot, that my whole existence is stricken by calamity" (Birrer 1979, p. 19).

Common speech is replete with body-mind metaphors. ("She's a dumb but beautiful blond," "My body feels like a lump today but for some reason I'm thinking well.") Some ideological phraseology also carries such metaphors: For instance, physical training teachers at the turn of the century used to invoke "a sound mind, in a sound body," and the Nazi ideology of the superman reflected the conviction that the mythical Aryan (biological) stock carried vastly superior capacities for performance by superior beings (selves).

The important theoretical point about such metaphors is that they are extremely varied. We have different experiences with our bodies and selves, and thus conceive of their relationships in different terms. The perspectives on these relationships, therefore the metaphors, are if not infinite then at least multitudinous. To make matters even more complex, there are as many metaphors possible for the same person as there are others who make objects out of this person's appearance or performances. ("She dives like a queen; no not a queen but like a seal; no like a champ; no . . . in fact, she doesn't dive, she just floats like a . . . Well I don't think she's so good, she has a long way to go, she's more like a half-matured but still awkward heron diving for fish.") For the theorist and researcher this implies a need to capture patterns of such in vivo imageries, attempting to spell out their significance for patterns of interaction.

SYMBOLIZATION AND THE BODY

As will be fully discussed in Chapter 6 on symbolization, symbols are created, maintained, elaborated, re-created, and sometimes destroyed through interaction. They have their life *in* and *through* interaction, not in some abstract realm of thought. At the same time, a given symbol does not stand in splendid isolation: It is part of a system of symbolization.

These systems of symbolization as well as single symbols are created, maintained, altered, indeed argued over and fought over, through interaction.

Like other objects, the body becomes symbolized. (The body-mind metaphors are instances of this.) The body can be symbolized in any of its aspects: parts, systems, gestures, movements. It could not be otherwise, since the body is an object whose many meanings necessarily emerge during the course of diverse actions and interactions. Marilyn Monroe, her gestures and the image of her body, still stands for glamour and sex, at least for the generation of males who saw her in the movies. Andy Warhol used this symbol of a certain kind of feminism to create still another symbolization, when he parodied American mass culture by creating ironic multiple images of Monroe in a set of brightly colored lithographs. Significantly, he used her face and particularly her lips to create his symbolization rather than the prevailing masculine imagery of her conspicuously capacious bosom. He also used her sultry eyes, but pictured ironically rather than invitingly.

To take the point about body as symbol further, I would argue that it is not necessary for the body to be obviously symbolized in order to affect action. Since the body as an object is constantly in interplay with the self within actions, it follows that body symbolization is literally embedded in every action and interaction. We recognize this implicitly when, say, we describe people's gestures and behavior by making reference to the body (he smiled knowingly, he sat down abruptly, he glanced questioningly). In our responses to these gestures and behaviors (and to our own also) body symbolization will also be embedded. This is not to say that interactants are necessarily conscious of that bodily involvement, but they certainly may be—as when driving a car, some other driver makes an obscene gesture to indicate how badly I am driving and so I make an equally explicit answering gesture. Note how this example exemplifies both the linkage of the gestures with interaction and with a wider system of meanings.

ACTION, PERFORMANCE, AND APPEARANCE

With regard to action and the body, there is action *on* the body, *toward* the body, or *with respect to* the body. It is analytically useful to conceive of these actions and interactions as involving the acting person or persons in *performances* or *appearances*. By performances, I mean carrying out an act. This may be done for oneself as well as for, before, with, or through others. However, any performance may include a combination of these subdimensions of interaction. Juliet Corbin and I have expressed the many aspects of performances in the following way:

> Performances may be routine or problematic, depending upon the nature of the [action] and the context in which it occurs. Playing scales on the piano is a routine and simple task for the concert pianist. However, playing a new and difficult piece may be problematic at first. Playing a fast piece may be problematic even for a skilled pianist if he or she has recently suffered from a heart attack. . . .
>
> A performance may also be simple or complex. It may require one person, or two people, or more. It may require more emphasis on the physical processes or on the mental processes, or it may require equal emphasis, as when one plays a difficult piano piece. Its duration may be variable. A performance may begin with a mental rehearsal about what one is to do in advance of the physical part of the act, or it may not. And completion of the physical portion of an act may be followed by a mental review of one's performance, or it may not. A performance may be conducted with one or more parties to the performance not aware of certain aspects of the performance—usually the mental processes that condition the physiological or visible aspects. Or a performance may be conducted with none of its aspects hidden. And it may be carried out because of a commitment to a person, place, or thing, or it may be done out of sheer desire. In addition the term *performance* denotes . . . the capacity for . . . appearance. *Appearance* is used here in a double sense: first, the appearance of action—what I or others think of what I did; and second, appearance in terms of physical features— the way I look to myself and others [including when acting]. Each of those aspects of appearance (action and person) involves the body (Stone 1962; Goffman 1959). Action and appearance relate to performance as conditions that define a person's perception of the purpose as well as to anticipated consequences of his or her performance. (Corbin and Strauss 1988, pp. 56–57)

It is well also to add that actors present themselves, deliberately managing their appearances, including appearances-in-action. These *presentations* of self (Goffman 1959) involve the body too, either self-consciously or simply as part of the action.

BODY PROCESSES

Consider next several *body processes*. These serve to enhance, promote, denigrate, destroy, maintain, or alter performances, appearances, or presentations. Hence it is through these processes that much of the shaping of interactions, selves, identities, biographies, and body features occurs.

When viewed from the standpoint of the actors themselves, processes look like strategies, or deliberate actions taken to enhance, promote, denigrate, and so forth. Wearing certain styles of clothing to enhance given performances or abusive actions performed to elicit information from prisoners are examples. When viewed from the standpoint of the researcher, these body processes are seen as more than an aggregate of strategies but as distinct phenomena. One such process is protection of the body, entailing a host of different kinds of actions but also analyzable into subprocesses like defining the potential threat, minimizing the likelihood of it materializing, and warding off damage when it does materialize. Among the other major body processes are abusing the body, shaping the body, presenting the body, living with the body, training the body, carrying out work through the body's actions, and "having an experience." These processes have different salience in different situations (torture for spies, gymnastic exercises for toughening bodies). Just as important, each process will have different sets of relationships with the selves of actors who are involved in acting them out, and with the interactional and structural conditions bearing on them.

Can there be any doubt that these should be of interest to sociologists, and that their description and analysis must entail significant interaction that ranges from the most microscopic to the most macroscopic in scope? Discussion of these processes should add measurably to what we understand about individual and collective interaction.

"HAVING AN EXPERIENCE"[2]

I will present next an instance of how a body process can be related to interaction in a relatively complex if brief analysis. Such a discussion is logically preliminary to carrying out actual substantive studies of body process–interactional relationships under various conditions and at different levels of interaction. However, I will only confine myself to suggesting how the more abstract scheme might be developed with one body process, namely, having an experience.

Which of us has not talked about having some special kind of experience that was either unforgettable, or if it occurred recently was so different or extraordinary that we are driven to talk or at least think about it? The experience can be terrifying (a near fatal accident, a rape, a hurricane, being lost at night in the mountains). Conversely, the experience can be "wonderful," "remarkable," "marvelous," "terrific," "fantastic," "never to be forgotten." The special experiences that I am interested in here are those occurring *through* the body or deriving *from* body itself, which sometimes are merged. Heightened sensations of the body, as through extreme pain or exhaustion, exemplify the "from" type of body experience. "Through" the body experiences can be illustrated by the unforgettable moment when you as a young tennis player win your first championship, or I as a young singer give my first concert singing Schubert lieder.

A vivid description by a forty-year-old woman about an event that occurred thirty years earlier will convey much of what I want to cover in my analytic commentary:

> This was my first public performance, and I approached it with all the serenity of inexperience. I simply don't know that I'm supposed to be nervous. [During the afternoon of the concert, she naps unconcernedly, and backstage, while waiting for her turn to perform, she and her friends giggle and comment on the other students' playing.] When I emerge to face the audience . . . I feel such a heady joy that I know nothing can go wrong. I am both half-conscious and hyper-conscious as I play—a state of grace in which my fingers become deliquescent, pure instruments of my will, and in which I am not really playing but listening to the lovely music as it pours out. When it is over and after I bow to the applause in a haze, [my teacher] looks at me and strokes my hair, it's a happy moment.
>
> But this is the last time that I enjoy such an innocent calm. From then on, performing becomes more self-conscious, more problematic and difficult. (Hoffman 1989, pp. 79–80)

Keep this description in mind, for it illustrates points made in the commentary below.

The basic process of "having an experience" is the *undergoing* of an experience. "Undergoing" is not just going through some everyday experience, but one that means something special: joy, humiliation, shame, perhaps a great achievement. Even if you forget your special experience by repressing it because it was so shameful or terrifying, nevertheless you have had the experience—and later it might be recalled, never having really vanished. In this instance, the experience is characteristically linked to a trajectory (cf. Schuetze 1992). Dewey distinguishes between these special experiences and ordinary ones, in this way:

> Experience occurs continuously, because the interaction of the live creature and environing conditions is involved in the very process of living. [But sometimes] we have *an* experience. . . . Experience in this vital sense is defined by those situations and episodes that we spontaneously refer to as being "real experiences" those things of which we say in recalling them "that was an experience." (1934, pp. 35–36)

You can see that the exceptional intensity of having *an* experience such as this young girl's is a certain wholeness, fullness, a boundedness of the experience, as compared with the flux and flow of the ordinary passage of events. Even if you are much interested in ordinary pleasurable events, like playing a lot of tennis, these are different than, say, the day you finally "caught on" how to serve the ball powerfully or the day you unexpectedly defeated, against all odds, a celebrated tennis star. When the experience is terrifying, horrible, painful, or in some other way memorably negative, then identity is in some degree injured or even shattered. Rather than losing one's self *in* the experience, one now loses self *because* of the experience.

There are several subprocesses involved in this undergoing of a special experience. Listing these subprocesses and a sentence or two of elaboration of each should be all that is necessary for understanding the gist of this part of my theoretical approach:

1. *Living through* the experience. That is, you are *responding to it*: savoring, recoiling, hating, trying to escape it, and so forth.

2. *Defining* is crucial. You must self-indicate that you are having *an* experience. This can occur during or after the experience itself.

3. *Characterizing* the experience. This can be done either very crudely or very elaborately.

4. *Interpreting* the experience, its meaning to you. This can happen also during, after, or very long after the experience occurred.

5. *Reinterpreting* the experience may occur, though certainly not always, if the experience continues to be important—positively or negatively—as its meaning is reworked. With successive reviews of the experience, layers of meaning may be added to it, as well as a *recasting* of its meanings.

6. *Biographical relocating* may occur if the experience is reinterpreted/recast in its meanings and set into a reinterpreted biographical context.

If having the experience has a lasting effect, then it will do so presumably through a change in identity, even if the change is small—perhaps more interest in classical music now that Mahler's second symphony has opened your eyes. ["Like some magic key, the revelatory moment opened a magnificent world to me. All of Mahler was now, if not instantly comprehensible, at least accessible" (Oestreich 1991, section 2, p. 1).] This changed identity will play back into future interaction and contribute to the creating of new meanings.

Among the conditions that precipitate having an experience are those at any and all levels of the conditional matrix. You cannot have that wonderful, exceptional, and unforgettable ski run at sundown without the full institutional ordering of the ski industry, the value of vigorous, active recreational exercise, the economic resources that permit owning ski equipment and paying for the weekend expenses to and at the ski resort. You cannot have the experience either unless without the standards and criteria for exceptional performance, let alone the training and months or years of self-training for your performance.

Among the other conditions that affect having an experience are other body processes. For instance, body abuse deliberately inflicted—as in concentration camps—is a condition for horrifying experiences. Primo Levi's books (1979, 1986, 1988) among many others make clear that these experiences were engraved forever on memory and affected identities in the most profound ways. Or another example: Recently I saw a documentary film showing lesbian women voluntarily undergoing scarification of various kinds, for reasons of personal identity. Some of the procedures were very painful, yet the scarification experience could also be joyous for what it expressed symbolically. So shaping the body (or having the body shaped) was a condition for having this particular unforgettable experience. The previous example of skiing, in its turn, exemplifies also the conditional body processes of training the body and performing through the body, as they impact on having the special skiing experience.

An equally important point about having an experience is that we not confine this phenomenon to single persons, because the undergoing of experience can be collective. Families treasure memories of certain outstanding events ("Remember the day that John fell out of the apple tree?"). More striking are the large-scale collective events in which entire social worlds and even nations have a shared experience—individual experiences too, but also shared: for older Americans, the day Pearl Harbor was attacked and the weekend of Kennedy's assassination; for older Germans, the night Hamburg was firebombed; for the French, the weekend Paris fell before the German attack, and the day that the city was retaken from the Germans. These shared experiences generate repeated retelling of the events and experiences, as well as the accompanying development of legends. Also, individual experiences become complexly fused with the collective one, and stay with the actors throughout their lives.

Having an experience can be paralleled by the active *creating* of these experiences. We plan to go to the opera to hear Pavarotti in person—a quite different experience than hearing him on TV or on a CD. In other words, we manipulate conditions so as to create, or at least make more probable the creation of, these special experiences. I suppose that, ordinarily, people do not intentionally create negative experiences except perhaps for experimental purposes, or as side effects of desired actions like scaling a difficult mountain peak and getting caught in a terrible snowstorm.

One last point, worth remembering: It is not just my own body but also the bodies of others that contribute to my having or creating a special experience. Indeed, as in competitive sports like football or in shared activities like lovemaking or ballroom dancing, it takes two to tango. As always, body and mind together make for the dance.

NOTES

1. This chapter is an adaptation of a book on body processes that I am co-authoring with Juliet Corbin.
2. The term is John Dewey's (1934), who used it with reference to having an experience with the making or viewing of art.

Chapter 5

Interaction, Thought Processes, and Biography

[T]he concrete leads to the general, but it is through the general that one recaptures the concrete, intensified, transfigured.
—O. Sachs, *Seeing Voices: A Journey into the World of the Deaf*

This chapter has two purposes. The first is to develop implications of two assumptions of the theory of action discussed in Chapter one. Assumption 6 was "Actions (overt and covert) may be preceded, accompanied, and/or succeeded by reflexive interactions. These actions may be one's own or those of other actors." Assumption 13 was "Interactions may be followed by reviewals of actions . . . as well as projections of future ones. The reviewals and evaluations made along the interactional course may effect a partial or even complete recasting of it." My developing of implications of those assertions will entail relating three phenomena: thought processes, biographical processes, and overt actions.

That is one purpose for this chapter. A second is that I hope to persuade you of some significant but unrecognized implications of Dewey's life-long contention that activity is ongoing, not episodic. He first asserted this in his 1896 paper on the reflex arc when attacking stimulus-response theory. If we take seriously that activity is ongoing, we should begin by asking what this means. It means exactly what James Joyce used as such an effective technique: the relatively continuous stream of consciousness. One doesn't have to be an intellectual or of rich imagination to have such continuous or continual streams, for we all experience them. Sometimes we notice particular images, bits of memories, passing reveries, daydreams of future scenes; sometimes we do not notice, or are not attentive to those items in the continuous flow, especially if they do not seem immediately, situationally relevant. In this chapter I will examine the more transitory phenomena, *regarded as action*, and consider their implications for interaction. In doing so, I will have elaborated important and ordinarily overlooked aspects of a theory of action.

Early in the history of sociology, a distinction was made between the objective reality of overt action and the subjective aspect of that action. Thomas and Znaniecki (1918–1920), for instance, based their explanatory scheme on "values" and "attitudes," and in general Chicago sociology has self-consciously balanced both overt and covert aspects of action. Other sociological and social science traditions have also, of course, decreed that explanations of action bring in subjectivity, although synonyms for subjectivity such as symbolization, meanings, intentionality, and cultural values have varied with the tradition. Social scientists differ in how essential they believe is the necessity for gathering data on interior action in order to explain the particular phenomena in which they are most interested. For example, systems of symbolization, culture, social structure, and language itself are often analyzed with scarce reference to the interior life of people who produce or use the symbols or words. Some specializations, like demography, tend to pay scant attention to anything other than populations as they are born or die at certain rates or as they migrate from one region or country to another (Maines 1978). Although demographers have crude, mundane ideas about what procreative action in families consists of, these ideas constitute underlying preassumptions for their writings and theories.[1] Neither an interactionist view of behavior nor its theory of action can ignore what is pointed to by this distinction between the more and the less visible actions, but we need not accept such a crudely dichotomous reification. A much more subtle analysis is called for than is represented even by the usual referencing in research publications to self-conceptions, identities, self-interaction, and other such concepts. Mead's analysis (1934) of self-interaction in relation to overt interaction, and Blumer's later one (1969), are among the most subtle interactionist abstract renditions of these phenomena, and of course these are widely cited and quoted. Perhaps this is because their analytic schemes provide general orientations for research in which individual and collective behavior are linked, but also because these provide legitimization for the use of "self" concepts and support a criticism of the more strictly deterministic (structural, biological, economic) explanations of behavior. Even noninteractionist sociologists may draw on Mead or Blumer in some of these respects. Other traditions, like the phenomenological, possess alternative analytic schemes about interior processes and their relation to an outer world.

What I offer here is intended to follow through on certain aspects of the Pragmatists' analyses, especially Mead's and Dewey's. In the pages below, I will make an extended general theoretical statement about thought processes in relation both to interaction and biographical processes—or more accurately, the relationships among all three phenomena. Then I will illustrate by commenting on the case history of a young woman who will be seen struggling with a series of identity issues. It is not the truth of my theoretical statement that I seek to demonstrate, but only to suggest a useful analytic framework that pertains to two matters. The first is my attempt to fill out yet other aspects of a theory of action. The second is my attempt to stimulate future, more complex analyses of the significant phenomena discussed below.

THOUGHT PROCESSES AS ACTION

Thought or thinking is commonly seen to be restricted to the more rational modes of inner action. When I was a college student, my generation was still taking classes in "logic" although by then our textbooks (cf. Cohen and Nagel 1934) characteristically presented a separate section devoted to classical logic (syllogisms) followed by another section on scientific method (hypotheses and testing their validity). Probably none of my readers needs to be persuaded that such classroom views of human thought processes are of little or no utility to scientists dealing with empirical complexities. Even textbooks in symbolic logic today are unlikely to aid the creative thinking of a scientist, and probably are of limited use even for systematically checking errors in thinking or they would be more widely used.

Quite aside from how scientists and philosophers think, I recommend observing the mechanics of our own thought processes when confronted with some common problems: How do you figure out in which direction you have been walking absentmindedly when lost in a maze of unfamiliar streets? (Check where the sun is at this time of the day; or in bad weather, at least try to retrace your steps in a doubtless faulty memory?) Or, how do you decide whether to buy a tempting ice-cream cone if you are slightly overweight or after you have read an anxiety-provoking article on the hazards of cholesterol at your age? What do you present in a speech and in what sequence, given an audience that probably will include both academics and laypeople, some of whom may agree with your position and others of whom may be dead set against it? How does a teenager figure out how to deceive his or her parents about where the evening will be spent away from home? Or, how does one of the parents, finally allowing him- or herself to think about whether or not to break up an increasingly intolerable marriage, over the next months think through and certainly explore his or her feelings about spouse, children, money, work, and life in general; as well as his or her own and others' reactions during and after the separation?

If modes of thought are not just a matter of syllogistic or hypothetical thinking, they are also not at all confined to carefully carrying out deductive and inductive steps. (This is so even when we are not acting with regard to people and social situations but with technology or impersonal situations.) These steps are accompanied by mental activities like "gut feelings," speculations, sometimes flashes of insight, and thinking with the help of metaphoric images. The popular jargon term *blueskying* suggests some of the looser but possibly quite creative modes of breaking through the more restrictive, if systematic, modes of rational thought.

Rational and systematic thinking, certainly with regard to interaction, is also abetted and supplemented by a number of other "mental" activities. These mental activities include images, imaginations, projections of scenes, daydreams, elaborate fantasies, flashes of insight, rehearsals of action, construction and reconstruction of scenarios, the spurting up of metaphors or comparisons, the reworking and reevaluating of past scenes and one's actions within them, and so on and on. One has only, as I have suggested, to observe oneself when traveling through the day. Whether struggling with particular problems, and whether one's inner life gives rise to as rich a stream of consciousness as, say, that of Leopold Bloom, Joyce's hero in *Ulysses*, if one has never taken a careful look at his or her own flow of thoughts and images then he or she is likely to be amazed at his or her own virtuosity. The play of inner life, as suggested earlier, goes on relatively continually if not always noticed.

All that I have written above has been very descriptive, but to this can be added more systematic remarks. First, however, I further suggest that a thesaurus be checked for the words *thinking* and *thought* but also *imagination*. You may well be astonished at the variety and complexity of thought processes recognized by this useful terminological instrument. Of course, if you pursue the listed synonyms, you may become even more astonished, though in general they parallel my descriptive offerings of thought processes. Novels, too, are replete with rich descriptions of varieties of thinking; for instance, here is Virginia Woolf's quick portrait of a poet observed at work: "He held a pen in his hand but was not writing. He seemed in the act of rolling some thought up and down, to and fro in his mind till it gathered shape or momentum to his liking" (1946, p. 6). Anyone who has carefully composed sentences before actually writing them, assessing and editing and searching for substitute words or phases, will understand that last sentence of Virginia Woolf's!

Whether the thesaurus is consulted, novels are scrutinized, or one's own modes of thinking are observed, it should not be difficult to recognize some of the quite varied characteristics of thought processes. (You can substitute *mental activities* if you prefer this more encompassing if possibly misleading term.) A simple listing of some dimensions along

which thought processes vary can render more specificity to their vari-
ance, as well as allow more precise location of grossly descriptive general
categories like "fantasies," "daydreams," and "pictorial images." I preface the list with the warning that such general categories should not be
identified with just one dimension or another. For instance, a particular
daydream can be playful or serious, consequential or not consequential
for the daydreamer, but so may other forms of thought.

The dimensions along which they may range, beginning with the ones
just mentioned, include:

playful	not playful
very significant	insignificant
short duration	long duration
voluntary	involuntary
controlled content	uncontrolled content
repeated	not repeated
very aware of	unaware of
quickly forgotten	never forgotten
maximal personal involvement	minimal personal involvement
spatially specific	spatially nonspecific
temporally specific	temporally nonspecific
pictorial	nonpictorial
"scenes" (drama)	no scenes
speech involved	no speech involved
coherent content	incoherent content
clear meaning	opaque meaning

In addition, of course, a thought form may or may not immediately
precede, accompany, or succeed overt action; and the time of the overt
action may vary from far in the past to far in the future. You can surely
supply your own illustrations to this partial listing of dimensions.

But why list such dimensions? Is it not apparent that mental activities
come in all shapes and sizes? So why add this kind of detail? There are
several reasons. To begin with, many social scientists pay almost no
attention to interior activity: ignoring it, taking it for granted, but leaving
it unexamined, or giving it the kind of abstract but not very detailed
analysis that can be found in the writings of Mead, Blumer, and Znaniecki
([1919] 1983). These analyses have been invaluable, for reasons mentioned
earlier, but not too much can be done with them other than to use them
as general orientation or as justification for a particular research stance.
Attempts to elaborate on them, as in periodic commentaries on Mead's
concepts of the "I" and on role taking, have been without significant
impact either on research or in further developing Mead's theory of action.

What the Pragmatist/interactionist tradition does insist on, however, is that these modes of thinking are themselves action. Mead discussed and analyzed his stages of the act (1938) in the context of interaction between actor and environment. He argued that projections of future consequences of the act become built into preceding stages of the act, well before its actual overt manifestations—overt in the sense that others can see the actor in motion and that the actor can observe his or her own completion of the act. When there is a consequence of the act, this validates the overt act, helps the actor to distinguish between a "mere" daydream (covert) and a "responsible" action.

However, an observer might also "see" thinking in the usual sense of the term as it takes place, for instance, in the quotation from Virginia Woolf. Of course, an observed poet might not be creating poetry just then but listening to the rumblings of his or her stomach or merely daydreaming. But then again an observer might make similar misinterpretations of the actual visible action that followed. The poet may not have just composed the lines he pretended to have just conjured up, quoting ones previously created; much as George Frideric Handel, known for his fabulous skill at improvising at the harpsichord, would weave long sections of previously composed music, or their variations, into the new material. You would have to be familiar with all of his music to know which was being composed on the spot and which was not.

Lest those above lines connote sophistry to you or my criticism of Mead's analyses seem too general, let me state my main argument about interior action more straightforwardly. The relationship of interior to exterior action is complex, but often likely to be analytically and behaviorally relevant. Even well-grooved, routine action and interaction may be accompanied by thought processes—not just casual or irrelevant ones like idle fantasies or thinking about personal problems, but directly relevant to the work at hand. As I vacuum the house, barely noticing my movements, still I give myself commands, think to myself, There's more lint than usual there, be sure and get it or "she" will complain. Similarly, the carpenter says to himself, Hit that nail again, as he assesses whether the nail is firmly in yet, or thinks, Maybe it needs another hit.

In a later chapter, routine action will be discussed in detail, but here in relating this to thought processes it is again apposite to point to Dewey's assertion that activity is ongoing—including inner action. Quite aside from reveries that might blessedly break the boredom of carrying out routine action, all routines are ordinarily not as fixedly automatic as those which occur in a machine-controlled mass-production line. Routines take continual vigilance. This is because tasks are not necessarily ordered to meet all the little contingencies that can and usually do occur while you are carrying them out. For instance, while vacuuming a carpet, you notice a spot, and so have to decide whether to remove it then and there or wait until later. As my colleague Juliet Corbin has said: "Routines call for monitoring, assessing, judging, making choices!" Except, I would add, under conditions where no new contingencies impinge or they go unnoticed, perhaps because you are thinking of something other than your immediate actions.

To continue with this discussion of interior action: Much like young children before their speech becomes inner speech—to use Vygotsky's phrasing (1939, 1962)—people may even talk aloud to themselves as they act, especially if the activity is new, difficult or problematic. Inner speech and thought succeed but also accompany and precede visible action. Only when viewing action from an analytic stance can we separate overt from covert action; in fact, they melt into and inform each other. In particular instances of overt action, it is possible to say that this specific action is either a condition or a consequence of invisible self-reflexive action. Yet, in general terms, the overt action is both condition and consequence of self-interaction. Also, again in general terms, the overt action is accompanied and accompanies self-interaction; particular instances, of course, may not.

As I wrote that sentence I began to laugh because I had an image of a colleague who, like me, frequently composes diagrams when thinking. In his office there is a chalkboard, always covered with some sort of diagrammatic pictures—circles, connecting lines, boxes—and with words and phrases peppered all over it. When I enter his office, sometimes I hear and see him talking to a student as he sketches his diagram, sometimes explaining the diagram but sometimes thinking aloud as he actually creates it. When he is alone, thinking through a problem and diagramming his thoughts, presumably he talks silently to himself, but if he is like me then he may even sometimes express some thoughts aloud. Where, then, to draw the line between inner and outer interaction?

Furthermore, just as Mead argued, individual action, whether overt or covert, is complexly linked with collective interaction. This must be, if only because it involves interacting with others. Also, since we are languaged beings, our thought processes can scarcely occur without connections with collective contexts. Indeed, it is quite clear that the content of modes of thinking, whether fanciful or serious, or along any other dimension, is deeply affected by the social worlds and social universes that we inhabit, including their ideologies, imageries, perspectives and other symbolic representations. Our social worlds also supply us with significant others who enter our judgments, projections, and other self-interactions (Shibutani 1955). Aside from content, it is also possible that the prevalence, frequency, and perhaps even the absence of the use of certain forms of thought are affected by the nature of group affiliations. Thinking in parables, or thinking with rich metaphoric imagery, or thinking in architectural forms, or thinking "rigorously" as when working out an engineering or mathematics problem, all these instances assuredly vary by occupational training and propensity. On the other hand, most thought processes must be universal. Who does not make judgments? Review actions? Experience pictorial flashes?

Universality is also assured insofar as action takes place in social situations, involving courses of interaction with other actors, each of whom is acting with respect to a perception of these situations. To assert this as characteristic of human action is not to succumb to the claim that only a dramaturgical view of behavior can capture its essence. Most assuredly, life has its dramatic aspects, but life is not played out on, or solely on, a stage. Yet the situational requisites of action do ensure that important aspects of the total sum of possible types of thought are pictorial, scenariolike, and do involve elements of drama.

I will mention a few additional other points before ending this discussion of thought processes as action. One pertains to the commonsense term, "emotion" or "emotions." Even the more seemingly sophisticated and technical treatments of emotion, as by sociologists of emotion, sometimes tend to conceive of this phenomenon in structural rather than in a combination of structural and interaction terms. For example, it is true that flight attendants, because of their work, tend to experience certain kinds of emotions, whereas football players experience other kinds. They have their respective emotional experiences because they are *interacting within* their respective structural contexts. In terms of thought processes, the point is that "feelings," "emotions," or any other synonym for these are truly inseparable from but can be analytically differentiated from forms of action, including pictorial images or daydreams or "ah-ha" hunches, judgments made, memories that spring up—even from dispassionate and "systematic" thinking. Analytically speaking, emotions arise in and accompany all of these: they are aspects of them. Emotions ought not to be reified—conceived of as separate phenomena.

My second point is only a reminder that thought processes as action are ultimately linked with the hard reality of the outer world and actors' interactions with it and its citizens. This point, of course, is directly relevant to any tendency to overestimate the dramaturgical elements of human action. To carry this particular metaphor further, we can say that the scenario, however well written and practiced, is influenced by the stage itself, which after all sets its own and often unanticipated conditions for action. Life and performance are more like what is experienced by the professional pianist who when performing out of town must choose a local instrument that, even if he has played it before, can offer its own surprises, as can the concert hall.

However the main point here is not criticism of a somewhat misleading and restrictive dramaturgical perspective. Rather it is to say that much of the enormous complexity of interaction rests on the interplay of exterior *and* interior interaction. The latter part of this interplay appears to be especially rich and significant for interaction, once it is looked at closely.

In *Mirrors and Masks* ([1959] 1969), there is a lengthy discussion of this interplay of interior and exterior interaction, but no examination of the thought processes except for daydreaming and fantasy. One passage in the book suggests why I failed to wonder how thought processes might *specifically* influence overt interaction. I will quote the relevant sentences because they fortify my conviction now that there was nothing unusual in my reasoning, because sociologists, including the interactionists, generally still make the same assumption as I did then:

> I choose to discuss fantasy rather than more fragmentary covert processes (such as visual and auditory images or spontaneous visual recollections) because *undeniably* these latter do accompany and influence the course of conversations [or other interactions]. Fantasy and reverie seem further removed from the course of action, and less likely to occur during conversational interplay. . . . My general position is this: fully conscious thinking directs action during, after, and preceding interaction, and so also do less reasoned mental processes. ([1959] 1969, p. 64, italics added [I now see, and am emphasizing in this chapter, that these too are forms of action.])

The questions of what specifically were these "less reasoned processes" and how they influence overt interaction—let alone how they might relate to a theory of action—were overlooked because of my too easily assumed premise. In the next section, I will attempt to relate these thought processes to biographical ones, and later in the case history analysis draw more specific connections between both sets of processes.

Before doing so, one last important point remains to be touched on. Ordinarily, most of us associate thinking with individuals; but thinking can be collective as well (Durkheim 1915; Halbwachs 1950). It is carried out in concert by committees, projects, family members, and other collectivities, including in times of national crisis by major communities within entire nations. Fantasies can be collective (two lovers constructing reveries about their future life together) and even institutionalized (ritual ceremonies involving visions, as among some American Indian tribes). The same general point can be made about collective thought processes in general—collective in the sense that through interaction the members of communities of all kinds construct, share, and interactionally sustain collective imageries, memories, emotions, legends, myths, ideologies, and other symbolic representations. Since this collective interaction is inseparable from individual thinking and from the conveying of this thinking to other persons, it follows that the usual thought processes are flowing into, accompanying, succeeding, and continuing to affect the shared symbolic representations. To appreciate this point, one has only to remember such dramatic and large-scale instances as the extended discourse since World War II among the vanquished French, or the ironically parallel discourse among the Germans and especially that between Germans of different generations. As I write this sentence (1991), Americans across the nation are sharing and creating thoughts, imageries, and projections that are fantastic as well as relatively realistic about possible consequences of the oncoming war with Iraq.

THOUGHT PROCESSES AND BIOGRAPHICAL PROCESSES

"Biography" is an enormous terrain and many people are busily exploring it. My aim in examining it here is only to look at biographical processes in relation to thought processes. The happy rediscovery of a case history that I recorded many years ago that pertains to changing personal identity allows me to build on the immediately preceding discussion. In the pages below, I will conceive of biography in terms of changing identities.

In *Mirrors and Masks* there is a section titled "The Sense of Personal Continuity" (pp. 144–47). Its opening sentence sets the problem: "The persistence of identity is quite another thing than its imagined persistence." My argument there emphasized conditions both internal and external to the person that would make for or minimize personal recognition of (biographical) change in his or her identity, though the discussion focused mainly on internal conditions:

> Awareness of significant change is a symbolic matter. A change must be deemed important before it and kindred changes can be perceived as vitally important. Everyone's behavior changes in some regard but not in all; and which are trifling, peripheral, irrelevant, and even believed spurious does not depend merely upon the appearance or disappearance of actual behavior. (p. 145)

Because my analysis emphasized the symbolic character of being or becoming aware of personal change, it emphasized the role of language in the "symbolic ordering of events" that lay at the heart of interpretations of one's own life:

> The sense that you make of your own life rests upon what concepts, what interpretations, you bring to bear upon the multitudinous and disorderly

crowd of past acts. If your interpretations are convincing to yourself, if you
trust your terminology, then there is some kind of continuous meaning
assigned to your life as-a-whole. Different motives may be seen to have
driven you at different periods, but the overriding purpose of your life may
yet seem to retain a certain unity and coherence. (p. 145)

It was, I wrote, the "terminal assessment" that was "crucial to feelings
of continuity or discontinuity. . . . The subjective feeling of continuity
turns not merely upon the number or degree of behavioral changes, but
upon the framework of terms within which otherwise discordant events
can be reconciled and related" (p. 146). My argument ended with "events
must be ordered to be comprehended at all. Like other events, the details
of any person's life may be conceptually organized and patterned by the
observer and thus understood, explained, and managed" (p. 147).

As I look at those passages now, I reason that what is missing from that
analysis is the mechanics provided by an interplay of thought processes
and the interaction with the outer world. True, I had captured the general
interplay of interaction and self-interaction, but the latter was analyzed in
the social-psychological ("self" or "identity") terms familiar to most interactionists and others, rather than in terms of the microscopic examination of thought processes and their interplay with outer events and
activities. It is this analytic gap that I aim to address next.

It is difficult, however, to formulate a simple statement summing up the
nature of these processes. One way to begin clarification is to ask whether
it seems possible for anyone to maintain a sense of personal continuity in
the face of experiential changes (external, bodily, or mental) without some
modicum of reflection about those changes. If you and I can agree there
must be reflection, then there remains only to recognize that to those more
rational processes there should be added the power of what, a few pages
ago, were referred to as the "more fragmentary covert processes" or the
"less reasoned processes." But alas for any expected simple statement of
relationship, there are several different thought processes—among them
judgments, reviews, projections, daydreams—and for each there are
doubtless subtypes related to my list of their dimensions.

So we might expect that as a person's life moves along, as he or she
encounters new and often different experiences and events, and as those
experiences are thought about, wondered about, fantasied about, replayed in imagination, compared with past ones, assessed, evaluated and
reevaluated, and so on, one would expect that the entire process of experiencing a sense of personal change and/or maintaining a sense of
personal continuity would be complex, multifaceted, and variable for
different orders of events and the meanings immediately or ultimately
given to them. The above very long sentence was designed to convey my

own sense of the intricate web of relationships that exist between thought processes and these particular aspects of biographical evolution.

In the case history presented below, you will see this abstract sentence illustrated. You will also see a variety of inner (thought) processes appear, although they do so in various combinations. It is true, however, that some combinations or appearances are clearly related to types of social situations, interactions, and personal problems. To use a common example that most readers will immediately personalize: Suppose that you are composing a speech. This will require at least some reasoning about and juggling of the points that might be made and their ordering or sequence; also considerations of amount of time for each point given the available total time; also the shaping and reshaping of sentences, the selection and ordering of words, during which you might actually hear (aural images) words and phrases; but you may also have pictorial flashes of audience reactions to this or that point or sentence, small daydreams of their reactions or your delivery of phrases, and so on.

I turn now to illustrating through a case history this view of inner interaction in relationship to overt interaction and biographical processes.

A CASE HISTORY

In the autumn of 1944, my first year of college teaching, I began a study of daydreaming. Its purpose was to show whether certain types of daydreams affected behavior, and if so how. A number of students volunteered for the study, and one by one I had them sit opposite me at a seminar table, responding to my request to close their eyes and to "drift" or "free associate" for several minutes. When they opened their eyes, or after I had interrupted them, I asked them if they had had anything that they would call daydreams, and if they did not then to continue with the free association. If they reported a daydream or reverie, then I would interview them in great detail about its features. For instance, did it have a story line? What were its images? What actors were in it? What did they say, do, look like? Were they themselves in the daydream, and if so then what were they doing and feeling? Also, what was now their reaction to the daydream? What did they think it meant, if anything? These sessions lasted perhaps two hours, and the students were willing and usually quite articulate subjects.

Among the students was a young woman who apparently was struggling with important personal problems having to do with religion, but problems that seemed quite typical of what men and women of that generation at her age and with her background were "thinking through."

So, mutually intrigued—I with the research possibilities and she with the opportunity to think and then talk aloud—we struck a bargain. From

November 27 until mid-December, when she went home for the Christmas holidays, then again on January 5 and 7, we had twelve sessions in all, every day or two except for the holiday period. In my recent re-reading of the typed transcripts written virtually word by word in shorthand "on the spot," I found in them various thought processes, biographical processes, and accounts of interaction in social situations. Their relationships to the personal identity issues were discoverable by close reading of the transcript.

Here are a few background items that should prove useful in your understanding of this case. The young women was about twenty years old, a sophomore in college, and highly intelligent. She also proved to be self-reflective, articulate, and candid about herself and her mental activities. She was not particularly anguished about her identity problems because she recognized that she was going through a developmental process of growing up into adulthood. She described her mother as a highly religious Protestant, who regularly attended church, and who exerted constant pressure on her daughters also to be churchgoing and religious. Her father, whom she much admired, was not very religious. Although he went each Sunday to church, he might even be an atheist. Not long before, her older sister had married a Catholic, to her mother's dismay. In their town, buried deep in a Midwest rural region, most people were churchgoers. Yet, during the week they were often, as my student conceived of them, acting in "immoral" fashions. They drank, were bent on making money in business, probably sometimes didn't obey the sexual mores, and often were not particularly kind or compassionate. So there was a strong "contradiction," she felt, between their Sunday and everyday conduct.

As the interview sessions begin, the first major issue that surfaced, both in free association and other mental activity, and in the discussion immediately afterward, was this large question: Is there a God, does he really exist? Over the course of the month's sessions, this question was joined by a number of others concerning religious issues. Here are some of them: What should she tell her children, when they were growing up, on Sundays when all the other mothers were going to church? Would it not be hypocritical to sing Christmas carols next Sunday or at home, when she thought this behavior inappropriate considering how little religious she felt? Was she becoming an agnostic? What would it be like to be an atheist? Could she live as an atheist? How would she find another atheist to marry? How should she act, and what would she feel during the Christmas holidays, when on Sunday her mother would, as always, expect her to go to church? How would she act when dying without any belief in God?

During the several weeks of this extended interview some issues become settled, at least more or less. The additional issues that keep arising do not necessarily seem (to her) to be directly connected with each other. However, near the end of the sessions she perceives (correctly) that all of them overlap, constituting a cluster of issues. She also realizes, as did I from the beginning, that these religious issues are linked with a more basic, and eventually clearly expressed, identity issue: How to become an adult who could become an "independent" person—a self-respecting one, with integrity, who expected to return to her hometown and live without too much conflict and self-damage in this not altogether supportive environment? In technical jargon, this deeper issue was: How was she to keep continuity with a personal past, while becoming a somewhat different person than when younger, and in the face of projections of future conditions that could affect a sense of personal continuity?

It is quite clear that the very activities of invited daydreaming when combined with fine-grained interviewing about it, and with lengthy concentrated discussions over a two-week period, inevitably increased the student's focus on herself and her attempts to solve her identity problems. We, the readers, do not know whether under ordinary conditions she would have reached the same conclusions by herself, but certainly then she would have taken longer to do so. Also, during the sessions she becomes strikingly and increasingly adept at recognizing and perhaps even at producing daydreams, as well as at noticing her more fleeting images and flashes of memory. All of this, I reason, only makes her interviews more useful, since the thought processes in them are highlighted, whereas ordinarily these are not much noticed but surely occur and with not inconsequential effects on overt behavior and presumably identity too.

Since my purpose is to use this case history solely to illustrate the theoretical framework sketched in this chapter, only a few focused quotations from it will be presented. These will be accompanied with brief commentaries and prefaced by some general remarks.

She had been concerned with her religious issues for many months. Because she had been mulling over them, worrying about them, the interview sessions provided her with an opportunity to confront them more directly and concertedly. By the third or fourth session, most issues have already appeared in reported mental activities during the sessions and in her discussions while reasoning aloud about these activities. The sessions vary in the number of issues that appear and in their combinations. Each issue keeps reappearing, however, until she senses or believes that it has been more or less laid to rest as a problem. At first, she does not sense the connections among these issues or how they relate to more complex identity issues; but early in the sequence of sessions she already begins to point to how issues that previously were separate seem now to have "come together" in this daydream or that. She draws diagrams to illustrate this. Previously the issues looked like separate circles: O O O but in this particular daydream they overlap and so look like ⊗ .

Reading the transcript, one can see her thinking—in the largest sense of that verb—through the issues, one by one but sometimes in combinations. Because my research procedures had her produce and discuss daydreams, these procedures are a prominent mechanism for her thinking through the issues. However, as the quotations will suggest, a variety of thought modes are brought into play quite as discussed earlier in this chapter.

Unlike perhaps a physician confronting a diagnostic problem, she has no standard methods to apply to her problems, nor anything that could reasonably be termed strategies for either tackling or solving them. Rather, we see her "working things out" (my term) through a complex interplay of thought processes, as she imagines or reasons about social situations and her own and others' actions in them. There is no lack of rational thinking—the asking of focused questions, the drawing of implications and so on; yet this alone is not sufficient to solve her problems. We find her quite deliberately calling up daydreams in order to see how she might feel or react in given situations. (This is not entirely due to my having her daydream for research purposes, because she had been doing this previously but with far less self-consciousness.)

As this general process moves along, as the days pass, we can see in the interviews the appearance of various biographical processes (Corbin and Strauss 1988, pp. 68–69). These occur not only because of her thinking and talking during the sessions but also because she is, after all, in her everyday life encountering situation after situation, engaging in interaction after interaction. Such situations and interactions have bearing on her thought processes and her changing positions on religious and identity issues. This is not only because real life sets conditions but because it provides opportunities, planned or fortuitous, for ratification, confirmation, and affirmation of what she now believes. Sometimes the position she has reached on a given issue is somewhat shaky—she is not certain yet; sometimes she is more secure in where she has arrived in her thinking things through.

The relationships of personal problems, thought processes, biographical processes, and interaction are important enough to call for a clear summary statement. From my reading of the case history—and from what I sense directly from my own experiences with identity changes and less directly from a lifetime of casual reading of novels, autobiographies, and sociologists' reporting of life histories—I draw the following conclusions about those relationships.

1. There is action over time, during which there is self-interaction and overt interaction. Others are involved: directly in the overt and symbolically in the self-interaction.
2. There are a number of personal problems, or issues of concern.
3. There are thought processes through which the problems are de-

fined, worked on, and perhaps partly or provisionally settled. I use the term *settled* with its interactional overtones of negotiation and persuasion rather than the more definitive overtones of rational, almost mathematical-like thinking.

4.   There is the tangible world in which the person encounters others and interacts with them, and which precipitates—directly or indirectly, immediately or slowly—the personal problems. But this precipitation of problems can only occur through the mediation of thought processes.

5.   There is also the counterinteraction whereby the person, having reached a position on a given personal problem, now carries out action in social situations. But again thought processes play an intermediary role since only through them can the situations and accompanying interaction become defined as the person thinks they "really" are.

6.   All of this interaction takes place over time, which means that the observing analyst, and sometimes the person, can note the occurrence of biographical processes. ("Things are coming together, now they all fit." "I felt something had happened so that there was no going back." "I thought I was free of temptation but now I see I'm not there yet.") Hearing such phases, an analyst might give each a name denoting respective processes, such as perhaps partial "crystallization," a "milestone" turning point, and recognition of only partial and still vulnerable "progress."

7.   Note the sentences quoted below that stand for biographical processes indicating mental activity. There can be no biographical processes without thought processes.

8.   Perhaps some biographical processes are linked with certain kinds of personal problems and not with others. The partial comeback from a disabling illness involves biographical processes like the recognition of performance limits, and the recasting of identity. These seem not to appear in the life of the young woman of our case history; but crystallization or "the coming together of things" is as prominent a biographical process in her changing identity as it is in partial comebacks from disabling illness (see Corbin and Strauss 1988, 1991).

9.   Biographical processes signal changes in the positions taken toward personal problems. Although the person may be completely unaware of biographical processes, he or she will be aware of changes in position toward an issue or issues—or if not aware, then probably will recognize the changes after finding him- or herself acting differently in social situations. Awareness, or recognition, will affect future overt action.

All of this complex interplay between and among the major phenomena just discussed, as it takes place over time, could be seen in the overall case history. This statement must be taken on faith, because without seeing the document my assertion cannot be checked. A few quotations and very brief accompanying commentaries should, however, give some sense of the usefulness of my interpretative framework. The interviewer's questions, directives, and occasional explanations are shown below in brackets.

* * * *

Quote 1, December 17: [Interviewer: What do you think is the possibility of your going back to religion now given a crisis? Drift (for two minutes).] Looking at it that way I don't think there is much of a possibility of my change. I suppose there would always be in the back of my mind a lot of doubts—I'm afraid I could never participate wholly without a feeling of insincerity. I think it would be perhaps easier to buck the crowd and stick to my guns than it would be to change and go through a reformulation of so many ideas. [Did you have any daydreams?] Yes—more the idea of people—a lot of people trying to force me to change and my refusing to change. I'm turning from one to another listening to people talking to me. And I'm trying to listen to know what they're talking about. I didn't make any decisions one way or another. It was more an idea—I saw myself. [Drift again (for half a minute).] I kept on thinking about how almost unbearable the thought of going through different feelings inside of you and being indecisive [about them]. Then just for a moment I saw myself being very miserable, dejected, kind of pictured the state of mind that I just described, of having to go through it all again. [How do you feel now?] As if I wouldn't want it to happen. [Drift (half a minute).] That gives me a real horrid feeling, I wouldn't like that. As a matter of fact, I think I'd fight it so it wouldn't happen. I was thinking now of how I wouldn't want to have to do it, go though it, have to reformulate so many ideas; and I was thinking back on some of the similar feelings I've had the last year or so. How disagreeable they were. And I thought that I would do as much as I could to keep from changing my mind once I made up my mind. I think I *would*.

Commentary: The foregoing passage has been quoted to illustrate how various types of thought process about a given problem can appear in combination or quick sequence.

Quotation 2, December 17: [Why did you choose to daydream?] Because I wasn't getting any place doing what I was doing—just thinking pros and cons and the way I wished things were, and the way I knew they weren't. Whereas I didn't consciously say "now you're going to daydream about this," I know there was the idea in the back of my head that it would seem a lot clearer if I would daydream about it. It seems as if I could put myself in the situation more in reality than just thinking about it in ordinary thoughts, that I'd be able to see it clearer. I think I've done that most of my life. When I wanted to decide how I could do a thing, how I could put a thing across, how I could make them see it, I'd daydream about it. And I'd follow after much the same pattern in reality as in the daydream.

Commentary: That passage was quoted to illustrate at least one clear function of daydreaming vis-à-vis acting in social situations; but the daydreaming certainly occurs within the context of "thinking" about the given problem.

Quote 3, December 24, excerpt from her journal: [She was at Christmas eve service, bored, going through the motions, mentally refuting sayings in the sermon.] I had a momentary feeling of conflict when Father K was reading the communion prayers and the choir was singing the responses. Here I had a short daydream—almost a remembrance, and yet it was happening to me right then and there as I looked. I saw myself kneeling and having these prayers meaning a great deal to me—and going through me—completely and absolutely—I had a momentary feeling of relief; but immediately asked myself how I could ever feel that way, and again had the feeling of conflict—followed by a series of reasonings that it [religious belief] is socially determined, and so on—then went back to my state of almost complete boredom.

Commentary: One can see there all the major components—personal problems, thought processes, overt interaction, and a biographical process (reaffirmation of her achieved position).

Quotation 4, December 17: I've been thinking that one could take it as a necessity for going to church, or belonging to the right clubs that had a religious tie-up. That you could go home and get right back in the old pattern anyway. I wonder if it's entirely necessary. It would simplify things so much. Your children would . . . be confused because you went to church and yet were an atheist. I think you'd almost lose more than you would gain. [Asked to drift: she mulls over trying to "pass" as a believer, but reasons this would be almost impossible. Then asked to drift again, she has a daydream.] I've been trying to put myself in a real situation and started out picturing going to a town. We were total strangers. And I was trying to think of what I'd do. [Drift (for two minutes). She daydreams of going indifferently to church but because it was a matter of necessity, but slowly felt that people were accepting her, she and her husband making their place in the town despite being atheists. While describing this to me, she reports images now of seeing a child being born, bringing it up, and of women standing and criticizing.] Yet I had the idea that our position was still the same as before, and that it had ceased to make as much a difference because we had already found a place and it was pretty stable. Eventually you could do things the way you wanted to. Now there's an example of how new parts make up a whole. It just occurred to me when I said this, that after taking it slowly instead of banging out with "I'm an atheist, what are going to do about it?" that you could do as you wished and it would have no effect on your standing. . . . The ideas all fitted together. [What's been linked?] The idea of social pressure—the fact that it exists. The desire to do as you wished, yet the necessity of establishing a position and standing among strangers. And the idea that a man's worth is not taken right away but when he proves his worth those little things don't make as much difference afterwards. The idea that once you make the contacts—they would stick. And of course the related ideas that radicals are not accepted. I think it's less of a big mess in my mind. And I *think* that would be a way of *solving* it. Since I couldn't see myself completely going against what I think—and yet see myself jeopardizing my husband's or my own standing in the community.

Commentary: That long passage is quoted to show "things falling into place . . . fitting together" through a combination of thought processes, although her position is still tentative. This biographical process might be termed "early crystallization."

Quotation 5, January 4: Before, the church seemed a place of—oh—kind of apart from everything else. Something that was a thing in itself, and all throughout the church there was a great deal of wonder, awe, and reverence. Now it seems more like a social obligation to go. A place where one doesn't necessarily need to feel this reverence. In the past it seemed to me that it was almost being sacrilegious to take communion and not believe in it, and now it doesn't bother me in the least, it doesn't seem the least bit sacrilegious. More of an obligation. The whole issue seemed so important— now it seems—oh—kind as if it's shrunk terribly inside, it doesn't make much difference one way or the other.

Commentary: The biographical process here might be called *devaluation*, or a dropping lower in the scale of values (of the church and what it stands for). She attributes, in the next sentences of this summarizing interview, which I will not quote, her change of position not only to thinking about the issue but various specific daydreams relevant to it.

Quotation 6, January 7: [I ask her whether her judgments made of herself after her daydreams then fade away shortly after the daydreams themselves.] No. And each time that I look back—meet a situation similar to my daydream and then evaluate it, each time it becomes more forceful and becomes a definite pattern instead of just a demand. That was very true, say, for the Christmas carols. At first it took a number of demands and actual thinking what I wanted but then toward the end [of the sessions] it got to where it was almost unnecessary to think of them. Take it as a matter of course. Even singing them at home as we used to, where the emotional tie-up started from, singing them but not having any feeling abut them whatsoever. Just like force of habit. The daydreaming is groundwork and the demands on myself are built upon it and they're reinforced as you progress—each demand that you make as a result of the daydream makes the next stronger. Then you meet the situation and you make the demand on yourself as a result of what you want to be—made very clear by your daydreams—you make it in the first situation; then in the second situation and it's even stronger because of the first situation; and it goes on that way. [She gives other examples.] And *now* I know the pattern, it seems a part of me instead of something I'm making a part of me.

Commentary: In that last session, she is pointing to how the social situations in which she now acts according to current positions serve to ratify her beliefs in those positions. *Ratification* is an appropriate name for this biographical process, one that she herself recognizes, but without having a name for it.

I will make one last remark: Although this section has been about a single individual, a similar analysis, though much more complicated, could be made for changes of collective identity. As remarked earlier, only individuals can experience self-interaction, but the members of a collectivity can share "what goes on in their [individual] heads" through their collective interaction. They can share their dreams, daydreams, images, visions, imagined projections, and selected remembering as well as ideas, thoughts, and systematic reasoning.

*   *   *   *

A FINAL NOTE

Now to bring all of this back to a theory of action, in a quick summary. Action *is* ongoing. If that assertion is taken seriously, then we have to ask: Of what does this activity consist for human beings? Obviously we are not always in physical motion, but for the most part our waking hours are full of a variety of mental activities or, as I have termed them, thought processes. These accompany visible action, as well as precede and follow in conditional and consequential modes. Sociologists' write about self-interaction in their research accounts, using this term directly or as a general orientation in quasi-explanatory ways; also in Meadian, Blumerian, or other analyses of self, self-indication, self-awareness, and so on, the thought processes are assumed but rarely and not closely analyzed as such. I have attempted to supplement both this descriptive and the essentially philosophical approach with a theory-of-action analysis. In it, I have linked thought processes with interaction, whether micro or macro, as well as both with the biographical processes of the interactants and the problems they confront. We need not at all confine these processes to those of interacting individuals; they pertain equally to interacting collectivities.

NOTES

1. Writing those last sentences, I am reminded of a comment made by a fellow graduate student, circa 1941, who was destined to become a well-known American demographer. As we were walking together discussing a classroom lecture about "the subjective side of behavior," he scornfully repeated "the subjective side!" and, reflecting this persistent behavioristic perspective, spat on the sidewalk in disdain.

Chapter 6

Interacting and Symbolizing

Symbol: a word, phrase, image or the like, having a complex of associated meanings and perceived as having inherent value separable from that which is symbolized . . . and as performing its normal function of standing for or representing that which is symbolized. . . . Symbolizing: 1. To be a symbol of; stand for or represent in the manner of a symbol. 2. To represent by a symbol or symbols. 3. To regard or treat as symbolic. 4. To use symbols.
—J. Stein and L. Urdang, *The Random House Dictionary of the English Language*

Africa's famous traditional art that is no longer made or used for its original purpose has a powerful presence in Africa today as it lives on in the memory and the museums. Art serves as a symbol of national identity, and its magisterial forms exert a strong influence upon International African artists. Replicas of "Extinct" Art can be found on postage stamps, decorations in public places and buildings, bank notes, and an infinite array of miscellaneous objects such as match boxes, calendars, posters, lottery tickets and the logos of universities, corporations and airlines. As potent symbols put to new purposes, some works are more famous and powerful now than they were at the time which they were created.
—Wall text used in the exhibition, "Africa Explores: 20th Century African Art," The Museum for African Art, New York City, 1991

Note the gerund form of the terms in the chapter title. No one is likely to regard interaction as a thing or substance: Surely the term refers to the act*ing* of two or more persons (or if self-interaction, then internalized acting) and of collectivities en masse or through their representatives. I use the gerund "ing" after "symbol" to signify that my principal interest is, again, in interaction rather than its products, for symbols are precipitates of interaction. Also, a bit of reification will allow us to say that symbols per se can constitute conditions *for* interaction, or that symbols are used and also generated *in* interaction, or produced as consequences *by* interaction. I will convert those usages of symbols also, below, into the terminology of symbolic action.

The discussion in this chapter will as usual follow implications of the Pragmatist/interactionist traditions, although you will find almost no analysis in either of symbols, symbolization, or symbolizing.[1] Mead's extensive philosophic treatment of significant symbols is a justly famous exception (1934). Yet "meaning" and "meanings" are central to both traditions: from Peirce to Rorty, from Thomas and Park to the youngest heir of the Chicago tradition.

One aside before I embark upon my discussion. The philosophic and social science writings about symbols and symbolization are vast, especially if one includes collateral materials on such phenomena as ritual, myth, legend, metaphor, thought, dreams, mind, culture and political symbols. Running the risk of appearing to ignore or be ignorant of such important topics, I shall sharply constrain my discussion in two ways: (1) Its main task is to relate symbolizing and interacting, (2) in the service of a theory of action.

LANGUAGE AND SYMBOLIZING

Fifty years ago, the philosopher Suzanne Langer asserted that "the basic process in the human brain . . . may be called *symbolic transformation* of experiences. . . . The material furnished by the senses is constantly wrought into *symbols*" (1942, p. 44). Langer adds that "some of these ideas can be combined and manipulated in the manner we call 'reasoning.' Others do not lend themselves to this use but are naturally telescoped into dreams, or vapor off in conscious fantasy" (p. 44). Without the human brain, doubtless there would be no symbolizing and no thought processes. Yet something essential is missing in that causal statement, and elsewhere Langer supplies this in the form of a detailed discussion of language as also requisite for symbolization of all kinds. (See her Chapter 5, pp. 10–44.)

She is quite right about the central role of language, as any number of students of child development, thought, culture, and society have argued. So if there is no language, then there is at the human level no thinking, no symbolizing. Yet one can also argue, as George Mead did, that speech and other forms of language arose initially out of gestural interaction. Thus, interaction has prior status. Recent research on deaf children (Sachs 1989) seems to demonstrate that those who have richly intimate interactions with parents, especially with their mothers, and also learn sign language, are light years closer in thinking ability to normally hearing children than are deaf children who have been deprived of such interactions. Even if the latter learn sign language, they are likely to remain lower in ability and performance. As for those who never learn sign language, they are the furthest below the normal standard, although many are gifted with visual abilities that apparently do not entirely rest on more than a rudimentary level of language acquisition.

However, we need not be concerned here with the priority of interaction or language. The crucial point is that interactions for human beings involve some form of language: including sign language, meaningful gestures, use of icons or insignia, or other signs or symbols standing for meanings. As languaged beings, we interact in symbolic terms with each other and with the world and its objects. All interaction is *profoundly* symbolic. This is true also for self-interaction.

All interaction is therefore interpretative; assigning meaning to objects, events, scenes, settings or contexts, and relationships. This interpreting certainly need not be fully conscious, recognized, explicit, but the symbolizing is intrinsic to action and interaction. Furthermore, symbols that "enter" into interaction are not separate items; they are related to each other (as the dictionary definition suggests) in symbolic systems: Christmas, Christmas trees and their decoration, presents under the trees or in stockings, and all those other traditional icons like reindeers, Christmas cards, and Santa Claus. Interpretations of events and actions with regard to these draw on the meanings associated with a network of meanings. (The implications of this will be discussed at length later.)

SYMBOLS, SYMBOLIZING, AND SYMBOLIC PRODUCTS

For a theory of action, three central and related questions about symbols are: (1) Under what conditions, and by whom, and with what purposes is some thing (act, event, object, person) made into a symbol—or used as a symbol? (2) How is this symbol confirmed and maintained? and (3) With what range of significant consequences?[2] Abstract answers to those questions would perhaps look like the following. First of all, symbols can be products or the consequences of interactions. A crowd forms, has a short history, but the event becomes a symbol of something— perhaps of resistance to the government, or memory of some fantastic experiences. At a more microscopic level, two school children get into a fight, one managing to run off finally with the other's cap—voila! a symbol of victory! Symbols can only be generated through interaction, sometimes deliberately, sometimes not. There *is* no other way. Of course, the interaction need not be face to face. It may also be self-interaction rather than overt.

Yet it would be difficult or at least not frequent to avoid carrying symbols into interaction itself. (It is difficult not to reify in a sentence like that; perhaps a more accurate phrase is "carrying products of previous symbolizing into further interaction.") When sociologists write about social structure or culture as entering into or affecting interaction, they surely mean this kind of symbolizing, at least implicitly. At public demonstrations nowadays, as those against "Desert Storm" (the war against Iraq) or nuclear energy, we can literally see the symbols carried into the fray in the form of posters, banners, T-shirts and other clothing styles, and physical gestures.

When stated more abstractly, what this means in part is that these symbols are used within the interaction itself. They become intrinsic *to* the interaction because carried into it as a component of this interaction. The demonstrators' posters are raised on high, then still higher in passionate protest; the banners are accompanied by taunting shouts, clenched fists, and other expressive body gestures. So the carrying into interaction of visible symbols melts almost imperceptibly into symbolic gesturing and speaking. Other symbols are less obtrusively carried in but also become intrinsic to the interaction. Women demonstrators may strategically use their gender identifications and attributes, or spontaneously and implicitly "cash in" on these. At the demonstration, a celebrity may also cash in on his public image in order to push one or more of the demonstration's causes, speaking to roars of approval not only for his words but his very presence.

This can be said in more abstract form. Objects, like posters or banners, are not symbols per se, but only because of the socially derived reactions they arouse. When a symbol is "used" in interaction, this can only mean that an interactant, whether person or some collectivity, brings it into interaction in some way. The way can be ritualistic (the American flag hung out on a national holiday), or at the other extreme it can be marked by spontaneity (a standard gesture of disrespect toward the stupid driver of another auto). So called "symbolic gestures," like either of the above, are not of course the only symbols that are brought into interaction but, in a more subtle sense, countless symbols are there in the interaction. The most subtle are not words or even standard gestures but body movements that are interpreted rather subliminally. We do not just react to those; we interpret them mostly unthinkingly as part of the ongoing action and interaction. Thus, symbolization gets confirmed, reaffirmed, maintained—as well as previously created or born— through interaction.

So, among the answers to those questions posed above is that there already exist symbolizations that are precipitations of previous and even traditionally based interactions; these function as conditions *for* and *in* the interaction. This interaction and future ones may or may not sustain or modify those symbolizations.

Yet another point has been adumbrated above. Interactions necessarily embody symbolizing: They cannot do otherwise since the interactants are immersed in language and its visual derivatives, whether or not they speak or write but only gesture during particular interactions. In a metaphorical sense, we live in a palpable world of symbols, we act symbolically, we make symbolic products. So, we must also add the symbolizing that is coterminous with the interactions themselves to (1) symbolizations as sets of conditions that are carried into the interactions, and (2) to the symbolic products of interactions.

Consider also that new symbolizations not only are generated in interaction but are built on those that are conditional to and carried into the interactions. The old symbolizations persist but perhaps in new forms. Previous ones can be analytically located at the most macroconditional levels: Gender status, for example, in any society has its source in the most general of societal values. Yet symbolizations can shift during the course of countless interactions among feminists, and between them and nonfeminists as well as between them and men.

In passing, I also refer you to Chapter 10, on arenas. Intersections "in" arenas involve disputes and disagreements over issues, often of very large scale. Hence, frequently there are disputes and disagreements over how events and objects are to be defined (that is, symbolized), and in the most public way generate social change in the form of new symbolizations and actions based on them. Also, some of these issues are old ones, perhaps in new form or phraseology (conservation changes to environmentalism); because of this we can think of history impacting on the present. That is, historical conditions are still relevant in current interactions, as will be illustrated effectively, I hope, in the latter part of this chapter and in the next one.

When thinking about this tradition of symbols triadically (as conditions, as symbolizations in the interaction itself, and as products of interaction) we should not overlook that consequences, as always, can become conditions for future interactions. This general point applies just as clearly to the phenomenon of symbolization as any other.

MOTIVATIONS, SYMBOLIZATIONS, AND INTERACTIONS

Before discussing the very important topic of symbolic universes, I will briefly touch on motivation, a concept not much used or discussed by sociologists of any tradition. Yet it should be, because it can be useful if couched in interactionist terms. Ordinarily motivation is cast into a causal framework, as in much of psychology or psychiatry. Usually also motivation is conceptualized in reference to the actions of individuals. Yet it need be neither. For several interactionists who have addressed the issue of motivation, the concept is neither causal nor individualistic in its reference (Burke 1936, 1945, 1950; Mills 1940; Foote 1951; Strauss [1959] 1969; Scott and Lyman 1968). These writers, who all follow Mead's conception of "the act" (1938), tend to convert motivation into "motivational statements" and "motivational attributions"—that is, an actor's statement or attribution of causal statements with regard to self and others' actions in given situations. Assessments of situation, person, and self all enter into the organization of an act and are *part of its structure*. Also these motivational attributions though they may (or may not) be made by individuals are linguistic constructions, not merely expressions of invention by individuals.

Phrased in terms of symbolizing and symbolization, consider first the sociological concept of "motivational statements" and then the common-sense concept of "motive." The former embody symbols; that is, when making such statements an individual or collectivity is symbolizing others' actions and the reasons for those actions. This symbolizing through motivational statements can be done during the action, after it, and on occasion before when predicting that "he will . . . because of what happened before."

The same points can be made about self-addressed motivational statements. Indeed, shifts of personal or collective identity (see *Mirrors and Masks* [1959] 1969) are likely to turn around or result in changes in how the person or collectivity now conceives of his, her, or its major reasons for acting. An instance is the conversion of someone; another is a radical change in national identity.

But what about the assumption that motivation is causal? There is a more interactionist way of addressing that issue. As discussed earlier (Chapters 1 and 2), an actor can project the end point or the future goal of an action. Perhaps even the means are imagined. Yet both end and means can change during the action, even when it is of brief duration. Said in terms of symbolization, the symbolizing can change along the course of the action. The initial symbolization of a desired end of action is part of the total action, although it occurs through self-interaction before an observer can see the overt part of it. The self-interaction is analyzable as a condition that precedes and in some sense precipitates or allows for the overt part of the action. Yet the symbolization is not at all the only relevant condition. If conceived as *a* condition, then it is also joined by other contextual conditions, as suggested in the conditional matrix discussed in earlier chapters.

By contrast, any motivational statement given to explain the action is a causal assertion directed at explaining why it has taken place; this, as noted earlier, can be made before, during, or after the overt part of the action has occurred. That is so whether the causal (motivational) attribution is made of others or of oneself, or by others or oneself. All of this an interactionist should think of as symbolizing. Symbolic processes are patently operative, whether the symbolizing is done by an individual or a collectivity.

SYMBOLIC UNIVERSES

Larger than the interrelated sets of meanings associated, for instance, with Christmas, or with the game of tennis, or with the world of classical music, are what Ernst Cassirer alluded to as "symbolic universes":

> [Humans live] in a symbolic universe, [they do not] confront reality immediately; [they] cannot see it, as it were, face to face. Instead of dealing with things themselves [they are] in a sense constantly conversing with [themselves]. [They are] so enveloped [themselves] in linguistic forms . . . that [they] cannot see or know anything except by the interposition of the artificial medium. (1944, p. 25; see also 1953–1957)

Or in the phrasing of Berger and Luckmann:

> [A]ll sectors of the institutional order are integrated in an all-embracing frame of reference, which . . . constitutes a universe in the literal sense of the word, because *all* human experience can . . . be conceived as taking place *within* it. . . . [T]he entire historic society and the entire biography of the individual are seen as events taking place *within* this universe. (1966, p. 89)

To live in a symbolic universe is quite like the situation of several goldfish living in the customary bowl of water, the natives of both habitats being unaware of the limits of their respective worlds. Of course, humans can recognize that other peoples' cultures and mentalities differ from their own, but the difficulty of standing outside their own symbolic universes, of totally transcending them, is monumental even in this one-world century. Thus, and with unfortunate and even disastrous consequences, government officials mostly hear and see what their own symbols permit, even when advised by the best-informed experts, usually misunderstanding the foreigners with whom they deal. While recognition of and some measure of distance from one's own symbolic universe are sometimes furthered by experiences with other people's, yet it is difficult to break out of the symbolic fishbowl.

This total if not at all necessarily consistent network of meanings pro-

foundly affects our interactions and provides justification for our interpretations. It provides the very motivational and evaluative terms for
interaction and interpretation. So the assumptions embedded in a symbolic universe function as fundamental conditions for interaction, opening up opportunities and challenges as well as marking off boundaries to
action.

A wonderful illustration of these last points is provided by some sen-
tences from an analysis of Rabelais's great satire by Mikhail Bakhtin, a
Russian philosopher and literary theorist, who in his *Rabelais and His
World* (1984) contrasts the medieval with the Rabelaisian world:

> In the medieval picture of the world, the top and bottom, the higher and the
> lower, have an absolute meaning both in terms of space and of values.
> Therefore the images of the upward movement, the way of ascent, or the
> symbols of descent and fall played in this system an exceptional role. . . .
> Every important movement was seen and interpreted only as upward and
> downward, along a vertical line. . . . The horizontal line of movement,
> forward or backward, is absent. [And] there was no conception of progress,
> of moving forward in time. (pp. 401–2)

During the time of Rabelais, this symbolic universe was disintegrating:

> The narrow, vertical, extratemporal model of the world, with its absolute
> top and bottom, its system of ascents and descents, was in the process of
> reconstruction. A new model was being constructed. . . . Not the ascent of
> the individual soul into the higher sphere but the movement forward of all
> mankind, along the horizontal of historic time, becomes the basic criterion
> of all evaluations (pp. 403–4).

Some symbolic universes in the historic past may have been relatively
stable, but today many are strikingly rapid in their disintegration or
evolution. One of the best theoretical analyses of the mechanics of disintegration, and therefore reconstruction, of symbolic universes is by Kenneth Burke in his *Attitudes Toward History* (1937, especially vol. 2). Burke
notes how every system of symbolization carries potentials for dispos-
sessing some of its believers who over time become less and less committed to it, placing increasingly less credence in its assigning of meanings to objects, events, and relationships. Burke's approach to
understanding the mechanics of breakdown is consistently interactionist,
although he is a literary critic, not a sociologist by training or identity. All
of his concepts are interactional, while some are even phrased as gerunds
and most of the others could be gerunds. Here are some examples: Being
driven into a corner, casuistic stretching [of meaning], discounting, earning one's world, stealing back and forth of symbols; rituals of rebirth,

repossess the world, symbolic mergers, transcendence. Note how this list of concepts carries connotations both of breakdown in a symbolic system and the evolution of a new one. Both processes are collective, although reflected in the inner struggles and overt actions of individuals.

COLLAPSE, LOSS, AND ESTRANGEMENT FROM SYMBOLIC UNIVERSES

Recently Eastern Europe experienced the partial disintegration of several previously Soviet-dominated political systems and command economies. Parallel to this has been the collapse of the worlds of younger people who have known no other symbolic universes or of older people who bought into these via belief, motivation, and commitment. Now these overarching systems of meaning are emptied of previous meaning. This collapse of symbolic worlds runs parallel to but is not identical with the political economic systems and arrangements.

Estrangement from previous official ideologies and systems of belief and commitment had already occurred for many Poles, Czechs, Hungarians, and other East Europeans. Of course, many persons were never committed at all, or only in part to communism. For others, losing the familiar, including rights to employment and free health care, was a shock, equivalent to simultaneous loss of a world and not yet having a believable new one. In these countries and in the former Soviet Union itself, the new belief systems are emerging, doing battle with remnant or resistent elements of the old. That is, respective proponents are fighting for their convictions with words, ballots, and more deadly instruments. The public turmoil is echoed by private perplexity, uncertainty, loss of ideals, disarray, despair, and intense feelings of being adrift in a senseless and profoundly insecure world.

This is not the only kind of symbolic dispossession. Strangers in a foreign land may experience that status forever, or until they learn, through interaction, not only how to act like, but to feel like and in a deep sense to "be" natives. Immigrant experiences as so often chronicled reflect this loss of an old world and the transition sometimes to the new one. As the sociological literature has taught us, first-generation immigrants to America often huddled in ethnic ghettos, minimizing cultural clash and retaining their identifications with old symbols—attending ethnic churches, talking familiar languages at least in the home, and retaining the customary gender relationships. Their sons and daughters, the second generation, frequently felt the tension between foreign and native ways of acting and feeling. "Bitter conflicts between immigrants and their children rage about language" (Smith 1939, p. 281), the children learning English at school and the parents either not understanding their children's speech or furious at it. Autobiographies and interviews of the second generation reflected painful conflicts with parents and their frequent experiencing of awkwardness, embarrassment, ridicule, and humiliation in their interactions with native-born Americans. Observing this, Robert Park called them "marginal men." Even when accepted and outwardly integrated into American institutions and social groupings, the second generation and their parents could feel subtle estrangement: the first generation perhaps from inability to feel at home in speaking English and in other forms of interaction—humor, play, gossip, easy familiarity with American ways and values.

As one young woman wrote recently, "my body is stiff, sulky, wary. When I am with my peers, who come by . . . lipstick, cars and self-confidence naturally, my gestures show I am here provisionally, by their grace, that I don't rightfully belong" (Hoffman 1989, p. 110). And here is a further expression of the anguish of her transition to a new language that involves not just awkwardness in verbal interaction but deeper self-interactions:

> [T]he problem is that the signifier has become severed from the signified. The words I learn now don't stand for things in the same unquestioned way they did in my native tongue. "River" in Polish was a vital sound, energized with the essence of riverhood, of my rivers, of my being immersed in rivers. "River" in English is cold—a word without an aura. It has no accumulated associations for me, and it does not give off the radiating haze of connotations. . . . [T]his radical disjoining between word and thing [drains] the world not only of significance but of its colors, striations, nuances—its very existence. . . . I have no interior language, and without it, interior images—those images through which we assimilate the external world, through which we take it in, love it, make it our own—become blurred too. . . . [Later] I discover something odd. It seems that when I write (or, for that matter, think) in English, I am unable to use the word "I." [When writing in my diary] I do not go as far as the schizophrenic "she"—but I am driven, as by a compulsion, to the double, the Siamese-twin "you." (pp. 106–7, 121)

This immigrant, brought overseas (to Canada) as a thirteen-year-old, felt in exile for many years. Not surprisingly, the chapter of her book from which the quotations are taken is titled "Exile," and the volume itself is titled appropriately: *Lost in Translation: A Life in a New Language*.

For the second generation, the major problem seems not to be with language, although ethnic-affected pronunciation may be a problem for some. The problem is acceptance by the other American-born citizens who have longer genealogical roots in the country, or who persist, as happens more frequently in European countries than in the United States, in refusing to accept these newcomers as genuine countrymen. These interactions then are replete with the symbolizing of respective statuses and their accompanying intolerance, passion, and cruel, hateful, damaging gestures.

SOCIAL WORLDS AND SYMBOLIZATION

Berger and Luckmann refer to *sub*sets of interrelated meanings, smaller than symbolic universes, as "socially segregated subuniverses of meaning." They note that "Like all social edifices of meaning, the subuniverses must be 'carried' by a particular collectivity, that is, by the group that ongoingly produces the meanings in question and within which these meanings have objective reality" (1966, pp. 79–80). Also, "With the establishment of subuniverses of meaning a variety of perspectives on the total society emerges, each viewing the latter from the angle of one subuniverse" (p. 80).

What Berger and Luckmann term "subuniverses" seem superficially to be equivalent to traditional Chicago interactionism's "social worlds." This tradition emphasized shared activity and communication, so it is not surprising to find an interactionist like Tomatsu Shibutani writing about social worlds that each is a "universe of regulated mutual response [whose boundaries are] set neither by territory nor formal membership but by the limits of effective communication" (1955, p. 524). (For Shibutani, communication really refers to communica*ting*, that is, to action.) It is important to understand that symbolic universes provide the most general conditions for *meaning*, and so *ultimately* for action, whereas social worlds provide the *contextual* conditions for *action* and its immediate meaning.

This concept of social worlds and their processes will be discussed in detail in Chapter 9, and in Chapter 10 the important related concept of "arena" will be elaborated. I wish here only to add apropos to symbolic universes that Berger and Luckmann have taken a somewhat cautious stance toward these subuniverses of meaning: "it goes without saying that this multiplication of perspectives greatly increases the problem of establishing a stable symbolic canopy for the *entire* society" (1966, p. 80). Note they assume that a society is more or less homogeneous in its basic perspective or perspectives. In today's climate of events, it has become more difficult to equate "a" society with a nation—thirty years ago, at least in Western nations, it was easier to accept such an equation. A symbolic universe can be a symbolic canopy for a very large population without being equivalent to an "entire society." In the contemporary world, most nations are heterogeneous—even clearly dichotomous as in Belgium or the former Czechoslovakia or multinational as in the former Yugoslavia—divisible by region, race, ethnicity, nationality, or religious affiliation; but also by the occupational, professional, recreational, social movement, and other social worlds. Many social worlds cross social class boundaries, while national boundaries prove less and less of a barrier to the development and persistence of international worlds and subworlds. Rather than think of the potential divisions of these subuniverses of meaning and activity as weakening a mythical total society, I would argue that they more often provide opportunities for cohesive action, often taken in conjunction with other social worlds (see Chapter 9). The interaction and symbolization are not necessarily in the national (nation-state) interest, but should be viewed as ranging along other fault lines of interest.

A CASE STUDY OF SYMBOLIZATION: URBAN IMAGES OF CHICAGO

Symbolization can be thought of analytically in terms of its location in space and time, but also it gets symbolized, or "represented" along other dimensions: geographic, economic, social, cultural. Here is an abbreviation of a long case study of Chicago's "urban images" that depicts some of the complexity of this city's symbols:

> All such representations form a characteristic system of symbolism; they do not merely constitute a bunch of discrete images. The whole system has historical roots, for it develops out of the contributed perspectives of various important sectors of the city's population as they have experienced this city during its past. Today's populations inevitably redefine the old terms, using them in new ways, thinking about the city anew but using old symbolism. They also add . . . elements of imagery to the city's total symbolism. Likewise, today's populations may stress or select certain particular images from among the total set, ignoring or denigrating the others—as some may wish to represent, for instance, their city as progressive and to disregard its slums. . . .
>
> Chicago has a particularly interesting imagery. Stripped of the superlatives with which admirers and detractors are apt to depict the nation's second city, Chicago can still emerge as recognizably "itself" if we glance at what is written about the place. Chicago is represented as a great midwestern industrial and commercial center. It is a cosmopolitan city, a world city, great in size and aspiration, in attainment and fame. It is the main railroad

and airlines crossroads of America. It is the home of so many and such diverse ethnic groups as to make it, as the journalists delight in writing, the second largest Polish city, the sixth largest German city, the second largest Swedish city. . . . It is unquestionably a town marked by a certain amount of violence, vice, graft, and those other unpleasant accompaniments of big city life. But it is also, by popular representation, a midwestern city which embodies something peculiar to the region that is not possessed by cities located elsewhere in the nation. A considerable number of Chicagoans appear to represent it also as a prairie city, and [others] imagine it to be a youthful, unfinished city.

Each of these representations of Chicago finds concrete lodgement in one or more urban icons or indices which can be pointed to (and frequently are) as proof or illustration. Especially meaningful are places, things, men, and legends. Crime, vice and urban disorganization are represented by "Capone," "gangsters," the famous Leopold-Loeb case, by juvenile delinquency, by the well known slums and the black belt. The cosmopolitan city is represented by the fabulous lake front—with its parks and wealthy apartment dwellings, its famous outer drive, its artistic institutions—and by such streets as State and Rush and upper Michigan Avenue. That the city is the unsurpassed crossroads of America is instanced by its many railroads, by its claim to the world's busiest airport, by a striking array of hotels, and by its deserved title of "convention city." To justify the city's industrial and commercial reputation, one has only to point to the steel mills (in older days, the stockyards), the department stores . . . the latest tall office building, the skyline in general; or to well known symbols like the water-tower . . . or to intone the city's motto of "I will" and the frequently quoted aphorism, "make no little plans." . . . All of these representations of Chicago's varied greatness are made visible in picture books and in popular descriptions of the city, in the tourist guides and by post cards; they are visible enough in the daily newspapers either as photographs or frequent points of reference. . . . [T]his entire group of images about Chicago . . . is a set rather than a series of discrete items. When Chicago's residents lay stress upon one or more of those images, they also systematically understress certain other images; e.g., when they point to the lake front with pride, they will carefully avoid mentioning, or visiting, the less palatable urban scenery that daily impinges upon lower-class Chicagoans. . . . To say that certain urban populations within Chicago link, stress, and avoid certain public images is already tantamount to saying that these images have functions and histories not immediately apparent. (Strauss [1961] 1976, pp. 32–34)

Among the structural conditions for these very diverse images of the city must be included membership in social classes and ethnic groups; the part played by icons, media, and popular histories in the continuing as well as changing symbolizations of the city; and implications of the symbolization for urban development, urban politics, esthetics, and urban identities.

LARGE-SCALE SYMBOLIZATION

In this section, I will highlight aspects of even greater ranges of symbolization and interaction, describing how imagery about immigration and social mobility has been subscribed to by citizens of the United States. Those aspects include:

1. The symbolization of the United States has a long continuity, though there is change in its specific symbolic forms (icons, rhetoric, and other specific manifestations) because the conditions affecting its believers and creators also change.

2. These complex clusters of symbols are deeply a part of native-born Americans' thinking, so much so as to constitute elements in their symbolic universes.

3. The structural and interactional conditions that sustain these symbolizations are part and parcel of their interactions as individuals as well as those of groups, organizations, and institutions. These interactions take place in economic, political, social, cultural, religious, legal, artistic spheres.

4. Individual and collective identities are shaped by adherence to these symbolizations and by acting in good faith in accordance with them.

5. When these symbolizations begin to break down, and before they are rebuilt in new terms, former true believers can suffer from the blows to their identities an increasing disillusion, shame, even alienation from the country and from themselves.

During the last decades, immigration to the United States has increased greatly, people flowing in from every quarter of the globe but most notably from Mexico, Central and South America, and from China and Southeast Asian countries (Takagi 1989). Echoes are heard of old debates about whether immigration will be the nation's death knell (those poverty-stricken Mexicans and Asians) or its savior (those gifted Asian students and their hardworking, successful entrepreneurial parents)(Hayes-Bautista, Schink, and Chapa 1988). Aside from its magnitude and the variety of its national, economic, religious, and political sources, the immigration has been relatively continuous. In the past, much immigration was planned in order to fill manpower needs. Manpower issues today include argumentation about whether current immigration should not be weighted toward highly educated immigrants. Another striking feature of American immigration has been its varied ecological distribution. Various immigrant groups ended up in very different frontiers, cities, countrysides, and regions. These properties of our immigration provide the broad context for the major symbolization, and as this appears in individual actions and in those of organizations, institutions, and social movements.

For illustrative materials, I will quote selectively from *The Contexts of Social Mobility* (Strauss 1970):

> The early decision to throw the country open to virtually all peoples of the world was fateful for the nation, and consequential for the development of American imageries [*symbolizations*], including those pertaining to . . . immigration and mobility. . . .

IMAGES OF IMMIGRANTS AND ETHNIC GROUPS

> Among the images of mobility are: (1) Each immigrant group tends to come in at [or near] the bottom of the ladder, and then rises; this tendency has helped to keep America an open society. *But*, despite the waves of migration and the obvious rise of various ethnic individuals, the society is not really open—especially at the top. (2) America is, in essence, a melting pot where each immigrant group becomes Americanized, accepting American ideals and values including those of democracy, where every man has a chance to rise. *But* the so-called melting pot is a myth; people mostly rise only within their own ethnic circles. (3) Some immigrant groups are natively more endowed than others; therefore some will rise and others will not rise very much. *But* persons, not groups, are mobile; mostly it is individuals who rise regardless of ethnic origin. (4) Some groups are so pushy that they threaten others' standard of living—especially that of the original immigrants (natives) or older (especially Protestant) immigrant groups. *But* the natives no longer contribute much—are no longer vital—to the country and will or should be displaced by more vibrant, more successful . . . descendants of recent immigrants. (5) By the third generation, the children are quite Americanized—do not suffer from the marginality of the second generation—and subscribe to American ideals of success. *But* the third generation is more relaxed than the second, and need not be so mobile;, or so obviously mobile, as the second. (6) Just as every other ethnic group, [African Americans] should rise through their own individual hard work, or through ethnic (black) political power. *But* [they] are not like other ethnic groups because they were slaves and therefore not really immigrants; so they need a hand up the social ladder by federal or other agencies. Besides these general images there are [many] more specific images . . . Jews stick together so they have been successful, or Mexicans are lazy so they don't rise, or Poles are stupid so they cannot rise. . . .

THE IMPLICIT CONTRACT AND ITS QUALIFICATION

> Between the immigrant and the host country . . . an *implicit contract* seems often to have operated. The country could accept him, and if he chose to stay and to work he would be rewarded in ratio to . . . skills, ability, motivation, and other relevant virtues. This contract could become harshly explicit, as when advocates of limited immigration argued that this or that class of immigrant ought to be refused admittance because . . . shiftless or ignorant . . . mentally deficient or mentally ill.

Despite the implicit contract, many Americans, immigrants and natives alike, knew or soon learned that it was neither automatically honored nor agreed to by all citizens . . . "Exploitation" was the epithet mostly commonly applied to [employers' recruitment and treatment of immigrants. Also workmen, seeing or experiencing competition, often] accused industrialists of attempts to lower wages or break unions through recruitment of immigrants; therefore, appropriate legislation and other activities were backed by these angry Americans. With just the opposite view of unions, conservatives might regard unions as threats to the social order, perceiving them as composed or led mainly by immigrants. . . .

IMAGERIES OF AMERICANIZATION AND PLURALISM

Assumed and claimed contributions of immigrant and ethnic manpower to the building of American society [also] rested on other assumptions. . . . [The imagery of the *melting pot* was popularized in the early years of this century. Doubtless] few . . . founding fathers held such roseate conceptions of the New American who would rise out as an amalgamation of diverse immigrant strains. Rather, the prevailing view throughout the decades of national history probably has been some version of immigrant *adaptation to American values and institutions.* The immigrant would become assimilated (a term that had great currency among sociologists in the early twentieth century). Indeed, he would become Americanized (the lay term for assimilation). . . . After 1885, when the numbers of annual immigrants so greatly increased, fears for the endangered American Way became greater, and the efforts to Americanize . . . grew all the more intense. Mass compulsory education and the public school system . . . the playgrounds and the settlement houses, were partial answers. So were the churches and prisons. So was the Exclusion Act of 1921, which set definite restrictions. . . . In the end, the beneficial effects of time, combined with education and the impact of mass media, are supposed to have worked wonders with the grandchildren and great-grandchildren of the original immigrants. . . .

One consequence of the emphasis upon Americanization . . . has been the development of a variety of individual responses, counter-ideologies, and institutional reactions. First generation immigrants perhaps huddled all the more closely together because they perceived or sensed the native insistence that they quickly abandon foreign ways and take on American ways. The novels and autobiographies by their sons and daughters are replete with evidences of the second generation's attempts to strip away ethnicity and adopt American styles, with all the accompanying stresses of that difficult process. . . . [T]here have [also] been . . . a range of collective or institutional attempts to retain at least some flavor of ethnic origins. These vary from rituals like the annual ethnic fair, through organizations like social clubs where ethnic gestures can freely be exchanged. . . .

Running counter to expectations that the descendants of immigrants, if not the immigrants themselves, would become Americanized has been the equally powerful assumptions that every . . . citizen has the right to become the kind of individual he wishes—within limits of course . . . may worship as [he] pleases, chooses the friends he wishes, elects to live among neighbors of [his] own choice . . . elect [his] own occupation and career. . . . The result is *pluralism* . . . evident not only in the [urban] ethnic communities but in the obvious ethnicity of rural regions within states like Minnesota. Other objective indexes of pluralism which often are pointed to are the existence of ethnic political blocks, the prevalence of in-group marriages, and the frequency of social mobility within the confines of ethnic groups themselves.

From time to time, Americans have celebrated or bemoaned the passing or diminution of pluralism; celebrated it in favor of the more civilized Americanism; bemoaned it because "conformity" to American "standardization" represents a loss of color (as in the passing of the ethnic ghettos) or of richness (the abandoning of psychologically satisfying ethnic customs and gestures) or of civilizational values (the yielding of esteemed cultural practices for the mass culture of America). Such judgments are made by "natives" as well.

THE NATIVISTIC ANIMUS

The nativistic animus against the "hordes" of new immigrants . . . has been marked by a continually evolving imagery. [This burgeoned in the late nineteenth century, when many Americans felt much threatened by the aliens and saw the social and economic order being much endangered. The native could] see the evolution of city machines, corrupt and dominated by foreigners, could see the possibility of America's embroilment in foreign affairs because of the nationalism of recent immigrants [and] the increase in illiteracy, pauperism, vice, crime. . . . Embedded deep in the core of nativistic reaction to immigrants, then, were queries about mobility, present or future. [This fear, fright, anxiety, and so on resulted eventually in the 1921 exclusion act, supported by the rationales of eminent social scientists of the day. Meanwhile the] presence of poverty-stricken immigrants . . . always had called forth a strong stream of reform. . . . Reformers essentially accepted the task of patching up some of the unfortunate consequences of the nation's need for immigrant manpower. . . . There were reform movements in virtually every area—religious, economic, political, medical, educational—and the resulting institutions and occupations had a profound impact on the texture of American life. . . . [T]he reformers were not always natives, but descendants of those who had profited from reform institutions.

Among the important mobility imageries of ethnicity [and mobility] are those which focus on the relationships of immigrants to their descendants and the descendants to American life. [There was the poignancy of the frequent psychological separation of second generation immigrants from their parents. The novels and media of the day are replete with what the sociologists termed "cultural clash" and "marginal men."]

THE QUESTION OF [AFRICAN AMERICAN] IDENTITY

One . . . questions . . . that perplexes many Americans, although most others only make unquestioned assumptions about it, is whether [African Americans] constitute an ethnic group. [Until Myrdal's redefinition, asserting

that their] situation and future was basically different than that of the
immigrants and their descendants. . . . most American sociologists had
assumed *the ethnic metaphor* for the [African American]. . . .

Stances taken on the question of [their] identity affect not only the actions
of individuals but profoundly influence the political, economic, and even
social policies of various organizations and institutions. . . . The very complexity of the American scene militates against consistent views even within
single organizations. Times change and so do the relative influences of
positions within organizations. (pp. 79–104)

In sum, on a massive national scale there has been an incredibly complex intertwining of images and ideologies, and their economic, legislative, and rhetorical manifestations. This symbolization continually enters
into and becomes regenerated by individual and collective action, including that by organizations and social movements. As noted earlier, interaction is inherently symbolic, the symbols functioning variously as conditions and consequences, and as integral to the interaction itself. The
foregoing description brings out also that though there is an overall national symbolism there is also great diversity in the specifics of how that
symbolization enters action. The specifics are linked with differential
social locations of the actors *and* the differential situations within which
action takes place.

DIFFUSE COLLECTIVE SYMBOLIZATIONS

As remarked earlier, anyone who wishes to study symbolization and
symbols is challenged by a vast number of possible topics, either theoretical or descriptive. I have limited my discussion to a very few, slanted
toward theoretical issues, and with the intention of staying close to elaborating aspects of the theory of action outlined in Chapters 1 and 2. There
is one other type of symbolization to which I have given time and
thought, and will address it now.

There are many collective symbolizations that cannot be in their total
gestalt precisely traced to specific social worlds, communities, cities, or
other social groupings. They are also not traceable to the "all-embracing"
frame of reference, which constitutes a "universe" (Berger and Luckmann
1966, p. 89). A symbolic universe is too general a concept, referring, as
both Cassirer and Berger/Luckmann use it, not only to something invisible to those living within its frame but something to which an analyst
cannot definitively trace particular collective symbolizations. The origins
of these symbolizations lie in more general conditions—economic, social,
political, geographic perhaps, and in the varying contingencies that these

conditions set for different collectivities or aggregations of people. Contemporary collective symbolizations that are widespread but *also* diffuse in this way would include—at least in the Western nations—various images, attitudes, passions, and actions taken with regard to the atomic bomb and its offspring of nuclear military power; they would also include the increasingly fearful imagery of "chemistry" as the destroyer of health and the environment. Similarly, in the last century, Americans evinced a mixed and varied palette of images and reactions toward "the railroad." These affected almost all aspects of nineteenth-century life in the United States (Chandler 1977).

Aside from not having their sources in specific social worlds but in diverse populations, such collective symbolizations tend to possess certain characteristics. They are constituted by a cluster of overlapping but often inconsistent or antagonistic symbolizations. They are global—many images that cover a lot of symbolic territory. The various symbolizations seem to get put together in different combinations, at different times and places, and by different collectivities; that is, the clusters are flexible. Though they have roots in past structural conditions, they are wonderfully adaptable to emergent new conditions. So they tend to have a continuity that an informed observer can perceive, with new versions of symbolization connecting up with older ones. Said another way, the cluster of symbolizations over the years is found useful by successive generations, who can find meaning in some version of it within their own lives. Its global, flexible, adaptable features, in fact, permit users to treat it like a smorgasbord, taking from it what suits their tastes. Legends and myths are very much part of this total symbolization, though specific ones get added to or altered or even forgotten from one generation to another. Last but not least it is important to note that a set of significant and changing structural conditions is likely to give rise to collective symbolizations that deeply affect countless interactions of individuals, organizations, institutions, and other collectivities, giving rise to ongoing sequences of consequences including on the national and international scales.

NOTES

1. See, however, Orrin Klapp's *Symbolic Leaders* (1964) and others of his books such as *Heroes, Fools and Villains* (1962).
2. This is a slightly revised version of wording by Hans-Georg Soeffner when characterizing my approach to symbolization, in his "'Trajectory' as Intended Fragment: The Critique of Empirical Reason According to Anselm Strauss" (1991).

Chapter 7

Representation and Misrepresentation in Interaction

To represent. . . . To act instead of or as authorized agent for; stand in the place of . . . ; also, to appear as an instance or illustration of. . . . To be the symbol of; typify.
> —Funk and Wagnalls, *The Practical Standard Dictionary of the English Language*

Things are seldom what they seem
skimmed milk masquerades as cream
highlows pass as patented leathers.
> —Gilbert and Sullivan, *The HMS Pinafore*

Representation, misrepresentation, and associated phenomena are integral to interaction. They have their grounding in our abilities to symbolize, and to develop personal and collective identities. These abilities make group membership not simply a physical belonging but a symbolic one. Members of collectivities of all kinds may choose to act as representatives of the collectivity; they also may be chosen or requested to do so; and they may be thought by outsiders to represent one even when this is not true. It is notable too that acting as a representative may change a personal style of behaving, as often evidenced in the strong leadership or confident public speaking of people who in their private lives know themselves as shy, though if representation continues long enough the shyness usually will disappear as personal identity changes with successful public performance. Identity, in other words, can be profoundly affected by representation of and to collectivities. Although representational activities are not entailed in every interaction, they do constitute a crucial aspect of many interactions. Moreover, the signs of representation can be manipulated so that misrepresentation constitutes the darker side of representation.

169

DIFFICULTIES IN INTERPRETING REPRESENTATIONS

But, more innocently, we should remind ourselves of the potential difficulties in interpreting representational interactions—whether of other interactants or even of oneself. The difficulties derive from three basic conditions. The first is that interpretations rest on "correctly" reading signs. Because they are signs, they *must* be interpreted, even when their readings are assumed.

Here is a striking cultural instance: At the close of a party in Tokyo attended by a group of friends, among them a young Japanese-American man, one of the Japanese women "turned and began to hug me [the man]. I was pleased" because usually the Japanese "show so little physical affection." But then the woman, sensing his response, said "No, no, you don't understand" and squarely kissing him on the lips, used the cross-culturally significant symbol of slipping her tongue through her lips. *Now* correctly interpreting the meaning of her hug, "I backed away gently, embarrassed" (Mura 1991, p. 273).

A more complex instance: One Japanese-American friend of mine, shortly after landing in Japan, was asked by a passing American tourist where a certain street was located. The tourist had mistakenly identified her as Japanese. My friend gave correct directions, but chose not to reveal that she was actually not Japanese-born. Note the phrase "chose not to." This means that she had an option to declare herself an American, correcting the misassignment of identity. Although her failure to correct the mistake was trifling, the incident speaks clearly to the issue of representation and misrepresentation. By choosing not to correct the mistake, my friend was misrepresenting herself. She was "passing" as a native, a Japanese citizen.

So the first condition that brings about difficulties regarding representation is the basic ambiguity of the signs of particular representations. Their interpretation is often uncertain, difficult; they may even be recognized as currently impossible, the criteria for accurate judgment being inadequate or unclear. Or as my Japanese-American friend's experience in Japan reflects, the reading of certain signs (her bodily appearance) may be so assumed that they obscure the disconfirming signs (her clothes and gestures). In addition, as will discussed later, the signs may be manipulated so as to make interpretation difficult and even erroneous. Signs may be hidden, disguised, or deliberately falsified, making the task of interpretation all the more—and sometimes indeed very—difficult.

A second condition for the difficulty in interpreting representational interactions is this: They rest on the multiple bases of representation that each social unit (whether an individual or collectivity) will possess. It follows that in a given interaction, it may act on more than a single basis.

It may also shift from one basis of representation to another during the course of the interaction. On this point, I will quote some lines from *Mirrors and Masks* pertaining to "structured interaction" of individual actors:

> both structured in the sense that the participants represent social positions; and at the same time is not quite so structured. [There is] an observation by E. C. Hughes that the person who represents a given status is supposed to possess one or more attributes such as skills, certificates, and even certain age. In addition some other attributes may be expected and indeed required, although no one says so openly. Thus American physicians are required to possess necessary skills and training but also, more covertly, are supposed to be men and white-skinned. [This was written in 1958.] . . . The sharing of secondary qualifications allows people of the same status to work together familiarly and with relative ease and lack of embarrassment; whereas when some of these qualifications are missing, or certain others are present, the interaction is upset. A woman physician in a clinic staffed otherwise with male physicians changes the atmosphere. ([1959] 1969, pp. 71–72)

Then I remarked that a male physician could act at different moments "in at least three capacities: as a doctor, a male, and a male doctor" (p. 72). So if a female physician were interacting with the male doctor, the possible combinations are multiple, are they not? "Actually one or more combinations may pertain during the entire span of an interaction. Which basis for relationship is operative during an interaction is problematic since more than one is always theoretically, and often practically, possible" (p. 72). Combinations of such bases of representation can be simple, such as doctor to doctor, doctor to male, male to female. "However, it is more realistic to say that the mode of interaction can change at any instant or phase of interaction and not remain the same through its entire duration" (p. 72). As for the matter of simultaneous multiple bases of representation:

> To make the matter more realistic, if more complex: any[one] operating as an institutional representative may act during any interaction, or interactional phase, in several different institutional capacities: for instance, as a physician, an oculist, a chief of the clinic, an old-timer in the hospital, a member of the hospital board. In which of these many kinds of status [the person] may be acting depends upon the many subtleties of what is said, by whom, in what context, how, and in what sequence. (p. 73)

In short, these multiple bases of representation set *many* possible difficulties of interpretation for the interactants.

The third condition that brings about those difficulties is that the representing social unit may, as touched on above, be standing for another, as well as or besides itself. Individuals may choose or be asked to represent families, organizations, a government, or a community. Organizations represent their members and sometimes social worlds; agencies represent clients; professional associations represent their members or portions of them as well as some segments of a profession. When I say that the individual or collectivity is representing others, it is important to understand that the action then consists of representing some person or collectivity to another person or collectivity. This is a triadic process of (1) a representing action, (2) with respect to some social unit, which is (3) directed at another unit (audience). The potential difficulty may be that the representing unit may not represent accurately (or honestly), or be judged as not doing so by the represented.

REPRESENTATION VERSUS "PRESENTATION OF SELF"

As a digression but hopefully a useful one for understanding these complicated representational phenomena—which are easily confused with presentational ones—consider a famous theoretical discussion about the "presentation of self" by Erving Goffman (1959). By presentation, basically he was referring to the self that a person or the collective identity that a team or small group *put forward* in an interactional situation. Thus the presentation made by a restaurant waiter (efficient, helpful, respectful) could be a deception, a mask that was removed the moment he moved through the swinging doors into the "back stage" of the kitchen—where he made a gesture of disrespect for his customers. (This is one of the most felicitous and humorous examples in Goffman's book.) Or, a person could present the self that he or she believed was wanted by others in the situation, acting in accordance with that expectation or was deemed appropriate by the actor. In both cases, these presentations reflect implicit interactional rules.

Goffman's analysis of presentation of self highlights some contrasting features of presenting and representing, as well as some similarities. Both of those sets of actions occur during interactions. Both can be false actions. That is, made deliberately to mislead the audience. Both require the others to interpret signs expressed in the actions. Both also usually involve interior personal or collective interactions.

However, there are important differences between Goffman's concept and the concept of representation. His presenting involves a very restricted time period: It is tied to one brief situation at a time, and often a repeated situation at that. Representing is more temporal: It has a past, present, and often is aimed at the future. The representing actor, as suggested earlier, is not necessarily an individual or a small group, but can be as large as a government agency or a business corporation, and either as formal in organization as those are or as informal as the hastily pulled together public demonstration described in the chapter on symbolization. Also, presenting as Goffman developed the concept seems to be limited to self-presentation, or perhaps representation of a small group through the person's or group's presentation. However, the concept surely also applies to, say, corporation advertising. Representation can be of another social unit: So as noted earlier an individual can represent another individual or an organization, and so on; and organizations can represent an individual, as in a court case, or a social world; a diplomat can represent his or her government, or just the president, or perhaps a particular social class that is powerful in the government. Goffman's actors present selves or collective identities, whereas actors can represent those but also statuses, perspectives, and positions on contested issues, as will be discussed later. Necessarily when acting, an actor does present some aspect of self or identity, but analytically speaking this is not identical to representing.

Goffman pays much attention to the micromechanics, especially the interactional rules, of and around presenting. Therefore he deliberately takes his analytic gaze away from structural conditions that affect the presenting process. He leaves these implicit and often omits consideration of them. To understand representing, however, one must focus on both the process and the structural conditions for it. Finally, it is important to realize that representing is a symbolic action. This is seen most obviously perhaps when the representing agent announces that he, she, or it is standing for the oppressed poor, or for feminist values or, like Jesse Jackson, for black Americans in a nation that offers blacks economic and social inequity and inequality. Presenting of self is also symbolic action, as indeed all human action necessarily is, but it lacks some of the scope and perhaps the range of complexity of the foregoing examples of representation. However, as will be seen later, interaction brings representation and presentation together in significant combinations.

REPRESENTATIONAL INTERACTIONS

Representational stances are assumed, claimed, attributed, proffered; they are also accepted, rejected, disclaimed; sometimes they have to be discovered because concealed; also mistaken attributions are disproved or fail to be disproved, and correct ones are successfully proved or fail to be proved. These representational interactions and their combinations lead to many interactional complexities. I am referring here to representation of collectivities and not to aggregates of individuals; the former inevitably entails the interplay of identities, but representing aggregates may not. Leaving until later our consideration of the more manipulative, concealed aspects of representation, let us look first at the nonmanipulative or open kinds.

As suggested by the listing of representational interactions, those adjectives do not necessarily mean that they are simple or unsubtle. During an interaction on a hospital ward (harking back to Everett Hughes's writing about the male white doctor), a physician can predominantly assume "the physician's role," acting as a representative both of that professional position and implicitly of the whole profession, with associated attributes of technical skill, knowledge, trustworthiness, reputability, and on this local terrain being in charge over all other health workers. If the nurses are women or African Americans, then either might rightly or wrongly attribute during a given interaction that the physician is acting inappropriately—as a male or as a prejudiced white. Patients who are women or African Americans might also make these attributions. Suppose then that neither the nurses nor the patients confront the physician or act openly in a negative way toward him. We can conceptualize this situation as one where the women must balance negatively attributed statuses against the physician's assumed status—not denying openly what he is assuming—and acting accordingly. The nurses are balancing their jobs, or perhaps just peacefulness on the ward, against rebuking him. And a patient may decide that medical expertise is more important right now than her dismay at his macho style or his racial prejudice. Otherwise she will presumably ask for another physician or at least object to those nonprofessional aspects of his behavior.

Suppose next that a physician steps more obviously out of professional status, as very occasionally have male psychiatrists who have persuaded female patients to have sexual intercourse with them. If this is discovered he probably will be deprived of his license to practice medicine. Yet, if he has convinced his patient that this is a form of salutary therapy, then she will have misread him as an honest, reputable representative of his profession. Such cases have not been unheard of, in which a physician falsely claims professional status, at least as ordinarily defined, and the patient has accepted his claim. If this breach of professional ethics is discovered, then the regulatory committee or board formally can ensure that he can never again represent their profession.

One of the additional complexities of representational phenomena is that other interactants can read an action as at least unwittingly representative when the actor is not acting actually in that capacity. "Stop acting like a typically oversensitive woman," says a male colleague, apparently a not infrequent attribution of status in the American business world these days. The accused may indignantly reject this attribution: "I am acting as a rationally thinking lawyer. When I actually act as a sensitive woman, believe me I will know it." Note the tug of war, the tension between the assigning and the disclaiming of representative status. His attribution may or may not be correct. In either case, if he does not choose to ignore her disclaimer then he has to argue against it—to convince at least his colleagues. Which strategy he follows will depend on the specific conditions bearing on this situation.

A variant of this is when someone is accused of unwitting representation, but rejects the accusation, only to eventually become convinced of its truth. Nowadays it is not unusual for a man to be told he is acting like a dominant male, to reject the accusation, only finally to be convinced by an elaborate argument that conceives of male dominance as a characteristic of Western culture—that he too is unwittingly representing this dominance. Thereafter he tries to "straighten up and fly right!" (As I look at these last lines while editing them, some months later, a controversy is swirling around the heads of American congressmen as to whether those public representatives are or are not insensitive to the issue of sexual harassment, which is a matter of immense concern to many American women.)

The following set of events illustrates additional aspects of representational interaction involving important political organizations. Some years ago, political witch-hunts were conducted by an infamous congressional committee in the form of public hearings, in which a number of American citizens were accused of belonging to the Communist party. Many of the victims were certainly not party members, nor had they ever been. In their formal testimony before the committee, they disclaimed the mistaken attribution of membership. If we assume that, in fact, some actually were party members but argued otherwise, then we would have to conceptualize this situation as one where although the committee's attributions were correct, and the accused were also disclaiming these, yet our same conceptual framework could be brought to bear on this different situation. The party members were misrepresenting themselves and claiming nonmembership or innocent status.

These were genuine events, but it is easily possible to imagine a situation that is just the opposite. For instance, when there is a devastating terrorist incident nowadays, with many persons killed or wounded, it is not unusual for several terrorist groups to claim they are the responsible party. In our terms, they represent the oppressed Arab people of the Middle East. Their claims set a problem for the antiterrorist departments of various interested and nowadays cooperating governments of discovering which group is actually responsible for this particular catastrophe, and discounting the propagandistic claims of the other claimants.

Another approach to these complicated representational interactions is to think not in terms of the representing actor but of the other interactants who proffer representational status to the actor. Then the recipient is put into the position of accepting or rejecting the proffer. Let us look at a formal but simple and frequent kind of such situation. Say, an organizations needs some member to represent it at a convention. A member of the board is asked to do so. Under varying conditions, the answer will be yes or no. However, proffering can be less formal, as once happened when a Chicago bartender lay dying from a gunshot wound inflicted by an angry customer. Realizing that death was imminent, he begged another customer, a known Catholic, to give him the last rites, a request granted by this impromptu representative. This odd incident reminds me of when I was once asked by a friend to act as a minister in his forthcoming marriage ceremony. He himself was a Universalist minister, and under California law could legally swear me in as a minister also, so that I could then marry him. I declined.

To sum up this section: These are a variety of representational interactions that include representational stances that are assumed, claimed, attributed, proffered; are accepted, rejected, disclaimed; sometimes have to be discovered; also mistaken attributions are disproved or not disproved, and correct ones successfully proved or fail to be proved. These may be components of interactions and may occur in various combinations They do so, as my examples suggest, under a variety of structural and interactional conditions, and they result in a variety of consequences.

REPRESENTING *IN* THE INTERACTIONS

All the foregoing leads to a dual question: What does representing look like as it appears in interactions, especially in relation to nonrepresentational aspects of the total interaction? and How does this relationship contribute to shaping the course of interactions and affect their outcomes?

Representational Aspects of Rituals

A useful place to begin the answers is to think of ceremonial rituals, whether religious or secular (cf. Turner 1982). Behavior in them is constrained, even dictated, by well-established rules. The actors in these institutional or collective dramas are not principally acting for themselves but as representatives of one kind or another: of God, the church, the community, the organization, the nation. In such ceremonies, representing actions are more or less strictly ordered. In some rituals, specific actors may be called upon to represent in visible form certain esteemed values—purity, humility, honor—wearing appropriate garb perhaps, or wearing facial masks, designed to reflect the values they are representing. (Eighteenth-century classical Italian drama and comedy sometimes imitated reality, using this format of representation.) Even in these closely scripted ritual interactions the outcomes are not necessarily foreordained, as the example of rainmaking or any other type of ritual prayer suggests. And no matter how carefully ordered the ritual actions may be, not every body movement or voice style or other individualist elements of carrying out the ritual can be prescribed. Though minimal leeway remains for individual expression, it does occur.

There are also rituals in which the action is less rigidly scripted. The minister who officiates at a marriage represents church and state, and may follow more or less customary ritual steps but perform the ceremony with wide latitude, especially nowadays. Also, some ceremonies involve contests in which the warriors representing their respective collectivities struggle against each other. Then the form of the struggle (the Trojan versus the Greek representative warrior; any event in the Olympics) is prescribed but its course and outcome are entirely open.

The paradox inherent in these ritual struggles over real stakes is their unpredictable outcome, reflected in such archaic epic poems as the song of Hildebrand, where father and son attack each other—unknowingly at first. These rituals do not reflect personal decisions, but in another type of situation free choice utilizes cultural or institutional mechanics for its ritualization. For instance, hospital staffs may decide to let a "hopeless case" die rather than keep him or her senselessly alive.

Another type of ritual, often combined with or sequentially flowing into nonritualistic interaction, can be seen in certain situations, as when the heads of various nations from around the world assembled at president Kennedy's funeral. They came to signalize respect; yet a bit of business probably got done after, or even before, the actual ceremony took place. This is expected when heads of state visit each other. The public sees the formal gestures of greeting and perhaps a glimpse of the evening's entertainment, but in private, the nations' representatives do their business. Of course, other representations may take place in these business interactions, as the interaction shifts to political party, social class, regional, or other bases of vested interest. Built into these Presidential events are even additional degrees of freedom, reflected in, for example, the more elaborate symbolic gestures of hierarchy made toward the queen of England or the president of France than toward a representative of an unimportant developing country.

Conversely, however, conventional everyday interaction is not at all devoid of at least bits and pieces of ritual representation. Ordinary conversations begin with ritual couplets ("How are you today?" "Fine") and gestures (handshakes). Or, a young academic rising up a career ladder may be concerned principally with personal reputation and amount of salary, but how often have we heard his or her parents claiming reflected glory in their own interactions with kin and friends?

To sum up the foregoing brief discussion of ritual representation, the actors' representations are expectable, are known. The actions of each actor fit together in at least partly prescribed or at least constrained choreography, and in the more closely scripted rituals the entire interactional course moves along more or less as scripted—unless there is a totally unexpected event, like someone faints or has a heart attack or a laughing fit.

Spectators at ceremonies are not simply spectators, it is worth noting, but are often likely to engage covertly in what Goffman termed "side involvements" (1963). At my high school graduation ceremony held in the school auditorium, the members of the graduating class were seated in rows on the stage behind the main adult speakers. Behind the backs of the adults, a considerable amount of stifled laughter and softly spoken wisecracking went on. These kinds of discrepancies are used by novelists, dramatists, and stand-up comedians, sometimes with devastating satirical effect. An unforgettable instance for anyone who has read *Madame Bovary* is the scene of the agricultural fair, at which an official is droning on and on about agricultural matters to the assembled audience, while Madam Bovary and her lover-to-be are engaging in intimate conversation. Flaubert's novelistic device is to alternately let us hear (and visually imagine) both sets of interactions, the public and the private. Of course, we have all acted out Flaubert's scene ourselves by running our self-interactions parallel to the overt interactions in which we are caught up, the covert interactions being entirely inappropriate to, and possibly even sarcastically at odds with, the public events.

Representations in Everyday Interactions

When we examine everyday interactions, we note that if representations are involved, they are likely to be interwoven with nonrepresentational aspects of the interactions. One way to begin to unravel this interweaving is to think of some interactions as not only preceded by representational conditions, but also as representing action that occurs during and often following upon given interactions. Before and as they enter a given interaction, the actors may have representational expectations of themselves and of the others too. Monitoring of the expected as well as emergent representativeness that often occurs during interaction indeed may be necessary, for otherwise the interaction can be hazardous.

For instance, a young woman answers an ad for a job interview. During the interview she needs to correct any mistaken expectation of what the prospective employer is looking for (say, a "well-mannered" black woman), and so should closely monitor the interviewer's actions and quickly adapt her behavior if she assesses the situation as otherwise than advertised. She adapts her behavior, that is, to what she suspects is "really" desired in an employee. Everyday interaction is full of such expectational traps, but aside from mistaken prior expectations, the representativeness can quickly and often subtly shift during the course of interaction.

In daily interactions, different degrees of representation are likely to appear during different phases of a given interaction. Thus interactions between organizations involve organizational representatives, whose actions during the interaction are partly guided by their representativeness; yet quite as in the instance of members of an organization who hold different position within it, the representational aspects may shift over the course of the interaction. As an instance of intraorganizational interaction, picture a scene wherein a subordinate is giving a verbal report to his superior. The opening phase may be totally representational in form and remain so until the report and its discussion are completed. Then the men may relax their formality, talk perhaps about the forthcoming pro football game; but near the close of their interaction they may revert to their more formal stances. Diplomats may also relax their representative stances during the course of their primarily official interaction, especially if the interaction is of long duration, if they find themselves liking each other, or if they have enjoyed working together before.

Everyday interactions are very much prone to this kind of interweaving of representational and nonrepresentational aspects. Here are two amusing and quite clear examples that I witnessed on separate occasions, each involving a customs official and incoming American travelers. Once when passing through customs, my wife and I, at the customs officer's request, listed the contents of a piece of baggage. In it, near the bottom, was a lithograph purchased overseas. "Oh," she said, "show it to me." So I dug down to the very bottom of this well-filled bag, totally disturbing its contents. When I lifted the lithograph out, she said in a very nonofficial tone: "So that's what a lithograph looks like! I wondered. I've never seen one. Thank you!"—and waved us on. At another time before a very busy customs gate, an incoming traveler and the customs officer discovered that they were both from Idaho; so they began discussing potato crops and cows, while an impatient and increasingly restive crowd of people piled up behind this talkative twosome. The conversation finished, the official turned calmly to the next (indignant) passenger. These are overly simple though perfectly real and commonplace examples of interwoven nonrepresentational and representation action that can be easily matched from your own experiences.

Representation and Presentation in Everyday Interaction

In thinking about everyday interaction, does it not strike you that besides a relationship between representation and nonrepresentation there is also one between representation and presentation? Perhaps we can sensibly phrase the latter relationship in the following way: Insofar as the action is *non*representational, the actor can be conceived of as presenting aspects of the self-in-action. Certainly he or she (or an organization) does this in ways that are more evident and expressed with more degrees of freedom than in more closely prescribed rituals. Insofar as the action is representational, however, the actor may be both "representing" and "presenting." No matter how prescribed the ritual action, something of the individual enters into the representation. If it is a deliberate "entering in," then there is surely at least a small element of self-presentation in Goffman's sense of the term. The same is true of the nonritualistic aspects of action that enter into carrying out the ritual: If the actor's body movements and other gestures are made with deliberate individuality, then think of these as a form of self-presentation carried out within the constraints of the ritual itself. In fact, the individuality can enhance the ritual effect. For instance, I am told that Protestant ministers in Germany are expected to have their own personal styles. To be expressive, one needs a ritual frame within which a personal style is developed. If the movements and gestures are unwitting, however, then there is no analytic point in conceiving them as even a small degree of self-presentation— unless one takes the risky step of saying yes unwitting, but subliminally or unconsciously asserting himself.

Complex Face-to-Face Interaction

Now what I want to develop is a conception of a more fluid interplay of representational and nonrepresentational interaction—a more complicated account of how representation may enter into interactions. Recently, in rereading *Mirrors and Masks* I found some of this complexity addressed. I will quote a long passage since it says clearly much of what I would repeat here anyhow. Before doing so, a few comments should be useful.

In the quoted passage the focus is primarily on identity in relation to interaction, rather than on representation as such. Yet the terms *represen-*

tation, representative, and *represent* are used as phenomena that are intrinsic to interaction, making interaction therefore impossible to analyze in overly simple terms. In the quoted paragraphs, I was criticizing the then currently popular terms *role* and *status,* and arguing that representing a given collectivity or social position would certainly affect a given interaction, set some of its parameters; but neither term would account for the specific actions within those parameters nor the outcomes of the interaction. This is because of contingencies that usually develop during the interactional course, which derive from unanticipated actions and their immediate interactional consequences. In other words, there is: (1) *a complex interplay* of conventional and emergent representational *components* (2) *with* nonrepresentational components (3) *in* the actions of each actor (4) *during* the course of the *evolving* interaction. What the quoted passage also brings out is the additional intricacy of representation in the form of visible and invisible audiences. The actors may or may not be appreciatively or painfully aware of some of these audiences; and this may be so for all the interactants—none of whom necessarily know what are the most significant audiences of the other interactants.

The actors may move in and out of representational action during the interaction, and at different times than each other. Yet they do this not necessarily in response to each other, but perhaps rather in response to imagined presences who are representative of one or another position, perspective, or social world. Moreover, in varying degrees they may even be unaware of the other's representational-nonrepresentational shifts. Nevertheless, they may be responding to the actions of the other(s) either on explicit interpretational grounds or by reacting quite subliminally. Furthermore, each is not necessarily aware of the full complexity of his or her *own* representations.

Here then is the passage:

> Face-to-face interaction is a fluid, moving, "running" process; during its course the participants take successive stances vis-à-vis each other. . . . [T]hey move through successive phases of position. The initial reading of the other's identity merely sets the stage for action, gives each some cues for his lines. . . . For certain purposes it may suffice to describe interaction as going on between persons who each enact a role or occupy a status. The actors, then, are said to perceive the situation, observe what is required with respect to the status of each, and carry out the requisite or selected line of action. . . . [T]his kind of description is often adequate, but for our purposes, it is not. The adoption of a general role [or representation] (say, a lawyer giving advice) toward a person [representing a status] of a given status (client) merely suggests the general framework within which interplay will go on. . . . But awareness of position enters into interaction in tremendously subtle ways. Actors "enact their roles"—but how? The terms . . . suggest but

do not come to grips with the complexity and phase-like character of interplay, nor do they emphasize the frequently unexpected results of interactional drama. . . .

To begin with the term "interaction" tends to obscure the fact that much
more than two flesh and blood persons are responding to another. . . .
[A]lthough there are only two main actors . . . there are also other actors
who are visible only to the audience, or to one or the other. . . . Thus, each
. . . while acting toward the other, may also be acting toward an invisible
third, much as if the latter were actually present. To make the matter more
complicated, if actor A is officially representing a close group with respect
to actor B then in a real sense the entire group should be there upon the
stage, so that when A makes a commendable statement they will nod in
collective approval, and then A will as much respond to them as to B. Or A
may view B as representing a group that he dislikes, so B should be standing with his group ranged about him. (Strauss [1959] 1969, pp. 55–56)

These last statements quite accurately describe the anguishing dilemmas of some representatives of social worlds that are contesting within
policy arenas. When studying the AIDS arena, my colleagues and I were
struck by the bitterness of certain leaders of AIDS organizations, who
alleged they were frequently being "misunderstood"—both by organizational outsiders and insiders—for policy stands that they had taken.

To continue, however, with the quotation about audiences in order to
emphasize the fluidity of face-to-face interaction:

If we wish to approach the complexity of real interactional events, we
would also have to make arrangements for the supplementary actors to
make exits and entrances and to fade in and out of the immediate circle of
conversation when they were and were not relevant to the main drama.
Their visibility might be signalized by their donning and doffing appropriate masks. These supplementary actors will represent a wide range of relationships: relatives, friends, teachers, and so on. Some will be persons
long since dead, or arising out of the actor's past. Many will represent
groups to which the actor belongs, and will appropriate gestures from him
during the interaction. Some of the invisible actors will be legends and
myths which enter the drama and affect the action. . . . The interactional
situation is not an interaction between two persons, merely, but a series of
transactions carried on in thickly peopled and complexly imaged contests.
[And, don't forget that some] of these transactions consist of each person's
responses to himself. (Strauss [1959] 1969, pp. 56–57)

Misrepresentation, Misunderstanding, and
Their Management

Here now are other facets of representation, also full of intricacies, but
more involuted. In *Black Like Me* (Griffin 1961), a white journalist described in detail how for some weeks he was able to pass, at least among

white southerners, as a black man while traveling in the southern states. He was able to misrepresent himself as standing for a member of "the black race" by darkening his skin with a chemical preparation and by then acting more or less appropriately when in public. The masquerade was not detected by the whites because he never engaged in extended interaction during which he would have had to be quite clever at disguising details of his biography. He carefully restricted his contacts with whites to allowing them to see him in public, walking, entering buildings, and talking with blacks. Probably some blacks did suspect his misrepresentation, because of some unfamiliarities of gesture or suspicious components in his conversations, but if so they did not challenge it.

Misrepresentation has some interesting properties. On the face of it, misrepresenting can only be done deliberately, that is, claimed either openly or, as with the journalist, implicitly. The intent is to deceive, to mislead, in short, to deliberately create misunderstanding. Yet as in the example, given some pages back, of the Japanese American woman in Japan, the attribution of representative status can be made, and then one has to decide whether to deny the attribution (the misunderstanding) or falsely accept it. On the other hand, if the other(s) suspects or actually knows that someone is misrepresenting and then makes an accusation of falsehood, then if the former chooses to deny this then there arises the problem of convincing the accuser, or perhaps some audience (like a judge) or both. The actors in such dramas need not merely be individuals but can be collectivities, or (true or false) representatives of them.

Misrepresentation would appear at first glance to be all bad, except for "little white lies." Of course, this is not so, since people and organizations misrepresent with perfectly good motives and with the best of intentions, either for what they perceive as their own good or for those at the receiving end of the deception. We know that the best of intentions do not always result in the best consequences, at least from the viewpoint of those who later discover "the truth," but the consequences may turn out to be salutary or at last positive for some of the actors.

A good example, albeit debatable in particular instances, is the "closed awareness context" (Glaser and Strauss 1965) found in hospitals that conditions staff action toward dying patients, and sometimes their relatives. Hospital personnel misrepresent themselves to those patients and kin as caring for someone who is going to live—leading the patient/kin to believe in this message—this same repeated drama that we studied thirty years ago and that still continues in American hospitals and elsewhere in the world. As described and analyzed in our monograph, there are at least three other awareness contexts in the hospital situation. First, there is a "suspicion awareness context" when the patient and/or kin begin to suspect the falsity of the representation; then they act strategically to discover whether their suspicions are true. *Discover* is the key term here, along with *disclose*, since the misrepresenting agents are unwilling to disclose the truth, strip off their misrepresenting masks, and stop acting out this fiction. A second context is "mutual pretense," where both the patient and the staff member know that a fiction indeed is being acted and the patient chooses to act it out with the staff member, to avoid embarrassment (and possibly other emotions) for either or both.

The third context is "open awareness," when there is no misrepresentation about the patient's perceived dying status and he or she knows what that status is. Then the interaction can be of staff members openly giving care to a dying person and the latter acting with knowledge of how they perceive and are acting toward him- or herself. Understandably, the patient can deny the attribution of "you are dying"—or accept it but outwardly and cleverly act as if it were not accepted. In that instance—and it does happen if only infrequently—and if the staff are persuaded, then a really complicated interaction is taking place, not quite as in Shakespeare's comedy of errors since the patient here is presenting him- or herself as accepting a dying status but secretly rejecting it (thus creating a closed awareness of another kind).

Awareness contexts with their associated misrepresentations and discoveries or disclosures occur at every level of interaction, from the most microscopic to the most macroscopic. Consider only the elaborate spy systems that nations develop in order to keep track of and ward off perceived dangers to national interests. The same representational actions occur here as touched on earlier: the claiming, proffering, denying, accepting, correcting, and so on. They just occur on a larger stage. The apprehended spy denies he is a spy, or accepts the accusation but his government denies he represents what he says he is representing. To make the interaction more complicated, the spy has often taken on his job knowing, or actually having made a verbal contract, that if he is discovered then his government (or foreign employer) will certainly disclaim him. Then the apprehending spy system has to determine, or guess, the truth; and even if it actually knows the truth, it may engage in mutual pretense with the employing nation for a variety of reasons; or it may pretend not to really be certain, releasing the spy who no longer has any other use than as this kind of pawn.

The *organization* of action in carrying out such misrepresentations involves a host of actors, and an infinite number of dovetailed actions. With regard to the operation of an effective spy organization, there is the recruitment and training of agents; the monitoring of their information and activities; the counterespionage tactics and operations; the interpretation of information, and convincing key organizational or higher governmental officials of its truth.

Such work, incidentally, can involve difficult moral decisions—misrepresentation often does. Keeping to our spy system example, during World War II, British intelligence officials and Churchill, after much debate, reluctantly decided to allow the Germans to bomb the city of Coventry unimpeded rather than to take protective actions, for otherwise the enemy would guess the vital secret that the British had already developed a system for cracking the German codes (Stevenson 1976). This decision was crucial for winning the war, but (mis)represented British intelligence as being far behind German cryptographic ingenuity. That the citizens of Coventry were kept ignorant of the secret and suffered the consequences of the bombing is not incidental, for the moral dilemma was clear to the officials who made this anguishing decision, as were many other similar decisions made during this war.

Another striking instance of a misrepresentation on a national level—in which we see mirrors mirroring mirrors—was the revelation, thirty years after the fact, that Hitler had been induced to declare war on the United States via a planted false document that had been fed to an unsuspecting pro-Nazi American senator, who, as anticipated, passed on the erroneous information *sub rosa* to the German government (Stevenson 1976). The rest of us, then and later, not knowing any of this history simply misunderstood what lay behind Hitler's declaration; and Americans or anyone else who do not know of this deception still have a misunderstanding about the actual declaration of war.

I will touch lightly on one last aspect of misrepresentation and misunderstanding, that of phasing or pacing. Everyone knows that many detective novels have some variant of the following structure: The hero detective discovers or cleverly elicits cues about who is the murderer, but does not reveal what or how much he knows, although he may drop false or vague cues about his suspecting of persons in order to lull the true murderer. At the close of the story, the detective either discloses his discovery or elicits disclosure from the murderer by a last shrewd tactic; or discloses in order to elicit an admission of guilt, which, in fact, he needs for actually getting a legal conviction. Lengthy interaction sequences in fiction and drama that centrally involve representational concealment, disclosure, discovery, establishing or breaking pretense, and so forth can be analyzed in similar terms.

Why should real-life interaction not also be similarly conceived in this way? Anyone doing research where such phenomena appeared might well think in terms of sequence, timing, duration, and other temporal characteristics. Even data about relatively brief interaction can be so examined. For instance, a skilled coroner in announcing a death to a kinsman carefully paces his disclosure, dropping cues by tone of voice, phrasing, gesture, so as to bring the listener more gradually into dawning recognition, thereby reducing the potential shock of the disclosure of this unwelcome news by this (initially disguised) messenger from the city or county (Charmaz 1975). Or another example, a husband or wife planning separation from the spouse often drops cues that the spouse overlooks or misinterprets, because she or he does not yet recognize how fragile the marital relationship has become. The actual announcement of intent to separate inevitably produces a shocked reaction (Vaughan 1986).

Larger-scale interactions, in terms of organizational scope and numbers of representatives and representing actions, lend themselves to the same type of conceptualization. An example rich in suggestive data is Schlesinger's (1965, pp. 266–97) descriptive account of the Cuban missile crisis, with its several phases involving the initial discovery of Soviet missiles in Cuba, the secret convening of high government officials acting in behalf of the nation, the keeping of the secret both from the Soviet Union and from the American public while the officials were working out strategy, the pacing of discovered information and disclosure of plans to the Soviet officials, and so on.

A particularly complicated combination of intentional misrepresentation and genuine misunderstanding is likely to exist among interactants who debate, manipulate, attempt to persuade, and otherwise position themselves in hotly contested arenas. They will accuse each other of deception when genuine misunderstanding exists; they will claim it is all a mistake when they have actually contrived at deception and attempted to create misunderstanding. This is so whether the arenas are great public ones, like the energy or environmental ones, or are arenas limited to specific social worlds.

I have dwelt on misrepresentation and its management because it is, again, intrinsic to a great many interactions. Sociologists have, in fact, created islands of substantive theory pertaining to misrepresentations. I say "islands," since each author creates his or her terminology to analyze his or her differing data. Thus we have studies, to mention but a few, of individual secrets, organizational secrets, lying, "passing," informational control; and studies of a host of substantive areas, including stigma management by epileptics (Schneider and Conrad 1980), concealed intraorganizational bargains (Dalton 1954), confidence games (Sutherland 1937), hiding mistakes at work (Riemer 1979), plea-bargaining arrangements (Skolnick 1966), sanctioned secrecy among scientists (Edge and Mulkay 1976), employee fronting before customers (Jackal 1978), privacy in various realms (Shils 1956; Warren 1974), deceiving the client (Glaser 1976), and so on. The conceptualization and its associated terminology put forward in this chapter might help to relate these apparently discrete studies, as well as bring them into more explicit relationship to a theory of action. The point is that the perspective reflected in each study can be rephrased in terms of the more encompassing general theoretical framework, which itself explicitly expresses a theory of action.

STRATEGIC INTERACTION

One type of interaction much referred to in the sociological literature (cf. Lofland 1978) is termed *strategic*. The concept refers to interaction directed at some purpose or purposes, which entail strategies of managing interaction itself, not merely (say) managing resources or attempting to control policy decisions. Probably the preponderance of interactional studies are directed toward this type of interaction. You will have recognized many instances of strategic interaction in this chapter's pages. To focus more directly on its major features, I will briefly allude to and comment on several case studies.

Consider again some of the complexities of interaction associated with various of the awareness contexts. The relevance to strategic interaction of the concealing, revealing, discovering, and so forth of how information should be readily apparent. Think also of misrepresentation and at least somewhat false presentation enter into the closed-awareness situation. Playing, as on the stage, also is called forth: the actors playing out scenarios meant to throw someone, or some collectivity, off the trace of discovering the concealed information.

However, misrepresentation is not inherent in all instances of strategic interaction. In mutual pretense situations, for instance, there may be an implicit negotiation about acting appropriately, or alternatively action is based on a quick assessment of a common or shared response.[1] Different scenarios are understandably characteristic of suspicion awareness contexts as opposed to open, mutual-pretense, or closed ones. Thus, representation, misrepresentation, and presentation can be complexly intertwined in these forms of strategic interaction.

To bring out further aspects and variants of strategic interaction, I will briefly discuss a well-known paper by Fred Davis ([1961] 1972) titled "Deviance Disavowal." The aim of this researcher was to analyze how his interviewees, visibly disabled men and women, managed their encounters with strangers during sociability situations such as parties. At the beginning of these "interactional situation[s] *per se* as a result of their being perceived routinely . . . as different, 'odd,' 'estranged from the common run of humanity,' etc.; in short, other than normal"—the disabled person will attempt to shape the unfolding interaction so as to move it to a more normal basis ([1961] 1972, p. 132). Davis's analysis is subtle, but the heart of it is suggested in his summary statement of stages through which the interactional course moves when successfully shaped. During the first stage, of "fictional acceptance," the normal person regards the disabled as inferior but acts politely as if he or she were normal. Here "the interactional problem confronting the visibly handicapped person is the delicate one of not permitting his identity to be circumscribed by the fiction while at the same time playing along with it and showing appropriate regard for its social legitimacy" ([1961] 1972, p. 140). Then in moving toward the next stage of "facilitating normalized role-taking" or "breaking through," a redefinitional process occurs in which the disabled person "disavows" his or her deviance and gets the other to accept this redefinition through a variety of tactics. Then "the problem . . . becomes one of sustaining the normalized definition in the face of many small amendments and qualifications that must frequently be made to it" ([1961] 1972, p. 145), because after all disablement is accompanied by visible handicaps to action.

We in turn can ask, What is going on during the phases of this interactional course in terms of representation, presentation, and misrepresentation? The disabled persons who do not want to interact on the basis of the other's stereotypical definitions of themselves are presenting themselves as something much more or quite different than disabled, correcting too the misattribution by the others of a "merely disabled" status, and gradually getting across their subtle claims to be normal just like the other—artists, baseball enthusiasts, brilliant scientists—a person much like you, and perhaps with similar interests; so your original definition of me was a false one, which I have had to rectify, and you are really not so wedded to stereotypes as to recognize the true person in me. Note that in this interaction, the disabled person's presentation is a corrective one and is carried out with great deliberateness and in fact with skill, since this kind of situation has been a repeated experience for him or her. However, no misrepresentation is involved in this strategic interaction.

However, more complexities are possible in this strategic interactional situation. For instance, the researcher did not interview the strangers, and so did not discover their possible roles in shaping the interactions; some may have experienced this kind of situation before and so might quickly establish an attitude during this particular episode of "I regard your disability as irrelevant to our conversation; you are a person who is perhaps interested in the same things that I am." Then the disabled person could quickly relax and not engage deliberately or at least pointedly in corrective self-presentation. A more striking interaction yet would have occurred if the stranger happened to be a physical therapist, who of course would then bring professional experience into this episode. This might further relieve the disabled person from having to manipulate the interaction, especially if the therapist signaled his or her professional status quickly and indicated expectations that a "perfectly normal" mode of interaction should occur between the two of them—although only if the therapist was genuinely trusted. This professional representation, and matching presentation, would ease the interaction quickly into other representational-presentational modes for both people.

Here is a third illustrative case that brings out still other aspects of strategic interaction. A few years go, some leading microbiologists realized that DNA experiments might possibly be hazardous to the larger community, but that whether hazardous or not it would be better not to provoke antagonistic public reactions by preceding with the experiments until more was known about their effects (Lear 1978). So they worked out an agreement within the microbiological community for a brief moratorium on DNA experiments, which would be maintained until careful guidelines could be devised and tested. These would cover levels of hazard possibly produced by different types of experiments. The argument put forward by the advocates of a moratorium was that if we continue to carry out such experiments without such self-review, then the general public, and the granting agencies, will regard us as irresponsible. So we must regulate ourselves!

This representation of themselves as careful, self-regulatory, thoroughly responsible citizen-scientists was "got across" to the outside world through a series of presenting tactics. Their moratorium and levels-of-hazard guidelines were publicized through public meetings and the media. Important microbiologists descended on Washington and gave informative lectures—as a type of lobbying—to congressmen, assuring their listeners of their responsible stances and the low level of potential hazard from their experiments. Further strategic action took the form of maneuvering to keep governmental oversight out of the hands of potentially hostile agencies, and successfully located in the National Institutes of Health, a friendly environment for biological scientists and an agency that for decades had represented the biological disciplines before Congress and the wider public. At the special hearings within this agency, hostile or suspicious nonbiologists sometimes accused the microbiologists of misstating the degree of hazard from DNA experiments, though on the whole the misrepresentation was rare. That issue aside, as the scientists increasingly established their credibility as responsible citizens, their presentation-representation strategies became less evident, and gradually this public policy issue faded away, becoming only of historic interest. So also did the danger to the social world of microbiology itself (Strauss 1978, pp. 230–40).

The main point of the pages immediately above can be summarized by saying that forms of strategic interaction will vary considerably in their mixtures of representation, presentation, and misrepresentation. These and their interrelationships need to be analyzed within specific situations, and doing so is useful for understanding the intricacies of strategic interaction as an important interactional form.

More generally these pages point to the central importance of representing and misrepresenting. No actor, whether a person or a collectivity, can escape the intricacies and significance of representational issues. Any theory of action that omits a close scrutiny of these issues loses considerable power to understand interaction and matters of identity.

NOTES

1.   There is an old humorous story that reflects how mutual embarrassment is avoided. At a boarding house, a woman forgets to lock the door of the public bathroom before taking a bath; while she is bathing, a man opens the door, quickly assesses the situation, then just as quickly closes the door, saying loudly "Pardon me SIR."

Chapter 8

The Interplay of Routine and Nonroutine Action

Outside the scope of habits, thought works gropingly, fumbling in confused uncertainty; and yet habit made complete in routine shuts in thought so effectively that it is no longer needed or possible. . . . [Yet] The more flexible [habits] are, the more refined is perception in its discrimination and the more delicate the presentation evoked by imagination
— J. Dewey, *Human Nature and Conduct*

A theory of action needs to take into account both routine and nonroutine types of interaction, but also to examine their relationships. In the next pages those matters will be explored. Again they are implicit in the Pragmatists' writings, couched there in philosophic rather than sociological terms. I say "explored" advisedly because of all the chapters in this book, what I will present here is the sketchiest, the most provisional, yet the issues are worth examining even in this form because they are of prime importance.

When I was of high school age, in common with many of my generation, I reacted adversely against the restraints of what was then called "custom," which we expressed scornfully as "inflexible" adherence to "habit," the "unthinking" following of "old-fashioned" rules that no longer fit contemporary experience. Adults arrogantly claiming the superiority of their outmoded "experience" nicely expressed our antagonistic motto. Only later in college when I read sentences like John Dewey's did my teenaged vision of an outrageously constraining world become modified. Routine behavior now began to look more reasonable and even useful as a springboard for the creative life to which I aspired.

After a year or so studying sociology at Chicago, I thought no more about routine behavior. Sociologists at that university, as elsewhere, were not concerned with this except perhaps in the sense of a more abstract terminology of rules and of status-derived roles. One of Robert Park's students (Doyle 1937) wrote an interesting monograph on southern racial rituals, although ritual was not, then and now, generally a significant topic for sociologists, as it has long been for social anthropologists. Park and other Chicago interactionists paid scant attention to routine behavior, either in and of itself or in relation to nonroutine behavior. Their orientation was expressed by Blumer, who once remarked that ordinary, everyday behavior sets no problems of explanation, whereas the new behavior precipitated by social change sets major issues for sociology. [Although he did not emphasize routine action, Blumer (1969) did, however, express in writing the view that action did generate both routine and change.]

The closest that the Chicagoans, then and until recently, came to careful scrutiny of how the routine and nonroutine might relate to each other was with Thomas and Znaniecki's famous sequence of organization → disorganization → organization (1918–1920). However, even there the intent was to develop sociological theory for giving an understanding of the drastic social changes that were smashing into the lives of immigrants and their children.

Much later, two other Chicago theorists came to grips with this very important sociological issue of how routine and nonroutine interaction reciprocally affect each other. Erving Goffman's intense examination of largely implicit interactional rules and their frequent breakage and repair in interaction is well known; indeed this was central to his work (cf. 1967, 1974). He would even use the term *ritual* when referring to interaction with reference to these rules. More recently, Howard Becker (1982) has examined the complicated interlocking of collectively shared artistic conventions as expressed in organizational forms, and the work of artists: work that can neither be efficient nor perhaps even take place without these supportive conventions. Conventions are also contributory to whatever creativity the artists may attain in interaction with the materials of their craft. Becker is less interested in the creativity issue as such than in demonstrating that a larger "collective act" involving artistic conventions, institutions, organizations, and even industries is essential if artistic endeavor is to take place continuously and professionally.

His research is pertinent to this chapter, but tends to be focused more on the contribution of routine social structures to efficiency and innovation than on their mutual interplay. However, his persistent use of the term *convention* to indicate cultural forms or formats, alternatively efficient or constraining, is very useful in terms of our own emphasis below on routine formats. These are either taken over directly as conventions or selectively adapted as individual formats or personal conventions.

Goffman's writing tends to focus on how implicit interactional rules both constrain and get broken, but ultimately become continually maintained through the interaction itself. Another limitation of his analysis is its very scope. It is restricted to face-to-face interaction with little emphasis on structural conditions other than interactional ones. Also it avoids temporal issues because it is focused almost wholly on repetitive episodes.

At the risk of being thought frivolous, I will next use the work of comedians as a thought-provoking illustration of the interplay of routine and nonroutine with which I am concerned. Clearly, comedians refer to certain elements of their public presentations as "routines." These are formats, such as Bob Hope's patter or rapid stream of quips, that give a structure to the presentation but that also allow for innovative comic effects. These formats have to be "just right," must utilize a niche in the market for humor and laughter, appealing to some segment or segments of the general public. Formats have to go through trial-and-error performances before the comedian can discover which parts of them are successful and which are not. Formats also may have to be literally discovered, in which the comedian experiments with several before finding one that works, or accidentally stumbles onto a successful one.[1] Will Rodgers, perhaps America's major comedian in the 1920s and 1930s, discovered his celebrated style through his wife's perspicacity. He had remained an unnoted comedian, until one day she said something like the following: "Every morning, Will, we sit at breakfast and you read the newspaper aloud, cracking wise about the things you read. You are really funny! Why don't you try that in your 'act?'" Before long such newspaper commentary *was* his act, or at least a large part of it. Once he had the format properly fashioned, then Will Rogers could play his audience effectively, and more than occasionally innovate with brilliance within the limits of his routines. His routine had become automatic.

ROUTINE ACTION

Before addressing the subject of routines, clarity requires distinguishing between them and routine action. Routine aspects are encapsulated in even an act carried out for the first time, in the form of bodily skills such as walking, culturally derived gestures, listening, and speaking. Stretching the term *routine,* perhaps, one could claim that perception and memory, which are thoroughly social in character and which enter into and make possible most if not all nonreflexive action, have been routinized through repeated experiences with the world.

Insofar as actions are repeated, they become over time so routinized as to fall mostly out of consciousness until something happens to call attention to them. The most striking examples are not such learned skills as driving a car or playing tennis but more fundamental cultural actions like eating with chopsticks or a fork.

Complex acts cannot take place without these usually taken for granted skills and abilities. Those certainly include modes of thinking and working. Yet to say this is to distort understanding of routine action. More accurately phrased, we should say that these routinized skills and abilities are *integral* to every action. Another way of conceiving of these routinized components is that they are resources, or assemblages of resources, built literally into the action. This is true even when, say, an aspiring Olympic athlete practices long and hard to perfect special skills, so that during the actual competitions he or she can rely on these aspects of performance to be automatically in the action. Metaphorically speaking, these routinized resources are drawn up or called up, but the metaphoric language obscures the reality that routine is part of the action itself.

Yet unless an action is totally routinized, as ideally it is in a perfectly performing mass production line, this is likely to consist of more than routinized components. Any specific situation in which action takes place will require some if only the smallest adjustment. When making repeated routine actions, say cutting grapes off a vine, a worker's actions will be far from identical, the additional nonroutine aspects constituting responses to the specificity of the angle at which a bunch of grapes is hanging or its height on the vine. The conditions that affect specificity may also be internal to the actor: When he or she is tired, then the repeated routinized action demands more care and attention—something is now occurring that makes the action less routine.

Combinations of internal and external conditions may also shift the balance between the routine and the nonroutine, as when fog descends on the highway or when rainy streets turn icy. Then driving and walking move from taken for granted to sharply attended actions. Those "same" actions move from predominantly routine toward what may even be elaborately new modifications of driving and walking. They are no longer quite the same acts.

So-called routine action thus is normally not entirely routine, and novel action necessarily has its routinized aspects. In short, one should not draw a hard and fast line between routine and nonroutine action. This is so whether the action or interaction is that of an individual or a collectivity. I turn now to the main topic of this chapter: routines.

THE COMPLEX NATURE OF ROUTINES
AND ROUTINE ACTIONS

Routines are standardized patterns of action. Without these, nothing much could be accomplished through action carried out on a *repeated* basis. Repetitive goal-directed action requires a patterning of action that does not need to be invented on the spot each time that a person or collectivity acts. During the course of encountering situations, unless an actor could quickly classify most with a standard definition, he or she would unquestionably become exhausted. When, however, a situation can be defined as slightly different, novel, or unusual, then although appropriate patterns of routine action are called upon, these will be supplemented with new actions or a slight adaptation of the routine. Even in the most revolutionary of actions, the repertoire of routines does not vanish; at least part of it becomes utilized in combination with the new. Many if not most routines are responses to problems, as my discussion below will reflect. However, some are not related to solving problems or acting in problematic situations. For instance, suppose someone has a set routine for reaching her office, that is, she takes the same route each day. She may have fixed on that route because then she can walk automatically while her mind is on other matters, thus making the walk unproblematic. On the other hand, she may have elected to walk this particular sequence of streets because they constitute the most beautiful walk. Likewise, foods served in American households are likely to be eaten in idiosyncratic sequence by different members of the family. One person will begin with a vegetable, another with a piece of meat; one may eat the salad before anything else, another afterward, and another during the main course. In this instance, no particular problems are being solved or eased by these individualized routines. Similarly for collectivities, some ritual sequences rest on preferences rather than on the confronting of problems, compared with such rituals as a rain dance, which is designed to break a prolonged drought.

If we think about organizations and other collectivities, it is apparent that routines operationalize arrangements, reached by virtue of explicit or tacit agreements between or among actors. How the members reach agreement is varied—through negotiation, persuasion, some degree of coercion and manipulation, and so on—but agreements must be there or the arrangements will not be arrived at or will be fragile. Those outside the agreements will ignore, cut corners, or even play fast and loose with the arrangements. Conflict within organizations is reflected in these discrepant behaviors toward arrangements and their associated routines. These arrangements frequently get hardened, at least for a time, into rules and regulations. As Gusfield phrases this: "To institutionalize a pattern of behavior is to make it recurrent and routine and to surround it with a norm" (1991, p. 10).

These arrangements should not be conceived of as involving only a few persons, such as the musicians in a rock band or a team of researchers in a laboratory. Participants in an agreement or sets of interlocking agreements may include representatives at every level of an organization, and indeed may include those outside the organization, or among many organizations even if scattered geographically. A convenient example is Joan Fujimura's (1987) study of what is entailed in carrying out research projects in cancer laboratories. There must be an articulation of work, based on arrangements supported by standing and ad hoc agreements that tie together the project, the laboratory, other research departments, supply departments, laboratories elsewhere including overseas, government funding agents, and so on. All of this interaction underpins both the tackling of problems and the routine actions that go into this innovative work.

The chief function, or consequence, of routines is their contribution to efficiency and/or efficacy. A felicitous phrase by E. C. Hughes that "One man's emergency is another's routine" is helpful here. By this he meant situations like a homeowner hysterically telephoning a plumber because a toilet is overflowing. To the plumber, this event is just a routine matter, a job to be done immediately only if there is no other pressing business; otherwise the customer is calmly told "we will be there just as soon as we can," which translated *sotto voce* means "according to our own schedule, not yours!" The plumber's scheduling of time and jobs, and the division of labor among workers in the shop, are all part of his and its daily routines. Hopefully these routines enhance efficiency and prevent clients from rendering the work less efficient by their urgent calls for immediate action. As we all know, there can be a clash between the requirements of efficiency and effectiveness. On a broad scale this can be seen in the American health care system today. With steadily rising medical costs, and pressured by the federal government, hospital boards and administrators have opted for greater efficiency (especially in financial matters); while their critics, including medical and nursing personnel, argue that this "all-out" focus mitigates against giving maximum or even adequate ("effective") clinical care to patients.

Built into routines and routine actions are technologies, developed for more efficiently and perhaps effectively, accomplishing the larger action. Technology can be "hard," in the form of tools and equipment; it can also be "soft," in the form of bodily and mental skills and procedures. Hard and soft technology feed into each other, with the hard embedded in procedures and skills or it will not work properly and the soft enhanced by the hard *if* one knows how to use it. Technology also may include materials, such as the supplies used in medical equipment and the psychologists' chimpanzees and white rats. By simplifying the materials so that they can be used broadly, in routine ways, the clinical or research work is eased. Likewise, the procedures used with these materials get standardized; otherwise efficiency and effectiveness will be less (cf.

Clarke and Fujimura 1992). The example of the chimpanzees and white rats also makes evident that a great deal of learning about the materials must take place, in this case by the psychologist, before those materials can be used properly.

All of this about routines is fairly obvious. Perhaps not quite so obvious is that routines, but not all routine actions, usually are the end product of solutions to problematic situations. We might usefully think of routines as only the quieter aspect of an unending sedimentation process. First let us assume a preceding set of routines, then the problematic situation or contingency that sets a problem, then figuring out what to do since the current routine solution is not working. If the trial solution is successful (more will be said about this below) then it gets added to or partly substituted for the inherited routines, and becomes an integral component of the total ongoing routine. Some of the new solutions are truly innovative, although if someone does not know their history then later they are likely to appear merely as integral to the routines. All of this is true of common activities like painting a wall with a roller instead of a brush, a practice with an infinitely longer history, as it is true of using a personal computer rather than writing with a pen or pencil if you are under, say, the age of ten.

Recent research in the sociology of science and more specifically ob-servations of how laboratory scientists actually carry out the work of solving their research problems (Law 1986; Star 1989b, p. 191) provides an interesting instance of the last points, but also adds a startling per-spective on these solutions. When confronted by their research problems, physical and biological scientists frequently borrow technology from another discipline or specialty. In doing this they ignore or are ignorant of the limitations of the technology as recognized by its originators and the assumptions that lie behind their own use of it. In essence, the bor-rowing and use of the technology "black boxes" this recognition of its limits and the originator's assumptions, though the technology enhances the borrowers' own creativity. For the latter, the technology represents a set of routines that enables the tackling of their own specific problems, making it easier or possible to solve them. The inventors of the technology, however, are likely to remember the routines as solutions to previous problems.

A point often missed when thinking about routines (and routine action too) is the symbolism buried in them. Why is it missed? Probably because of the very ordinariness, lack of excitement, even dullness associated with them. Yet let them be challenged and you cannot but notice annoyance, anger, indignation, and other signs of passion. At stake are statuses, interests, identities, and ideologically driven convictions. Examples abound, including the persistence of, and argumentation over, musical conventions and routine formats as well as accounting or other business practices. True, some routines are easily changed because actors are already disenchanted with them, discontented that they no longer work well or in fact mitigate against their particular interests and identities. If so, the routine arrangements and actions have lost some of their symbolization or, perhaps more accurately said, the symbolism is less freighted with passion or positive feeling.

However, routines often seem to be maintained long after they become inefficient or ineffective, and deemed so by their critics. Vested interests, and symbolism also, of powerful interactants may keep these in place, backed by punishment for infringing on the organizational rules that symbolically have replaced previously consensual or negotiated agreements. Yet weakened symbolism for some actors may lead them to break organizational rules or find their ways covertly around them, discovering as they do so new ways of acting and working.

But I have observed another more subtle set of conditions that sustain at least some portion of the network of routines found in organizations. Organizational routines are always linked in complex sequences and combinations. The procedures and other standardized interactions of nurses and physicians on a medical ward represent such an intermeshing. Around the clock on these wards, and over three eight-hour shifts, a multitude of tasks need to be done, a large proportion of them being standardized for efficiency's sake; but strictly clinical tasks also are routinized to increase their effectiveness.

Now, from time to time a patient arrives on the ward whose behavior causes such problems for the nursing staff that he or she becomes greatly disliked, is avoided as much as possible, and consumes an inordinate amount of time and energy, as the personnel seek to control the deviant behavior and as they talk endlessly about their problems with this patient. For some time afterward, among the hundreds of patients whom they easily forget, they remember him or her well and with anger or disgust. This patient has become what I call "the patient of the month" or "the patient of the year." The nursing personnel even compare the current problem patient with a similar previous one: "He's just like Mr. Smith, remember him!"

Despite those vivid memories, rarely are changes in the usual routines made to prevent comparable future days and weeks of furor. Why? One answer lies in the staff's belief that these are, after all, only occasional behavioral incidents in normally uneventful daily work. Another and perhaps deeper reason is that to avoid such episodes would require a considerable reworking of the ward's arrangements, constituting major organizational changes. The implicit trade-off is less-than-excellent care for these particular patients, and also the ward's upset, as balanced against major or minor changes in a complex of organizational routines. These processes are generic to organizations.

Routines are more likely to get changed under other *sets* of conditions. For instance, after a catastrophic incident, measures may be taken to change or supplement standard industrial safety procedures because these have proven inadequate. However, if not everyone defines them as inadequate, especially those who can bring more power or influence to bear on this situation, then the routines are unlikely to be substantially altered. Or if influential interactants judge that a mere few accidents scarcely warrant extra expense or the degree of structural changes needed, then on balance few if any great changes in safety routines will be instituted, although a few official regulations may be added or substituted for cosmetic effect.

Yet when rules or regulations are changed "upstairs" by a government agency or within an organization, and will be closely monitored, then the affected interactants need to adjudicate between the efficiency/effectiveness of some extant routines and the necessity to build or add or substitute new routines. We have observed the beginnings of this adjudicative process in hospitals. An administrative command came down to the head nurses that the current system of using "floating nurses" would no longer be operative. Each nurse would be assigned permanently to each ward, rather than occasionally being reassigned wherever there was a temporary shortage of staff elsewhere. Now each ward would somehow have to manage to cover for its personnel who were temporarily absent. This change resulted in a great deal of "figuring out" by the personnel on each ward, with much negotiation among the personnel, and also among the various head nurses who foresaw difficulties for which they could ease each other's problems by swapping personnel. Presumably wards in close geographical proximity and that were not too specialized in their work could make such new (and eventually) routine arrangements for meeting temporary staff shortages.

In short, this kind of incident, or when there is an annual review that changes organizational rules, highlights the processes whereby one part of the total network of routines passes out of existence and becomes replaced by new interactions that eventually become equally routinized. I might add also that in becoming routinized, sometimes a routine's origins are forgotten or become lost in the labyrinth of organizational history or through the turnover of personnel, except perhaps when there had been such a radical change in the organization's administration that the impact of its new policies could not later be easily forgotten. Organizational memory tends anyhow often to be evanescent, depending as it does on a stable and long-lived membership or work force (Engestrom 1984). Yet each generation inherits the sedimented routines without necessarily knowing, and usually not caring about, their origins.

All organizations and persons have routines for managing anticipated or expectable problem situations. Even when unanticipated events occur, it may be possible to rely on standard procedures, techniques, and other reactions, even on secure skills, that will function automatically when facing the unexpected contingency. On the other hand, reliance on current routines gives rise to what Veblen long ago termed "a trained incapacity," which refers to skills that are no longer appropriate because new circumstances are being confronted. In order to solve the new issues, new routines must be invented—sometimes very quickly! Trained *in*capacities must be abandoned in favor of learning new skills.

As an extreme instance of trained incapacity, think of those unfortunate Europeans who during World War II were overrun by the Nazis, and could not cope with the profound alteration of the routines of their lives. Aside from the question of the upset in their valued activities and to their identities, some of the conquered could not generate the necessary flexibility to live successfully under the new regime. Their ingrained capacities for living in their old but extinguished world now hindered or incapacitated them for maneuvering in the new one. They had literally lost much of their symbolic universe, and its elements of stability that were so much part of their lives. Other conquered individuals, and populations too, though never accepting the Nazi values showed great capacities for establishing new routines with respect to acquiring jobs, food, clothing, information, and other survival necessities.

ROUTINE, INNOVATION, AND CREATIVITY

Routines can block or make possible innovative as well as more creative action. For this particular discussion, an arbitrary distinction will be made between innovative and creative actions. Innovation is usually the making of a successful solution to a problem; eventually in its turn it too will lose its novelty and become routinized. The innovative solution can be minor or judged later or at its inception as brilliantly innovative (albeit the same is true of innovation that is the result of play or playful fantasy or other nonproblematic interaction). Creative action I will define as innovation at its greatest, and that additionally results in very major changes in collective perception, values, and action, whether it be Picasso's and Bracques's "discovery" of cubistic drawing, painting, and sculpture, Newton's formulation of his radical and profound principles, or the development of modern business procedures in the nineteenth century that were prompted by the difficult articulation of many different and complex types of railway systems (Chandler 1977). There is creativity in all fields where innovations shake those particular terrains and perhaps will spread into others. Yet what is judged as greatly creative and what is merely innovative or only ingenious can be reversed in later years, when the extent of its lasting impact on perception, values, and action is assessed and reassessed.

Too great an adherence to routines, whether commitment to their symbolism or convenience, or too great a pride in the hard-earned technical skills embedded in them blocks both innovative and creative action. However, standardized interactions are indispensable for both. Standardization gives support *and* provides a springboard for important novel actions. I have already touched on skill and technology as aspects of routines. These aspects are requisite for meeting the new problems or the contingencies that in fact may get defined as challenges rather than merely troublesome or as creating crises. Such challenges are literally built into scientific activity, though alas not every competent and ingenious scientist can be a major innovator or a creative giant. The same is true of any other field of endeavor, though some fields have been much more written about than others and so creativity and innovation in them has been rendered more visible to outsiders.

Another crucial but easily overlooked feature of routines vis-à-vis innovation and creativeness is that they set limits. Not only do the limits provide challenges but they give anchorage for potential innovators and creators. During the Renaissance, patrons specified details of paintings for which they contracted, such as subject matter (Christ on the cross), size (the larger were more prestigious), colors (azure blue was the most expensive), whether they themselves were to appear in the painting, and so on. Despite *and because* of such severe limitations, an insistence on conventional topics, materials, and traditional style, the great Renaissance painters were able to create masterpieces.

One of the problems confronting contemporary artists and writers is the widespread ideology that to be truly creative one must, like Matisse or Joyce, create a radically new style. Many have pursued this holy grail, abandoning traditional routines that might have served as ballast against the perpetual instability of shifting from style to style in search of *the* style. Conversely, they may be bound too tightly by adherence to routine procedures and perspectives, but tinkering, say, with new materials—though only to use them in usual formats, thus creating fashions or fads but not being genuinely innovative. The same is true for fields not so obviously animated by fashions and fads as are the fine arts.

Every innovative or creative interactant develops a style, whether personal or organizational. This is composed in part of novel perspectives and procedures and in part of inherited routines. In time, the new itself becomes personal or organizational routine, from which further innovation or creativity will "take off" (or if it doesn't, into which further action gets "frozen").

These styles are not simply styles but pieties. They are ways of action, orientations toward living, and declarations of authenticity to which actors are deeply committed (Soeffner 1992, pp. 78–82). As Kenneth Burke has remarked, quoting the philosopher George Santayana, "piety [is] loyalty to the deepest roots of our being." Or as Burke himself has emphasized, "piety is a system-builder, a desire to round things out, to fit experiences together into a unified whole. Piety is *the sense of what properly goes with what*" (1936, p. 95). In the *Random House Dictionary of the English Language,* there is a list of twenty or so definitions for *style* that reflects this complex phenomenon. Explicitly or implicitly these definitions point not only to the symbolism but to the personal or collective identity inherent in creating or adopting "a" style: the commitment to modes of acting, living, and in a deeper sense perhaps "being."

The editors of my dictionary seem less aware that styles embody routine or settled ways of interacting, as well as being springboards for novel and sometimes creative action. On the other hand, commitment to a style can be so great as to blind its possessor to new possibilities of action. One interactional process that furthers or hinders these possibilities is that commitments to differential styles often bring their possessors into heated disputes over how or what is appropriate or proper ethical, esthetic, efficient, or effective action. Such disputes and resulting arena activity can lead to the continuation or change of old or new styles.

So the interplay of routine and creative acts is highly significant, although perhaps this interplay is easier to grasp conceptually if the action is only slightly innovative or merely ingenious. In the latter two cases, the limits and relevance of standard procedures are, on the face of it, more visible. Yet the most creative individuals or groups utilize existing techniques, equipment, and modes of thinking. Even if the techniques and equipment are virtually brand-new and the modes of thinking are recently formulated, nevertheless soon they will no longer be novel but constitute standard ways of carrying out the work (Becker 1982; Clarke and Fujimura 1992). They too will be standard operating procedures. Usually the actors will not think of them as being part of the creative process, but they surely are. Only when the routine aspects of the process become unduly taxing or boring do the routines jump into prominence. Then, as in business firms or in laboratories, the executive or scientist either "grins and bears" the boredom of this necessary work or, having power, delegates it to a lower-level executive, assistant, or graduate student.

Consider now some conditions that promote a maximum of creativity or innovation. For instance, is it better to work alone or in a team or some other form of collectivity? Arguments for each view can easily be adduced, with examples to fit, depending on the field of activity. Artists who become famous for their creativity are likely early in their careers to live and work in close proximity to other artists, which provides a rich texture of interaction, a crucible within which artistic styles are born or further developed. Later, having formed those styles and found their markets, they may retire to the relative solitude of their homes in the countryside. In contrast, the requirements of physical and biological science virtually rule out too much working alone; this is not likely to happen anyhow in this day of computer mail and telephones. The same is true of innovators in large business firms.

To my way of thinking, the question posed above is misleading. The question really is, What conditions generally promote creativity and innovation, and how are they maximized by the person or organization? It is banal to assert in this regard that very different conditions serve various actors well or badly. Whatever the general conditions that support creative or innovative action, I believe that actors who would be or actually remain creative or innovative, have to judge their own gifts and capacities and assess conditions as in some degree genuine or as potential barriers or aids to their goals.

In my own discipline, as in academia generally, taking paths that divert overly much from the main goal of research—engaging in a lot of administrative work, getting immersed in building research institutes, working constantly to keep research funds flowing in, becoming a specialist and consequently responding to frequent calls for speeches and consultations—all such activities not only take time and energy but shift motivation away from "staying productive." Most every academic recognizes those hazards to research creativity but may find them difficult to avoid, either because of a sense of obligation or because of the tensions and uncertainties of a divided identity. Academic organizations suffer from similar poor judgment about their lines of activity.

Actors who were previously creative or innovative but no longer control the conditions that would allow or promote continuance of this activity—which take them increasingly into the realm of the routine—are doomed to lose some of their creativeness or innovativeness regardless of their gifts and skills. They may lose these anyhow if we can believe the physiological reasons given by scientists in certain fields, like physics, when talking about the great discoveries being made primarily by young minds, which are less trammeled than older ones by conventional concepts and theories. Yet the accomplishments of some outstanding older scientists seem to fly in the face of this conventional wisdom, which leaves uncontrolled in its speculation many potential social and cultural influences on scientific activities.

In order to stay creative or innovative, individuals and organizations restrict their agendas. They select, seize upon, or develop activities and settings that renew their sources of successful activity, to keep themselves alive to possible challenges, and to prevent their settling into even the most satisfying but ultimately stultifying of routines. Moreover, unexciting and routine types of settings and activities are unlikely to provide the necessary interactional stimuli for creativity or innovation.

An important aspect of the settings and their activities consists of appropriate or inappropriate audiences with whom to interact. An appreciative but informed audience, sensitive to the meanings of an actor's actions and its products is vital to creative and innovative interactions. This, perhaps, is one of the main consequences of young artists living in close proximity to older artists, and to take creative ones—alive or dead—as role models. The same is true of research engineers who work together on "hot" problems, and who present and listen to papers at various kinds of scientific meetings. On the other hand, too much stimulation can lead to an inability to make sure choices of direction.

Oddly enough, certain routines also help in this continual refreshment, just because they break the inevitable stresses of creative or innovative action. Routines here provide a kind of oasis, much like episodes of calm sleep. So some great minds read detective stories and others play musical instruments; but all find the time to do this, indeed have scheduled times or moments for these respites. As we all know, collectivities utilize the same social mechanisms in the form of celebratory occasions of various kinds, breaking the routines of everyday and work life. Such special occasions have double features: While contributing to the pleasurable side of social life, they also entail peaks or even sustained periods of activity when participants will work to the utmost to ensure success for the upcoming festival, feast, picnic, or parade. Symbolism of the anticipated event as well as images of pleasure motor this preparatory action.

These scheduled periods of recreation and relaxation link with the important contributions that pacing makes to innovative and creative action. Some people need schedules to "produce," whereas others are inhibited by them. Beyond schedules, however, is knowing when to engage in routine behavior and when to throw oneself into more innovative interaction. Innovative or creative people drive their spouses and friends a bit crazy, because they tend sometimes to go on extended bouts of work (not at all properly labeled as "psychologically obsessive"); it is just that these people are not stopping for anything more routine in their lives until their idea, conception, or insight is worked out (at least in the head). If they stop too soon, as they have discovered, momentum will be lost.

This point is related to another. There is a great difference between having an exciting idea, or being struck by an insight with radical implications, and actually working it out. Work *is* entailed in being innovative or creative. (Even as a college student, studying esthetics, I did not believe the idealistic philosopher Croce, who theorized that having an aesthetic conception was sufficient in and of itself.) Both getting an insight or idea and working it out may take a great deal of time. An insight, say, may come rapidly but discovering its implications, and perhaps proving them to others, may stretch out over many months or years. In working out an idea or insight, the innovative/creative person does not "force things," but allows subliminal processes to take place as a prerequisite to more conscious interior and overt interaction. While these latter processes are going on, all kinds of routine actions will occupy the actor.

The same subliminal processes sometimes surprise him or her; the scientific literature is replete with accounts of famous discoveries made in front of the fireplace by drowsy scientists or when stepping off streetcars or doing mundane tasks. However, these insights do not come from nowhere, but are properly prepared by much previous thought and overt work. And quite like the next steps of working out their implications in the real world, intuitions cannot be forced, but again, to use the garden metaphor, their roots are buried and emerge from paced routines. In this regard, my colleague Barney Glaser (1978, pp. 18–35) also adds an identity aspect, advising young social scientists that they need to discover the unique pacing that suits their own temperament and focused energy and should not imitate either other people's mode of pacing or their assumptions that these are universally valid.

Innovative or creative action embodies a continued radiance of spirit, engages the actor's identity so profoundly that his or her actions cannot be but immensely expressive. This is as true of organizations and other collectivities as of individuals. The material worked on may look inexpressive, impersonal, remote, but built into these acts is the sense of adventure, excitement, and challenge. You can sense that the actors cannot, in the deepest sense of the term, remain unaffected by the outcomes of their actions. They will not necessarily become radically changed persons, but some change there will be. If you have read James Watson's (1968) account of the final months and days before he and Francis Crick discovered the key to the double helix, then you will know what I mean.

John Dewey has written an eloquent passage describing this expressive interplay of time, self, and action. He was writing about artists and artistic activity, but we need not restrict his description to these. He writes:

> The act of expression that constitutes a work of art is a construction in time, not an instantaneous emission. And this statement signifies a great deal

more than that it takes time for the painter to transfer his imaginative conception to canvas and for the sculptor to complete his chipping of marble. It means that the expression of the self in and through a medium, constituted in the work of art, is *itself* a prolonged interaction of something issuing from the self with objective conditions, a process in which both of them acquire a form and order they did not at first possess. (1934, p. 64)

Here in a letter from Matisse to his son, this great and thoughtful painter expresses the same interplay of self and created object, and something of its intensity, making Dewey's points more concretely and vividly:

When I attain unity [of a painting], whatever it is that I do not destroy of myself which is still of interest . . . I am not absolutely certain. I do not find myself there immediately, the painting is not a mirror reflecting what I experienced while creating it, but a powerful object, strong and expressive, which is as novel for me as for anyone else. When I paint a green marble table and finally have to make it red—I was not entirely satisfied, I need several months to recognize that I created a new object just as good as what I was unable to do and which will be replaced [later] by another of the same type when the original which I did not paint as it looked in nature will have disappeared—the eternal question of the objective and subjective. (Flan 1973, p. 90)

One final point: Individuals need to know or discover their "true" gifts, and organizations their most innovative or creative agendas, otherwise they waste their best efforts and irretrievably so. Most nonprofit organizations, for example, have relatively routine, uninteresting, or unexciting programs, whereas the world is greatly indebted to the foresight of Warren Weaver, who as director of research at the Rockefeller Foundation some years ago persuaded his colleagues and the foundation's board to unequivocally and massively back new trends in biological and biochemical research, along with less novel or risky ideas. And the other night, re-reading an editor's introduction to Fielding's long-lived novel, *Joseph Andrews*, I was delighted to learn that this great novelist previously had launched many undistinguished although sometimes commercially successful plays before he wrote his great novels (*Tom Jones* is another). It was a further delight to recognize that *Joseph Andrews* is replete with scenes constructed in such a way as to be a constant silent reminder that while Fielding was creating a new literary form he was also drawing directly on the routines of the contemporary theater. In its turn, the novel undoubtedly had its impact on the next generations of dramatists—creative and otherwise.

In short, there is a cyclical process whereby routine plays into creativity and innovation, which in time flow back into the realm of the routine. In the literal sense, routine is not merely "routine" and creativity or innovation is in *no* sense divorced from its roots in routine. A theory of action should take both kinds of interaction into account, and most certainly investigate their interplay much further than I have here. Routines and routine actions should not be taken for granted or ignored, as does much social science literature. Neither should they be viewed in isolation from their consequences both for the maintaining and changing of organizations and identities.

NOTES

1. A major structural condition that supports this trial-and-error sequence is the existence of many nightclubs and other sites at various levels of reputation and sophistication, in which comedians can present their acts.

Chapter 9

Social Worlds and Society

Society as a whole . . . can be conceptualized as consisting of a mosaic of social worlds that both touch and interpenetrate.
—A. Clarke, "Social Worlds/Arenas Theory as Organizational Theory"

All theories of action embody sets of assumptions, and together the theories and their assumptions lead to at least implicit answers to a set of absorbing questions: What is the nature of *contemporary* society, and how can it best be conceptualized, talked about, and studied? I will address these questions in this chapter, giving some possible interactionist answers. These will be provisional in the sense that no one should be so arrogant as to believe that any formulation can capture the nature of the entire earth's "society," or so confident of predicting the next steps of its destiny. The best that can be expected is that some degree of fit to the social universe out there as one conceives it can be suggestively formulated.

My view of that universe was expressed in a passage quoted at the beginning of Chapter 1. It is appropriate to reiterate it:

[W]e are confronting a universe marked by tremendous fluidity; it won't and can't stand still. It is a universe where fragmentation, splintering, and disappearance are the mirror images of appearance, emergence, and coalescence. This is a universe where nothing is strictly determined. Its phenomena should be partly determinable via naturalistic analysis, including the phenomenon of men [and women] participating in the construction of the structures which shape their lives. (Strauss [1978] 1990, p. 237)

This perspective is not at all a purely personal one. It has its roots squarely in Chicago interactionist intellectual and research history. First of all, there is an animus against considering structure as more than

the enduring "given aspects" or conditions of situations, the aspects we can
bet with relative safety will remain "in place" and predictable for some
time . . . the consequences of prior actions and experienced as obdurate . . .
the enduring temporal conditions of situations. (Clarke 1991, p. 129)

The author just quoted, Adele Clarke, then correctly attributes to me the
view that:

structures ultimately are based in the commitments of individual actors to
collective action—to work of some kind—be it state-building, international
capitalist development, social movement organizing, drug carteling, or doing sociology. . . . [I]t is commitment to collective action that ultimately
structures social life. (p. 129)

The early Chicago tradition also focused on the emergence of new
structures through collective behavior and social movements (Park 1972;
Blumer 1946; Turner and Killian 1987) but also on studies of various
groups and social worlds. For my own thinking, Mead has been especially influential for his views of social change and communication. These
views imply an enormous, unlimited, and ceaseless proliferation of
groups that do not necessarily possess clear boundaries or tight organizational organization. The implications of Mead's conceptions, especially
of the endless formation of universes of discourse, with which groups are
coterminous, suggest an imagery of groups emerging, evolving, developing, splintering, disintegrating, as well as pulling themselves together,
or segments of them falling away and perhaps fusing with segments of
other groups to form new ones—often in opposition to the old groups. It
is this general perspective that I will develop here. I have called it elsewhere "A Social World Perspective" ([1978] 1990a) because it leads logically if not inevitably to an elaboration of the old Chicago concept of
"social world" (see also Shibutani 1955). So a conception of social worlds
will be used to give some answers to the questions with which this
chapter opened. Herbert Blumer (especially 1969), following some of
Mead's conceptions, had a somewhat similar interactionist view of society, though like Mead's perspective this view lacked a specific set of
concepts to make it more analytically useful. I believe he needed a concept like social worlds to make it so. But first I should address a related
topic.

ASSERTED OR PRESUMED DOMINANCE OF SOCIAL
CLASS, RACE, GENDER, AND OTHER SOCIAL UNITS

Certain social science conceptions of contemporary society assert that
among its principal features are one or more items such as gender ex-

ploitation, racial subordination, and corporate capitalism. I am wary of such assertions because they are so encompassing and clearly evaluative; also, I am wary of generalizing to cultures and nations around the Earth on the basis almost wholly of studies and observations of contemporary Western civilization. I assume that even under a seemingly overwhelming international corporatism, for instance, there is a very great variety of responses to it, quite as occurred with the dominant colonialism and imperialism of yesteryear. At the very least, local and regional conditions (economic, cultural, political, nationalistic, religious) will interact with the presumed main condition to influence what is going on at particular locales. Blumer's effective criticism (1948; 1990) of widely believed theories of industrialization and modernization makes the same general point; he argues against their advocates' failures to be sufficiently specific about the interplay of industrialization and the local-regional-national conditions.

The concept of social worlds in the sociological and interactionist sense is where I would begin thinking about contemporary society. I shall argue that if the concept of social worlds is made central to a conceptualization of society, then a radically different view of society emerges. This view is at odds with predominant models of society. Most social scientists, certainly most sociologists, think in terms of social structures, such as the state, social classes, ethnic groups, families, institutions, agencies, and other organizations. These structures or social units are viewed as palpable powerful presences at work in all nations. I do not disregard these, since they can indeed be very significant, consequential forms or patterns of collective action. Reexamining the discussion in Chapter 2 of the conditional matrix, recall that many analysts' favorite variables if they have any (say, social class, race or gender) are not at all dismissed as an important influence. But the matrix insists that anyone who asserts the primacy of a particular variable must provide evidence of *specific* connections between the all-significant variable and various other phenomena (such as institutions, agencies, social movements, social worlds). This evidence must be grounded in research, not merely claimed, nor must it consist merely of implications drawn from some seemingly self-evident ideology.

So I am not dismissing out of hand popular variables that seem relatively grounded, some of them in years of social science research and theorizing. I am only suggesting that they can be major or insignificant conditions, depending on the specific contexts of social life that they may or may not much affect. In tandem with that, I shall suggest that the concept of social worlds be considered as one of the major features of contemporary society, that the implications of this supposition be explored, and that this exploration not be equated with an insistence that social worlds are the only major influence in modern life. Let it be enough that we consider here their relevance to the variegated actions of people and institutions on this planet.

A SOCIAL-WORLD PERSPECTIVE

But why then elevate social worlds to such a central position in the discussion below? My reasoning is that this concept, and others associated with it, like "arena," can be of very great help for studying and understanding contemporary society in collective action terms: its complexities, diversities, boundary permeabilities, intersecting groupings, and its speedy changes. The concept makes it easier to avoid customary modes of thinking about society and nation, and can free us to conceptualize and do research about contemporary society in less trammeled ways. Yet it will not permit us the unwarranted freedom to dismiss or miss other important collective forms, like social movements or governmental action, which are so obviously related to the political and economic ordering of our era. This concept incorporates all the elements of *trajectory* discussed in Chapter 2: Thinking in its terms one inevitably utilizes, even if implicitly, most and probably each of the assumptions embodied in an interactionist theory of action. The concept does require that we conceive of persons in modern society as characteristically having membership in a multiplicity of worlds, ranging from a few memberships to a very great number indeed. Thinking in terms of social worlds, their activities, and their members is, I am arguing, immensely useful in understanding the nature of the contemporary world.

Social world is a much used lay term, commonly referring to environments such as the "worlds of" the theater, the military, baseball, horse racing, national politics, and both national and international banking. For our purposes, a useful working definition of social worlds is "groups with shared commitments to certain activities, sharing resources of many kinds to achieve their goals, and building shared ideologies about how to go about their business" (Clarke 1991, p. 131). I once elaborated the concept in this way:

> In each social world, at least one primary *activity* (along with related clusters of activity) is strikingly evident; such as climbing mountains, researching, collecting. There are *sites* where activities occur: hence space and a shaped landscape are relevant. *Technology* (inherited or innovative modes of carrying out the social world's activities) is always involved. Most worlds evolve quite complex technologies. In social worlds at their outset, there

may be only temporary divisions of labor, but once under, *organizations* inevitably evolve to further one aspect or another of the world's activities.

These features . . . can be converted analytically into subprocesses: for instance, site finding, funding, protecting, competing for sites. Technological innovation, manufacturing, marketing, and the teaching of technical skills. . . . Organizational building, extending, defending, invading, taking over, and converting. ([1978] 1990a, pp. 236)

Among the properties of any social world that will be of particular significance are its size, duration, origins, histories, rate of change, type and amount of resources, and relationships to technology and to state power. Social worlds also can be related to gender and social class, for some are composed only of men or women, just as some are composed of members drawn almost solely from one social class or another (the worlds of polo players or bowlers) while others cross over social classes (baseball) and/or gender. Some worlds are quite local, others regional or national, while an increasing number are international in scope of activities and membership. Some of these worlds are highly visible both in activity and in their internal affairs, while others are relatively closed to outsiders.

Additional properties are that some are linked with certain physical sites while others are much less spatially identifiable; some are well established and others are newly emergent. Some are very hierarchical; some less so or scarcely at all. The activities that are central to given worlds vary greatly: These activities can be around matters that are principally intellectual, commercial, occupational, political, religious, artistic, sexual, recreational, and so forth. In some social worlds there are complex formal organizations (most industries and major scientific disciplines), and some have many organizations but only one or two are dominant (IBM in the computer industry before the days of the personal computer) although, in general, organizational power is competed for or shared. As we all know, a few worlds induce their participants to make major commitments to their collective activities, or even almost solely as in religious or political cults. Most contemporary social worlds do not make such exclusive demands. In consequence, we all have multiple memberships. Since memberships can vary in intensity of commitment from very intense (virtually total absorption) to very peripheral (barely involved), in many social worlds there is a core of highly involved people but also marginal participants.

One property that seems particularly difficult for some sociologists to imagine is that of the relatively fluid boundaries characteristic of many worlds. This failure of imagery is because they are accustomed to thinking about organizations or other social units, about which usually it is possible to specify at least approximately who belongs and who does not, who are the responsible or accountable leaders, what is the range of duties, what are the rules and regulations, what resources are more or less available, where their activities take place, and of what these activities principally consist. Social worlds often are not quite like that, or even much like that. Perhaps we can answer such questions concerning the core participants in the worlds of professional sports, like football or basketball, and certainly their teams. But how to do that for all the spectators and the occasional TV viewers of games who are also potential customers for the accompanying objects: footballs, basketballs, sports journals, equipment, T-shirts, posters, pennants, and various other icons?

My experience when talking about social worlds to colleagues is that the first critical or quizzical question they ask is about boundaries, sometimes dismissing the concept of social worlds as just too fuzzy because "there are no boundaries." They do not think in terms of variation—for them all social units must be bounded. Furthermore, if not, then they are not worthy of or possible to study. The first attribution is nonsensical, and the second is an empirical question, not a matter for dogmatism.

Indeed, one of the more striking features of many worlds is internal dispute and decision-making concerning conceptions of their own boundaries. If these are in question, then their members ask and debate whether a given activity, person, or product is "really" representative of themselves and their world. That uncertainty links with the issue of representativeness discussed in Chapter 7. It also links especially with the issue of authenticity as it pertains to behavior that stretches standards beyond accepted limits. If these are stretched too far, expulsion of the standard breaker(s) may result, the boundaries then being rendered less blurred—at least for a while. (Perhaps it would be better to discard the concept here of boundaries and substitute something like peripheries, and thus avoid arousing irrelevant imagery. Alas, "boundaries" is too well established.)

Definitions of the boundaries of some social worlds are very conflicting or ambiguous—say, the world of fine arts painting. Was Remington, widely known for his paintings and sculpture of Indians, really worthy to be shown in fine arts museums, or is he just a celebrity in the wider popular culture, or perhaps in a subworld of fine arts painting? And what about the painters who have contracts to mass-produce paintings for galleries that sell principally to tourists? Or consider the instance of a world that seems clearly bounded: American medicine. The political elite and the more politically conscious of this world have had a long history of fighting to maintain its jurisdictions, for it also has been marked by battles over who and which "medical" movements should be considered authentic. Psychotherapy, for example, at one time was on the American Medical Association's list of medical cult quackeries; and more recently, acupuncture in the United States has achieved an ambiguous status, some of its practitioners being approved for referral by physicians and some not.

If the boundaries come to be perceived as too restrictive by enough members of a social world, this can result in the creation of new worlds (or subworlds) complete with their own standards, boundaries settings, and maintaining mechanisms, and subject to the same potential debates and challenges or drifts that lead in turn to their own segmentation. Jurisdictional disputes between social worlds (or subworlds) can be usefully thought of also in terms of the segmenting and intersecting of worlds. Outsiders may never know about most of the in-world debates, as within scientific disciplines or relatively esoteric occupations, although the government may step in as umpire or regulator—but many are fateful for the careers of participants and the unfolding histories of the social worlds themselves. Some of the disputes are about boundary issues.

Inevitably, participants in these worlds and, if we are careful not to reify the term, their organizations too become concerned with issues as these arise in the course of their activities and histories. Issues signify what I have discussed as arenas and these inevitably bring social worlds and subworlds into contact and relationships with others, if they have not already intersected. As we have seen (Chapter 7), the complexities of representation arise largely in terms both of multiple social world memberships and the necessity to take positions on issues.

SOCIAL-WORLD PROCESSES

Among the social-world processes are three already mentioned: segmentation, intersection, and legitimation or the issue of authenticity (Strauss 1982, 1984, [1978] 1990a, [1978] 1990b). Since each is linked with the others, this renders what transpires in social worlds all the more complex. Let us look briefly at segmentation first.

A most important feature of social worlds is their inevitable segmentation, or differentiation, into subworlds. This is the "pervasive tendency for worlds to develop specialized concerns and interests within the larger community of common activities, which act to differentiate some members of the world from others" (Kling and Gerson 1978). So a focus on social worlds quickly raises the issues of subworlds and their relationship to each other as well as to the larger unit. Segmentation subprocesses refer to how these subworlds originate, evolve, maintain themselves, distinguish themselves from others, break apart in further segmentation, also decline and vanish, and so on. Subworlds become differentiated

around several different sources or sets of general conditions, for example, space (regional or national, beaches for surfing); objects (child psychiatry); technology and skill; ideology; recruitment of types of members;
intersections (African American artists, Catholic sociologists). Segmentation processes include defining and building a legitimate core activity or
activities; differentiating the subworld from others; the writing and re-
writing of history; competing for resources; debating and maneuvering in
arenas; and further segmenting.

To give a sense of the linkages of segmentation with the other social-
world processes, I will quote from an earlier paper of mine:

> The defining of different types of activities and the building of organiza-
> tions for engaging in them, is often motored by a growing conviction that
> what "we are doing" is more legitimate than that assumed or promoted by
> some other, more established and powerful SSW [subworld]. Social move-
> ments are quite as characteristic of social worlds as the reform/revolution/
> religious or intellectual movements usually studied by social scientists.
> Movements and schools within art, poetry, science, education and a variety
> of other SWs reflect the initial formulation of subgroups within their re-
> spective larger worlds, whose members are reacting strongly against and
> strongly for. Their assumptions about the nature of the activities and per-
> spectives of the parent SW or SSW can be very different indeed; though, of
> course, they may be very little different, and so regarded by both later
> generations and by contemporaries who view the fight as a tempest in a
> teapot.
>
> However, the emergent SSW need not be bellicose about some or all
> rivals, but only assume that its own activities are equally legitimate. It will
> need to differentiate its own core activities, otherwise its members will not
> be able to claim anything special about their activity and their collectivity.
> Indeed, its own members need to believe that, or they will soon defect; also,
> potential recruits will not be attracted. So, whether antagonistic or not to
> other SSWs, a differentiating process will occur early, and continue. . . .
>
> Emergent SSWs . . . tend to stand between opposing tensions: there is a
> pull toward being distinct from neighboring SSWs, but not so distinct as to
> be defined as outsiders altogether. . . . This situation is complicated by the
> frequency with which defectors from one SSW will associate visibly with
> genuine outsiders, and adopt some of the latter's styles and technologies
> and activities; so much so that they can be accused of leaving the parent SW
> altogether—despite their claims that they have merely incorporated vital,
> fresh ideas and techniques. (1984, pp. 128–30)

Or consider the matter of competition among worlds and subworlds for
resources:

> Since SSWs bud or splinter off from other SSWs but remain within the
> parent SW, and intersecting others enter from outside into the SW, they will

all compete for resources *within* the encompassing SW. The nature of the competition will understandably vary according to whether the SW is relatively rich in one or another resource, whether its SSWs share organizations, media and sites, whether it has few or many SSWs competing, is declining or expanding or stabilized in its resource base, and so on. As for the resources themselves, they vary in salience for the particular SW. . . . Newly differentiating SSWs, quite like the more established, need to present claims to authentic activity and identity; must demonstrate that they are worthy members of the larger community. . . . When governments are involved in funneling or withholding resources from a SW, the implicated SSWs will compete for resources, seeking to persuade, negotiate with, and manipulate the relevant gatekeepers—both within the SW itself but quite possibly with executive and legislative representatives themselves. The SSWs do not necessarily trust SW representatives to truly represent all the SSWs and especially themselves. . . . [On those points, see Chapters 9 and 10.]

As for the relation of resource competition to intersecting: insofar as any given SSW may also be intersecting cooperatively with other SSWs, it may draw resources from those allied SSWs—places to meet, space in journals, money . . . manpower. . . . The expansion of a SSW unquestionably is linked with increased control over cumulative resources. To spread over more geographical territory, to recruit additional members and hold old ones, to engage in more activities or better versions of them, to engage in more diversified activities. . . . [I]t is necessary to get the related resources increased amounts and to keep them coming. (1984, p. 131–33)

This complexity of the segmentation process can be matched by that of legitimation/authenticity (Strauss 1982). Here the subprocesses seem to include discovering and claiming worth for the subworld; distancing the segment from others; theorizing to establish authenticity; setting standards, embodying them, evaluating them; and setting and challenging boundaries.

The social-world process of intersection is, I sense, an especially important characteristic of contemporary society. What happens when members of one social world/subworld meet members of another or others? Primarily, it may be information, skills, or resources that are transmitted. Or it may be ideologies that affect each other, with particular members being especially significant transmitting agents. As we have seen, the issues that constitute arenas also produce intersections; they further suggest that intersections not only can involve more than two social (or sub-) worlds but are of varying degrees of intensity, duration, and significance.

Perhaps the most important consequence of the process of intersection is that it fosters the knitting together of sections of society in cooperative (if sometimes reluctant or temporary) action. Perhaps the most strikingly consequential and large-scale intersectional knitting takes place not within large arenas, despite the multiplicity of intersecting organizations/worlds, but among all those worlds via arena participation within the "domains" (as described in Chapter 10).

It is important to note that all of the major social-world processes imply and traverse one another. Thus, legitimation issues arise not only from segmentation and intersection but also from technological, spatial, and organizational considerations. Within social worlds and their subworlds, we can often note rapid and extensive organizational building, expansion, and consolidation that has to be legitimated. Important technological processes such as innovating, manufacturing, and distributing though they seem relatively rationalized are not free of disputes that touch on questions of legitimacy, and are certainly in relationship to intersection and segmentation processes. In a sense, this complexity of reciprocity and mutuality of the processes is "what makes the world go around."

Even a phenomenon that seems as far removed from social worlds as "the body" is also related to such processes. You have only to think about the international feminist movement in terms of authenticity/legitimation issues or the intersections of feminist subworlds with those of completely different social worlds. Or think of the different ideologies and public debate about diet, body appearance, medical treatment, abortion, the management of dying, and any number of other body issues. It is almost inconceivable to me that these can be understood without taking into account that people of different social (sub-) worlds take different positions on these issues, act on those positions; but also that some issues do not at all engage every social world. And every issue concerning the body can be usefully analyzed in terms of the social-world processes. (Think of the intersections around the prochoice and antiabortion issues; or recollect the years of segmenting that have taken place over the question of proper diet.)

This example of the body in relation to social worlds also brings out another aspect of the social-world phenomenon. These social worlds are linked with larger society through their activities and technologies. Not only do they use the services of outsiders but also the products of industries that were not deliberately made for their use, though they may be. Entire industries, for instance, are related to the bodily concerns of people who engage in social-worldly activities, whether those concerns be around health, sports, appearance, or something else. Traditionally, such matters have been analyzed by sociologists in terms of social class, fashion, cultural or social movements, and so forth. Social worlds produce their own fashions and adopt those put forth more generally in the economic or intellectual markets, while as noted earlier the concept of social class is often relevant to social-world membership. A social-world perspective offers a fresh and alternative approach to phenomena ordinarily interpreted in those more usual terms.

Think also of political, religious, and cultural movements. These are a striking feature of modern society. I conceive of these social movements as congeries of social worlds and subworlds that generally are joined in diffuse and perhaps spatially scattered cooperative action. Resource mobilization approaches (Zald and McCarthy 1979, 1987) to social movements have focused attention on resources, politics, and power, whereas the older Chicago tradition and its newer versions (Turner and Killian 1987) emphasize the relationships of social movements to collective unrest, collective action, and reform. Both emphases I believe are needed (as events in Eastern Europe and the former Soviet Union are surely reflecting), but connected more explicitly to their roots in social-world activities, symbolizations, and processes that presumably affect their activities and fates. In the usual discussions of social movements, one can find ample descriptive materials bearing on significantly implicated social worlds. Yet there is little conversion of this description into an analysis of their significance.

SOCIAL WORLDS AND THE NATION-STATE

Next let us look at this concept of social world in relation to "society" and to nations. Rather than conceive of any nation—let alone society—as a unity, conceive of it as a vast number of social worlds, varying greatly in their properties, and linked in a variety of complex and often patterned relationships. If one does not regard the nation-state as a powerful social *unit*, as is maintained by structurally oriented sociologists, then what is it? For an interactionist theorist, the question is not what is "it" but how can we alternatively conceptualize the actions *of* governments and their representatives as well as the actions taken *toward* them?

Taking a social-world perspective on governments means refusing to assume homogeneity in any government or governmental agency, except perhaps only around certain issues and then probably not for very long. It is no news that even dictatorships are riven with factions, feuds, and struggles for control. In the more open forms of nation-states, particular agencies or their departments might be recruited from, captured, or heavily influenced by particular social worlds or subworlds. For instance, the State Department for many years was almost the private preserve of the East Coast elite; while for decades the Department of Agriculture essentially has represented the wealthiest farmers and farm corporations, whose policies as expressed by their major representative organization,

the American Farm Bureau Association, have been practically identical
with the department's (McConnell 1953; Busch 1982). Yet even within the
association there have been disputes—internal arenas—over which specific policies should have priority and which issues should be pursued
through their governmental ally. Competing social worlds also attempt to
influence various departments of the government and their officials. The
latter have diverse interests and disinterests in the different governmental agencies. Although the agencies may declare themselves neutral in
battles among the various pressure groups and lobbying organizations,
they cannot be neutral. They too are embroiled in the public arenas. In
turn, the agencies' own tensions, disputes, and internal maneuvering
reflect the outside turmoil and the positions of conflicting social worlds
within these public arenas. All the arena processes will be operative in
these internal interactions, just as they affect the external ones.

Courses of governmental action (including programs, plans, and implementation) evolve quite as described in Chapter 2 in the discussion of
the concept of trajectory. Actors in the evolving drama are those "others"
to whom I referred above. Others can be other governmental units, foreign governments or their units, and of course any number of external
organizations that in turn are representing one or more social worlds or
subworlds.

A wonderful example of what I am alluding to occurred in 1991 during
the abortive coup attempted by members of the Soviet Communist elite.
During the three days of the failed coup, members of internal social
worlds used their fax machines and e-mail to inform each other of the
developing events: scientists communicating in almost instantaneous
time with other scientists, and no doubt some Soviet officials who dis-
avowed the coup were communicating with their American counterparts.

Under more usual conditions, members of social (and sub-) worlds
communicate with and act together to influence, subvert, or get around
their own or other governments. A massive instance is the alliance of
organizations within the international AIDS community that succeeded
in changing the proposed site (Boston) of the 1992 worldwide AIDS meetings to another outside the United States, because of the American government's intractability about its immigration policy as it affects foreign
visitors with AIDS.

I am saying here only what is obvious: namely, that governments have
to engage in interactional processes (persuasion, negotiation, coercion)
with their citizens, and with organizations and other governments. Yet, to
understand both the actions of governments and the outcomes of that
action, a general theory of action would not take that obvious phenomenon for granted but make it central to understanding the various emerging forms of the nation state, whether in the most or the least economi-

cally developed parts of the globe. Descriptions of the new forms abound; sociological analyses do not, and they are often encumbered by older interpretations of the state. An interactionist theory of action should be useful here too.

GENOCIDE AS A CASE ILLUSTRATION

As an illustration, although perhaps a risky one because the social-world aspects perhaps seem not immediately apparent or of only peripheral significance, I will address briefly some issues that the concept can raise about a striking and frequent phenomenon: genocide by governments of nation-states. Genocide has characterized a fair number of them in the twentieth century. It has been much written about and eloquently described by survivors, bystanders, and occasionally by its perpetrators. Accounts and explanations of the Nazi-precipitated Holocaust alone doubtless fill many library shelves. The explanations are largely causal ones—attempts to say why particular cases of genocide occurred—just as some of the literature consists of attempts to judge whether genocide has actually occurred or is occurring, and to determine the truth or falsity of claims made about its existence or extent. As for the descriptions, they are just that, rather than sociological analyses of interaction during the genocidal events.

In his thoughtful book on genocide, Irving Horowitz (1980) argues that this phenomenon could not have taken place without the full coercive might of the nation-state. While there have been societies aplenty where mass murders occurred before the rise of nation-states, it is only in this century that national governments have had the technological resources necessary for quickly wiping out virtually entire subpopulations. About this, however, one can ask: Who is in command of the nation-state and who is it that becomes the genocidal victim?

After reading some of the literature on genocide, I drew the conclusion that there is not just some abstract government that acts but that representatives of specific social worlds are sufficiently powerful in the government to control significant actions of it. Not everyone or every clique or social circle in the government has genocidal power or wishes it. Indeed they may argue against it, or at least until they themselves are disposed of or banished or neutralized. The Nazi elite were certainly not a homogeneous group of people. They surely did not all know about or agree to the Holocaust. Of course, not every European grouping was slated for genocide but principally the Jews, Gypsies, "deviants," and political opponents. Gypsies might be conceived of by social scientists as constituting a cultural group, but they could just as usefully perhaps be thought of in terms of social worlds and subworlds, and Jews even more appropriately. Or consider Cambodia: The governmental elite who put genocide into motion were, Simmel would probably say, "a social circle" within the more heterogeneous party whose ideology, derived in part from European radical sources, led them to kill off anyone outside their relatively small and homogeneous social world—or at least those they believed were capable of effectively opposing or disposing of them.

I make no claim that this concept of social world is the only means to analyze such events. Yet at least it gets away from the usual political analysis and from the predominant social structural assumptions, and might afford a fresh approach to understanding this dreadful phenomenon. One can see the social-world processes in action, for instance, in the intersecting of Armenian refugees, decades after their genocidal experience, with newer and nonethnic social worlds that had learned lessons from the Armenian genocide—kept alive by vigorous Armenian refugee publications and propaganda. The most notable recipients of this long-lasting memory were from the human rights movement, a cluster of related social worlds. One of its main organizations is Amnesty International. Anyone who even contributes regularly to that organization is at least nominally or marginally a member of "the movement." If they read its literature they are less marginal; if they work for the organization, then like any "more inner" social-world member they are more central to its activities. A social-world analysis would necessarily go much further and examine, for instance, the intersections among human rights circles (genocide, governmental violence of any sort, civil rights for many different groups, and so on). Its analysis would also explore the other social-world processes, including legitimation and segmentation. Such studies would not neglect historical changes in these processes, nor their probably quite differing contexts and consequences from country to country.

In shocking truth, one of the major gaps in the analysis of genocide pertains to its long-range consequences, just because most of the writing on it is descriptive or causal. Descriptively we certainly know a great deal about the impact of the Holocaust on post–World War I Germany—right down to the variegated German responses to the Gulf War—and its continued reverberations in the Israeli psyche and in Jews everywhere. So, to mention the nation-state again, there are significant consequences for its citizens and also for its governments. I have just alluded to the consequences of the Armenian genocide for the human rights movement, and of course the other more contemporary instances of genocide have also had cumulative impact on Amnesty International and other human rights organizations.

Again, such consequences have been well portrayed and are well known, yet the corresponding analytic studies are generally lacking. An interactionist theory of acting could scarcely overlook the need for such studies, embodying as it does social worlds and *courses* of interaction. In this case, included are genocidal episodes that not only have indirect and precipitating causes but also long-run as well as short-run collective evolvements. These are *trajectories* into which are drawn not only the victims and murderers and governmental decision-makers, but the by-standers and avengers, and those who seek to prevent or limit genocide. Collective memory and collective action are part of all that.

Apropos of genocide, Irving Horowitz, mentioned earlier, has expressed a strong doubt that a "'symbolic interactionist' perspective" could account for genocide, because "it seems to move the discussion of genocide away from its promising roots in political economy into a softer theoretical plane of social psychology" (1980, p. 49). In saying this, he had an image of a somewhat or completely social-structureless interactionism, as reflected in, or as could be construed from, some of the symbolic interactionist literature. I trust any reader of this book on a theory of action will not close its pages with that view. Surely its theory of action, with its inclusion of interactive social worlds, can help us to understand the variegated, fast-changing, and complex nature of contemporary society. Said another way, and to repeat what was said earlier: Social worlds are not social units or "social structures" but a recognizable form of collective action.

Chapter 10

Social Worlds and Interaction in Arenas

The single most important opponent of localization research was thus not established physiology per se. Instead it was the antivivisection movement. . . . Ironically, however, antivivisection succeeded in uniting English physiologists rather than eradicating them. . . . The [antivivisection] act of 1876 helped vivisectionists to form alliances with researchers from other sciences, particularly from evolutionary theory. This is reflected in the roster of charter members of the Physiological Society, which included many prominent evolutionary biologists. [After a trial of a famous researcher brought about by the antivivisectionists] medicine, including the freedom to conduct and evaluate research, was symbolically intertwined with both localization theory and vivisectionist physiological research.
—S. L. Star, *Regions of the Mind*

Central to the Pragmatists' formulation of a theory of action was the necessity, when ongoing routine action was blocked, for reflection and the consideration of alternative paths of action. A broader Pragmatist reading of "reflection" was that discussion would occur when group, rather than merely individual, action was blocked. These philosophers were, after all, part of the reform movement known as progressivism, and though Dewey was a logician and so analyzed the concept of reflection or deliberation in his writings on logic, his other side was equally involved in social and political action. As reformers, the Pragmatists knew perfectly well that discussion could turn into bitter argumentation, and dissensus rather consensus might be its result. Consensus and discussion were idealized and desired, but to be worked out rather than assumed. In fact, Dewey's well-articulated theory of political pluralism was an effort to suggest how, in a political democracy, citizens could live with the reality of disagreements and yet reach effective consensus on particular issues. Curiously the Pragmatists did not build these insights and positions into their theory of action, thereby leaving it incomplete, and I believe thereby not elaborated through their social and political theories.

A logical step in elaborating their theory of action is to follow through on a not unreasonable implication: When two people confront an issue, then it is not unlikely that two discordant positions will be taken—at least temporarily. (There is an old Jewish joke that if three rabbis landed on the moon, at least one would assert the sky was blue and the others black.) Mead's strong concept of multiple perspectives surely implies the likelihood that disagreement about an issue will result in argument, debate, and not entirely harmonious discussion before equable decisions are reached about options and their consequential actions. Since discussants do not always agree even on the formulation of an issue—or that there *is* an issue—it follows that sometimes no settlement, or perhaps a very delicately balanced one, will be reached.

If the issues are difficult to resolve, and especially if disagreement about them persists, then we have what is commonly referred to as an *arena*. I will adapt the term for my own purposes, and in the next pages aim to show how action in arenas—involving disagreements within and between social worlds—is central to the phenomena of social order and social change. (See Chapters 9 and 11 for further development of this point.)

ARENAS AND SOCIAL WORLDS

The concept of arena will refer here to interaction by social worlds around issues—where actions concerning these are being debated, fought out, negotiated, manipulated, and even coerced within and among the social worlds. It can be individuals who do the acting, but for sociological purposes we want to locate them in some sort of social unit. Given the character of the social universe remarked on in an earlier chapter, the concept of social worlds is invaluable for understanding arenas, albeit social worlds act most visibly through organizations but also through actions of their participants. Social worlds and their constituent sub-worlds point to the shifting, problematic character of even well-developed and long-persisting arenas (see Chapter 9).

Social worlds and their segments have their internal issues around which their members or organizations debate, maneuver, negotiate, attempt to persuade, or coerce. Small arenas are likely to arise around each and every question that does not get settled fairly quickly. In addition, the social-world processes of segmentation, intersection and legitimation inevitably include thorny issues pertaining to value, status, loyalty, commitment, and other such matters capable of arousing deep passion (Strauss 1982, 1984). Arena action around issues ultimately signifies disagreement about directions of action—that is, in the broadest sense of the term, disagreement about the policy steps to be taken by the social world or subworld. Yet the term *policy* is usually associated with governmental units and *policy arenas* for those broad areas of argumentation that call forth images of struggles over legislation and executive action concerning energy policy, environmental policy, or civil rights policy. Though these policy arenas are national, regional, statewide, or local in scope, they are simply broader terrains where issues are fought out.

Within these arenas, characteristically the participants consist of a large number of different social worlds, and their representative organizations. When a new policy arena arises or additional issues evolve within an older arena, then the individuals or organizations belonging to social worlds have to decide whether to enter this particular arena or if already within it whether to opt out. In any event, they will not be involved with *all* the issues in any given broad arena, but only those perceived as pertinent to their own interests. Furthermore, an entire social world may not be involved but only those segments (subworlds) whose interests are involved. This means that subworlds are involved in broader arenas where other participants not only represent other subworlds but also sometimes the overall social worlds themselves.

There are two general points. First, arenas of any scope, large or small, involve questions of policy about directions of action. Second, the source of issues and debate can be both external and internal to the participating social worlds-subworlds. A major difference between the conventional, larger arenas and some of the smaller ones internal to social worlds, however, is that issues in the latter sometimes get resolved, or at least enduring arrangements made that keep disagreements more or less in check. In policy arenas, the issues seem to persist or are succeeded by generations of new ones, and sometimes to the participants seem almost to have a life of their own because they produce so many related issues.

I turn now to a discussion of these larger policy arenas in order to bring macroscopic phenomena more explicitly into my theory of action. Before doing so, I will make my major point. Arenas exist at every level of organizational action, from the most microscopic to the most macroscopic. As whirlpools of argumentative action, they lie at the very heart of permanence and change of each social world. By the same reasoning, arenas are central to the creation and maintenance of social order, in the traditional sense of that sociological concept.

POLICY ARENAS[1]

Social worlds and subworlds ordinarily deal with other social worlds and subworlds through *organizations*. They do this through relationships within a given organization or more formally by organizations dealing with each other. This immediately creates for them the problem of representation, since some organizations will represent or claim to represent the social world (social subworld) in external arenas. But who *is* "them"? This is one reason why the subunits fight for influence in these representing social-world organizations. Furthermore, many organizations are composed of members from different social worlds or social subworlds (like occupational or professional associations). So, whom does this complex, multiworlded organization represent? And when representatives claim representation, how are others—both inside and outside the social world or social subworld—to judge the representativeness? Or to be linguistically mischievous, how in the world are the implicated worlds going to judge representativeness (see Chapter 7). In these policy arenas, governmental agencies often claim to be neutral. Yet they are scarcely so. Nevertheless, unless they are relatively stable captives of certain organizations, be it business, labor, or whatever, then their participatory role may be more difficult to discern or prove, as arena participants well know. This nonneutrality adds to the turmoil of the arenas, by itself generating a jumble of issues. What is true of government is also true of science (as I shall discuss below) and its "findings." In arenas there are no neutral parties, no neutral government, no neutral scientists. However strictly objective they may believe themselves, they are embroiled in what is generally called the "politics" of the arena, and are unlikely to be able to stay out of controversy. The larger point is that *representation (i.e., representing) is not simply an issue but a process* that is basic to arenas.

There are other important processes. Arena participants ordinarily do not think in terms of processes, but see their manifestations as strategies, strategic action (as with representation). It is not so important to list these arena processes as to show them in operation. We would want to know under what conditions they are operative, including which specific broader conditions are relevant to the given process, as well as the actual interaction that takes place, and the specific tactics of the interactants along with some major consequences of the planned and unplanned interaction.

First and foremost in any arena is probably *the defining of issues*. For instance, in the AIDS arena, the initial definitions of issues changed rapidly; and new issues arose, issues clustered, issues splintered into several issues; and issues waxed and waned in seeming importance to various participants. Given the multiplicity of perspectives of the participants, much of the disputation, maneuvering, persuading, and negotiating has to do with defining the issues, that is, with getting the others to see these issues as you do. The "others" can consist of organizations, representatives of those organizations, or people within your own social world but belonging to another segment of it. Prior to that, there may be much disputation within a given social world over how, in the first place, to define an issue, as well as whether it is *our* issue and in what ways it does or will affect our world.

Another arena process is *the evolving of issues,* for if the policy arena endures very long, then new aspects of issues are likely to proliferate, or new issues are likely to bud off from old ones. These developments are precipitated by unforeseen contingencies that now face the participants. Developments are also brought about when additional participants who are concerned with entirely new issues or with new aspects of old ones are drawn into the arena.

This process is accompanied by another: *the matching of social worlds* and their representing organizations *with the issues.* Matching is an active process, carried out by the participants. They select and reject issues, and reshape them in accordance with their own images and aims. For example, in the AIDS arena at the present time, an image of AIDS held by many blacks is of AIDS as a white genocidal strategy; other blacks perceive AIDS as of far less consequence than other pressing issues like poverty and control of crime. In turn, the arena participants are shaped by the consequences of their actions vis-à-vis the issues. This matching process is generic to arenas because every grouping in an arena is engaged in such action. Seen from the participants' perspectives, matching is an organizational process: "We've got to do this right—so what's the proper strategy here?"

Another process is *the getting involved with alliances,* which brings a continual tension that exists between the perceived advantages of joining coalitions and the tendency toward pulling back into your own terrain. Although the participants may have very different and even conflicting perspectives toward a given issue, nevertheless they may conceive of themselves cooperating in some actions taken toward that issue. Even concrete events, like demonstrations that may involve multiple social worlds and organizations will reflect the potential fragility of arena alliances around specific issues or clusters of issues. Probably this is true even in the more stable arenas that involve long-term alliances concerning many related issues.

The intersecting of arenas is certainly also among the most consequential of generic arena processes. It is evident that each arena whirls around within a galaxy of other arenas. An analyst must take this into account even if studying not the galaxy but a single arena, just as the participants in each world must take this into account. When, for instance, AIDS organizations joined with organizations for disabled people in the lobbying of Congress, then the intersecting process was seen in highly visible operation. Some organizations that are engaged in combating illness such as cancer or cardiac diseases argue vociferously that too much money is being poured into AIDS: This ill-concealed competition for resources is also an instance of intersecting arenas. Presumably the intersections come in many shapes and forms, cooperation and competition being only two subprocesses.

To make the concept of intersection a bit more complex yet, it is also useful to take into account what Adele Clarke (1993), writing about social worlds, has termed "domains." A domain constitutes larger social space (or pictorially a kind of galaxy) *within* which particular arenas, and their implicated social worlds, have arisen and continue to exist. Her detailed example is taken from the field of reproductive biology in relationship to the domain of biology. Over several decades, vast changes have occurred in relationships between old internal arenas within the biological domain and the establishing of new relationships between it and newer arenas. In fact, she "discovered" domains when attempting to analyze the changes in this particular arena over several decades. Similarly, the long American disputation over drugs—mostly carried out in medical versus moral terms—can be usefully conceptualized as occurring within overlapping illness and criminal domains. The vigorous entry of AIDS into this domain has dramatically altered many relationships among the extant arenas within this domain. So, of course, it has also affected relationships among organizations and social worlds that are participants in such arenas. In this particular domain, one can easily see the more dramatic changes, but to track them systematically would require careful research. Lest you lose the main point here, given the inevitably changing conditions, both external to and internal to the domains, these domains evolve, and this evolution profoundly affects the evolution of particular arenas within domains. The reverse is also the case, especially by influential arenas. But further out on the fringes of the domain galaxy are other galaxies with which it interacts. Yet, how much and how significant the interaction actually is must be discovered, not assumed: the illness domain and which others, and interaction in what ways, with what major consequences? The research questions posed here are daunting but fascinating.

At this juncture, a brief summary of my main points and concepts should be useful. To begin with, there are *no* arenas without social worlds; conversely there are *no* social worlds without arenas! Subworlds are segments of social worlds. Organizations variously represent single or multiple social worlds and/or their segments. In the larger sense, arenas are situated within domains; also between intersecting domains, since there are also interdomain arenas such as between religion and medicine (abortion, reproductive technologies, definitions of death). Interaction among domains deserves notice for the interactional effects on each domain also, as well as on the encompassed arenas, on social worlds and social sub-worlds and their representing organizations. I made also the key point that arenas exist at every level of organizational action, from the most microscopic to the most macroscopic. They are central to the maintenance and change of each social world.

Interaction is a key concept here, not in the interpersonal sense but in the sense of conditions leading to consequences *through interaction*. Fur-thermore, variation in conditions, from the most macro to the most micro, gives rise to variation in structural and processual consequences. The various sets of structured process—in arenas, social worlds, organiza-tions, and possibly domains—give a kind of physiology to the structural anatomy that we have sketched.

Processes give the physiology but not without two more general sets of processes. The first consists of interactional processes (negotiating, per-suading, etc.; see Chapter 2, and Strauss 1978). As elsewhere, these pro-cesses go on within arenas. The second set consists of work processes, like the carrying out a division of labor, and the supervising of work (see Chapter 2; see also Corbin and Strauss 1988), because very explicit work is entailed in actions like the building of organizations and the mounting of campaigns, demonstrations, and other forms of lobbying. Policy is shaped through all of this structurally influenced interaction, albeit some organizations and social worlds have more influence than others, and over different phases in the evolution of the issues that lie at the heart of arenas.

It is important, also, to recognize the temporal dimension of arenas. They don't stand still even when they appear to be at their most devel-oped, stabilized moments. As conditions change in other domains, other arenas, and internally within the given arena, repercussions will be felt throughout all these social units. Moreover, there is the high drama and narrative appeal to policy arenas, which is often seized upon by the mass media, especially when they are at their liveliest. We are all familiar with the turmoil and clash of positions within arenas, whether these are over health, wealth, energy, the homeless, the elderly, or what to do about Eastern Europe in this decade. (These characteristic features of arenas are related to the participants' commitments both to immediate and to deeper or "ultimate" values about the nature of life and society.) As scientists, we firmly believe our disciplinary obligation is to interpret in analytic theoretical terms what transpires within and between these value-laden arenas, especially perhaps the more complex and seemingly significant ones. At the same time, it is essential to convey the ambiance of the arena: its tensions, conflicts, passions, furor of the struggle that goes on beneath diverse ideological banners, the dashed hopes as well as hopes realized. I remind you also of the inevitably dreadful or at least fateful consequences for some of the actors in these dramas. This injunction to capture as well as to interpret the drama is only a special instance of our dual commitment as social scientists: to describe and analyze in balanced tandem.

SCIENTISTS IN POLICY ARENAS

In order to highlight the interactional features of multi-issue policy arenas, I will next discuss some of the interactions between scientists and other participants in these arenas. These important and large-scale instances of "problem solving" and the struggle of divergent interests cannot be understood without a close look at their interactional features.

Scientific Arenas

Scientists are visible in virtually all policy arenas and strikingly so in some (cf. Hilgarten 1990; Horowitz 1988; Nelkin 1987; Whitley 1985). They are contributors to and often active participants in them. Just as many social worlds and their constituent segments debate issues important to survival and other goals, so do the social worlds within science. The latter form around disciplines and their specialties, but the social subworlds form mainly around specific clusters of interdisciplinary issues. Scientific controversies and their resolution lie at the very heart of scientists' work and their research organizations. Settling disputes over theoretical, procedural, and technical issues is observable at the local level of the laboratory up to the most monumental disciplinary debates around theories and claims about critically important findings. Since scientists like all other humans have no lien on the truth and no direct line to reality as such, they must, as recent studies of scientists at work have shown (Fujimura 1988; Gerson 1983; Star 1985, 1989b; Star and Gerson 1987; Latour and Wolgar 1979), negotiate theoretical and research claims by discussion, debate, and further research.

In addition, there are the more pragmatic controversies about priorities of discovery, about how to get, maintain, augment, and distribute resources, about whom to recruit to the department, all reminiscent of nonscientific fisticuffs. I am not, however, posing an equivalence between the ideological coloration and passion of mass public arenas with the generally more measured and deeply thoughtful ambiance of scientific ones. Accept only the essential characteristic of controversial issues and attempts to resolve them, and you have a scientific arena. But let the controversies spill out into the general public, largely through the mass media—as with the Gallo and Montagnier disputation over priority rights to discovering the AIDS virus, or as with public statements by an otherwise esteemed biological scientist, Duesberg, who claims there is no proof whatever of an AIDS infection per se—and then you are seeing some sort of connection between scientific arenas and policy ones. (For this debate, see Fujimura and Chou forthcoming). It is here that their respective boundaries become blurred, and not incidently set theoretical and research issues for the sociologist.

The Intersection of Lines of Work

It is crucial for conceptualizing the interaction between scientists and nonscientists to understand that this interaction takes place within a context of ongoing action. Prior to any transaction, both parties to it are engaged in their own lines of action. Scientists are attacking scientific problems while also involved in such activities as obtaining and maintaining resources, administering laboratories, pursuing careers. As for the arena participants, they are plunged deeply into situations, whether mundane or dramatic, that demand practical and sometimes speedy action. Some of their action (as action often does) consists of work, though it contrasts with the research and theoretical work of scientists. After all, plenty of work is entailed in fund-raising from either the public or the supporting social world, handling the media, designing brochures, writing grant proposals for re-funding demonstration projects, and managing personnel problems.[2]

Interaction between a community organization and a group of scientists is much affected by simultaneous transactions that the agency is conducting with other agencies, or with other scientists who may be giving them conflicting information. Ongoing discussion and debate within each organization can also affect the interaction between agency and scientists. Indeed, very often the agency members will differ in assessments of scientific information or its specific sources. The scientists, in their turn, are also working with contexts, in their instances contexts embracing other scientists, scientific organizations, funding organizations, and possibly more than just one community organization.

Processual Reciprocity and Lines of Work

In Bruno Latour's (1988b) book on Pasteur, the emphasis is on how Pasteur manipulated opportunities within various economic, social, and medical arenas (the term is ours, not Latour's) to advance his own work and career. Analytically, every study may legitimately focus primarily on one side of a bargain, Pasteur in this particular study. Ideally, however, a fuller analysis demands that all parties to a transaction be taken into account, although that is not always possible. Both the scientist's and any arena participant's lines of action must fit the other's, though not necessarily equally well, or else an exchange will not occur, be quickly tried and rejected, or finally break down or be only partly accepted.

The scientific information, for instance, must be perceived in terms of "It fits my needs," "It is just what we are looking for," "We can use that," or some such receptive terminology. In turn, if the scientists offer information or other services, they must believe in the usefulness of whatever they expect or actually receive from the other person or organization in this exchange. The trade-offs are often repeated or continuous, so an interactional history evolves between the parties. For it to continue, the reciprocities cannot stand still with respect to the changing requirements of the respective parties, whose own histories are also evolving.

However, the reciprocities are not necessarily identical nor equal in perceived value or types of service, nor in any other way comparable. An exchange may be comparable, however, as when the careers of both scientist and director of an organization become enhanced by their mutual cooperation. Usually, however, the stakes are different for each party to the transaction. Also, scientific information is usually not being traded by the scientist for information about some aspect of the arena, though it may be. Thus, if an AIDS medical researcher does not possess local knowledge about a potentially useful study population, like homeless IV users, then he or she may be willing to exchange some research information for this local knowledge. The researcher may also trade for reciprocities other than or in addition to giving scientific knowledge: money, prestige, or access to a population useful or necessary for a study. An exchange may not even involve scientific information for the arena recipient, but yield legitimation, jobs, and so forth. Furthermore, the parties to the transactions may not be aware of all they are giving to the others and certainly not of what the others will make of what they receive. So such trade-offs between scientists and arena participants can be complex.

Reciprocity around Arena Issues

Different social worlds are concerned with different issues, as may be their constituent subworlds. This means they need different kinds of information but also other services that scientists might provide. So there is *a matching of reciprocities* between these arena participants and their respective scientific partners or sources of scientific service. For example, AIDS organizations call on epidemiologists for some purposes and pharmaceutical chemists for others, just as environmental organizations call on geologists for some issues, economists for others—but not just any specialty in these disciplines, and not the same scientists for all arena issues in which the organizations are taking action.

Through this pragmatic logic—in which far more is at stake than merely the transmission of information/knowledge or even prediction of events—probably every discipline and a great many specialties are linked with policy arenas. Scientists' need for resources is so great, sometimes urgent, and continuous, that even those engaged in research of only remote practical relevance seek funding that is directly or indirectly concerned with arena issues. This, of course, had been true for nineteenth century science (viz., chemistry with industrial issues, economics and sociology with economic and social issues).

There is often an intricate, complex knotting of public and scientific interests, including governmental involvement that may be linked tightly with one or the other side of that equation. A striking instance can be found in *The Politics of the Ocean* (Wenck 1972), whose author, a geographer, had worked at a high level of the federal government. He describes his long and complicated campaign to enlist scientists from a staggering array of specialties, the White House itself, other governmental agencies and officials, congressmen, and potentially useful public groups in support of a program of oceanic investigation. Without the complex web of negotiation and persuasion that he wove this program would never have been brought into existence.

Cross-linking of the participants in an arena may be so complex that it takes a perceptive historian or sociologist to unravel the tangle, and the chronological story that lies behind it. For instance, Leigh Star (1989a) in a study of the mind-body scientific-medical arena in the late nineteenth century has traced the very complicated connections among the scientific laboratories and traditions within the context of connections among philosophers, physicians, theologians, and others of the interested "general public."[3] Both the conflict and the alliances between participants in such complex and overlapping science arenas and policy arenas reflect a multitude of interconnected interests—in careers, in disciplinary and institutional fates, as well as in specific programs and projects.

Scientists and the AIDS Arena

In the AIDS arena, some AIDS organizations, frustrated at the Federal Drug Administration's (FDA) slowness in conducting clinical trials of experimental drugs, and furious at their being withheld from people dying from AIDS, initiated a drive to enlist physicians in clinical drug trials outside the usual FDA channels for testing new drugs. Many of the physicians and medical researchers in these original extralegal (but now legally permitted) projects were gay, but certainly not all. The subjects of the trials are still mainly gay males. Experimental drugs and some possibly effective alternative substances were obtained from outside the country, and tried out in these trials. Pressure continues to be put on the FDA, both directly and by lobbying the other medical scientists, congressmen, and the general public. As this issue has unfolded, it has grown into a complex cluster of issues: the rights of pharmaceutical companies to charge such high prices, whether people with AIDS should be given free treatments, the effectiveness of the FDA, the question of personal survival versus maximal scientific accuracy, the legitimacy of the clinical trial sequence as such, and there is even some advocacy of placing more grass roots–derived controls on medical and pharmaceutical research. This array of subissues has bound increasing numbers of physicians, pharmaceutical firms, lawyers, governmental officials, congressmen, gay communities and their organizations, scientists and their organizations all into one large and rapidly growing political snowball. Yet not all scientific disciplines and specialties, drug companies, governmental officials, or even AIDS organizations have become embroiled in this particular set of issues. The matching of parties is always issue oriented.

In the AIDS arena, epidemiology, AIDS organizations and communities are inextricably linked. Epidemiologists do the research that yields the incomparably important numerical data, predict the rate and amount of disease spread, and estimate the incidence of AIDS in various populations. Also, virologists and immunologists are integral to understanding the basic bodily mechanisms bearing on HIV-AIDS. The respective specialties of each of those disciplines have profited greatly in gaining resources and furthering their knowledge by entering into AIDS studies. Yet in doing so they have had willy-nilly to get involved with some of the arena's most central and hotly debated issues.

One implication of this reciprocity—as well as conflict—between scientists and nonscientists in such policy arenas is that over time neither can remain unaffected by their interaction. To greater or lesser extent, scientific specialties become stimulated, expanding in additional directions, developing into new lines of research and innovating new technologies, and splitting apart into further specializations that form relationships with other specialties.

Here also is a specific example of complex reciprocities from the AIDS arena, not very visible unless looked at closely. A black community agency took the lead in attempting to convince blacks that the entire local black population soon would be at great risk from the spread of AIDS. The agency backed its warnings with epidemiological facts and figures about current and future rates. Between the agency and certain other black influentials there is an alliance, partly the result of persuasive efforts by its director. The organization also has an alliance with the city's Department of Public Health, whose AIDS department acts in various ways to further the agency's fight against the widespread indifference or skepticism in the black population ("Only white gays get it," "It's just a white genocide plot," "We have many more pressing problems"). The Department of Public Health helps this agency, among others, in several ways, including the following: Its research staff does local studies of AIDS distribution and projects AIDS trends; funnels scientific and other information from elsewhere to the agency; sends speakers to meetings initiated by it; steers funds to it for training staff, educating the community in starting its own small studies; and further the agency's obtaining of state and federal funding both by informing its staff of funding opportunities, and in the writing of research and other grants whenever experience in grant writing is lacking. In turn, the agency and its allies cooperate in ways that furthers the research of the Department of Public Health, whether by opening doors to subjects for research or in the wider political sphere.

Services of Scientists and Arena Processes

There are further questions about scientists' contributions to arenas: What, why, when, how are they given, and with what consequences to the arena? Here, briefly, are a few answers. First, consider the generation and use of information in scientific arenas, then how the same information is used in policy arenas. The information that scientists produce for themselves results in different types of products, notably data, facts, findings; concepts, conceptual relationships, models, theories, and information about techniques, procedures, and technologies. The whole point of the scientific enterprise turns around the production and utilization of these products in continuous interaction both of scientists among themselves and with these products. Unless the specific activities of individual scientists are seen within this interactional context, they cannot be understood.

If we contrast this situation with how scientific information is used in policy arenas, the latter situation runs parallel but pertains to pragmatic utilization. Again, we cannot understand how arena participants discover, select, and incorporate scientific information unless those actions are seen in an arena-interactional context. Scientists also engage in their own arenas in a host of activities that do not constitute actual research but nevertheless are linked with research and research activities: getting and maintaining a flow of grant funds, building departments and institutes, negotiating with deans, maneuvering for space.

If we follow scientists into the policy arenas, we immediately see the overlap in their activities within both types of arena. They lobby congressmen for the university when its budget is threatened, testify or give speeches in behalf of the environmentalists when their research seems relevant, raise warnings about atmospheric damage if society does not curb its energy consumption, talk on TV about one side of a public issue or another when approached as experts in the area. Aside from being committed arena participants themselves, they may just believe that their own expertise or information should be used in the public forum. So they engage in types of arena activities that are, of course, well recognized. They testify, counsel, warn, predict, legitimate, and on occasion even mediate. They get into the mode or habit of doing these things through various paths; by invitation, persuasion, manipulation, negotiation, even coercion, but also through conscience and a sense of morality. Under specific arena conditions and as issues change, scientists may engage in one or another or several of types of arena activities that embody scientific knowledge or skills.

More important probably than a list of scientists' arena functions, or pathways to them, are the social mechanics of the selection and utilization of scientific services. Selection and utilization are related to the generic arena processes touched on earlier. As remarked there, these processes are analytic constructs that point to actions that the arena participants perceive in terms of strategic action. Around the issues that concern them, they have to figure out what to do. This means devising strategies that pertain, say, to lobbying effectively or persuading people in another arena that "our interests overlap here, so we can cooperate on this issue," or trying to work out the meanings and implications of an event in relation to issues when that is not clear. They can also act strategically just as citizen-participants in relationship to these same arena processes, as when marching in demonstrations. The specifics of how, what, when, and with what consequences are affected directly by situational conditions in combination with such arena processes.

Attacks on Scientists, Sciences, and
Scientific Procedures

Conflict between scientists and nonscientists certainly is not new. But lay opposition to science and scientific work is something quite different than in the days of Galileo or even Darwin. Contemporary policy arenas probably engender more complex and varied antagonistic reactions from nonscientists.

In policy arenas, there seem to be three predominant types of tension between nonscientists and scientists. The first type is the most obvious: Particular social worlds and their representatives disagree with, criticize, even reject the evidence of specific scientists or groups of scientists. Each social world or social subworld will choose certain scientific work as explicitly or at least implicitly supportive of its positions and reject the evidence put forth in other investigations. Certain individual scientists are chosen as the darlings or villains: Among DNA opponents, one particular nonmolecular biologist was greatly admired for his stubborn fight to increase regulation for minimizing potential public hazards from DNA research; whereas Edward Teller was the bête noire of Americans who fought against the Star Wars concept during the Reagan years. When important individual scientists openly advocate a policy position, then in bitterly contested public arenas they open themselves up to adulation or vilification. In local policy arenas, as in the controversy over Love Canal, the individual scientists who first call attention to public hazards are likely to become local heroes to some social worlds and anathema to others. The research of such scientists becomes publicly visible, at least the part perceived as relevant to the arena, and receives various degrees of positive or negative publicity. Furthermore, if any dissensus among colleagues becomes bruited about sufficiently, it may be used as ammunition by nonscientists within the policy arena itself. The media, of course, are avid for such human interest studies, and some scientists are not loath to give or leak them. The front page priority dispute between the American Gallo and his French rival Montagnier, for instance, both claiming discovery of the HIV virus, was "settled" by their respective governments becoming involved in public negotiation, though the dispute is alive once more, and Gallo's claim is currently being reviewed by a panel of his American peers. Scientists who work in industry or government or are members of think tanks are perhaps even more suspect in some social worlds just by virtue of their affiliations. This is true in the AIDS arena for scientists who work for drug companies and even in the Centers for Disease Control.

The attack on science is probably the most significant type. Aside from human propensity to choose sides in favor of one's own positions, there is so much research in lively policy arenas that is inadequate, incompetent or barely competent, rushed and doubtless sometimes descending to "cutting corners," or apparently sometimes dishonest, that distrust is engendered about certain individual laboratories, research agencies, and centers. Upon entering a policy arena, the pressures to produce, and to produce quickly, can be so great that conditions increase for producing less than adequate research. Also, officers of agencies and foundations who are granting funds for research in an arena may have vested interests in obtaining results from even "quick and dirty" research, whether for reasons of emergency action, pressure from further up in the organization or even from the White House or just for personal career reasons.

AIDS research is again an example. As in other bitterly fought mass issue arenas, much of the government-funded research has probably more than usual built-in expectations of quick and useful results. This set of conditions increases the probability of second-rate and even sloppy research: Understandably, some inadequately trained researchers, but also opportunists, have jumped into the shower of AIDS dollars, producing research that is sometimes of dubious value by most scientists' standards. Though there is certainly some recognition of this in the AIDS arena, that does not mean the research findings are disregarded, since information is at a premium. In this particular arena, as probably in others, one can also observe some curious phenomena: For instance, outreach street workers being used as collectors of field data and being regarded as "field researchers" in a research project; social workers affiliated with sexual abuse clinics being trained by government representatives, at a workshop, in administering research questionnaires to be used with clients, and urged to get this data collection done despite some murmurs from these practitioners about the impracticality of the task; or methadone clinics being given government funds to carry out evaluation studies of their own intervention efforts. Evaluation studies of various programs (training, education, and intervention) are a striking feature of the AIDS scene, because government agencies have generally made such studies a condition for obtaining program funds. The old motto, "No taxation without representation" has been replaced by "No funding without evaluation" in this policy arena, as doubtless in many another.

The second type of tension probably is far less significant. It consists of the rejection or acceptance of information or other services from certain disciplines or scientific specialties. Since many scientists themselves attribute different degrees of credibility to other specialties or disciplines, this disagreement among nonscientists is entirely expectable. However, the very character of policy arenas means that some participating social worlds will suspect or trust the motives or judgments of certain fields. Advocates of nuclear energy are unlikely to have any confidence in sociological research, however pertinent it may be even in terms of adverse market reactions to build more nuclear reactors. Yet, rather than rejecting entire disciplines or specialties, a social world/organization seems likely to seek or happen upon, or be sought out by, a reputable scientist or scientists whom it judges can speak to its needs.

The third type represents a more radical critique or conversely an acceptance of science in general. While certain scientists and sciences are less relied on or will generate confidence or sometimes antagonism, nevertheless science generally is unimpeachable in today's world. It is that very reliance on science that gives public reaction (demonstrations, lobbying, and other political pressure) its potentiality for profoundly affecting some of the institutional procedures that are traditional in scientific or science-related work.

Thus, at the outset of the DNA controversy, a few farsighted molecular biologists foresaw a possibly strong public reaction against their experiments, which could have resulted in the imposing of restrictive regulations on their experimentation. Their alarm convinced a sufficient number of influential colleagues of the danger to their social world and its customary practices. Subsequent to vigorous in-house debate among these specialist colleagues, they mounted an effective lobbying-educating campaign, convincing enough congressmen that the public hazard from their research was minimal, and anyhow could be contained without undue and potentially harmful external regulation. Not surprisingly, the fight against the molecular biologists in this DNA arena was supported and even led by other biological scientists who were from other specialties, because in their own lobbying-educating they could claim to match some of the expertise of the other experts.

The AIDS arena is much more complex, involving as it does a great number of passionate institutional and social-world actors—ethnic groups among them. In consequence, it should not be surprising that certain rules of the scientific game have come under attack. Particularly vigorous has been the drive by AIDS organizations to change the established sequence of basic research to mass application that pertains to medical drugs. As of current writing, the clinical trials part of the sequence has been altered and the lay reformers have got themselves directly into the review process. There have also been criticisms of the sampling methods used in the trials, because these have ruled out women and some ethnic populations, with strong support from the latter and from feminist groups. Recently a reputable black public health researcher spoke out against white, male, university-dominated AIDS research. In doing this—and calling for a great expansion of the populations studied, as well as for the recruitment and training of researchers drawn from people of color, especially to do community-based research—she was in effect attacking the institutional structure of medical, biological, and social science, which she believes leads to gravely biased research.

The Blurring of Boundaries

In all of this, one can see or sense a blurring of the normal lines of demarcation between the expertise of scientists and the questioning of this expertise. The boundaries between the two realms of being—science and nonscience—become smudged. The boundaries are still there, but they are far from sharp and clear. When science enters policy arenas—when science and policy arenas overlap—even when the actual research is done far away and at the back of the laboratory, some of it becomes visible, for better or worse depending on your view of things. When science becomes visible, it does not so much become vulnerable as have to prove its claim to be called responsible—that is, it becomes an arena actor and gets recognized as such. Even if not understood by avid consumers of scientific findings, there is no such thing in policy arenas as neutral science.

SUMMARY NOTE

It should be clear that interaction around arena issues is central to the confronting of contingencies and problematic situations. Social worlds and the actions of their members cannot be understood without intensive consideration of arenas: both those internal to the social worlds and external arenas (primarily discussed here) in which they participate. Arenas can serve as a microscope for arriving at a clearer understanding how social worlds change—in what ways and directions—and how their members experience that change too. In a broader sense still, arenas can be thought of as at the heart of any organizational order regardless of its particular scope. In that sense, arenas are central to an understanding of "social order." Certainly they are a central kind of interaction and therefore significant for any theory of action.

One last comment may be useful. Recollect that this chapter opened with a discussion of Pragmatism and progressivism. The concept of arena and its many and subtle implications means that progress as a form of action is much more complex and disorderly than the Pragmatists imagined. In fact, my editor and colleague David Maines writes that "In effect, you have made the notion of progress problematic by politicizing it." To this I amend "problematic but not hopelessly so for all issues."

NOTES

1.   The next two sections of this chapter, dealing with policy arenas, are shortened versions of unpublished papers coauthored with Shizuko Fagerhaugh, Barbara Suczek, and Carolyn Wiener. All of us (and Frances Strauss) worked together on a project whose focus was the shaping of policy in the AIDS arena, with field

observation and interviews gathered especially in the San Francisco Bay Area. This research was supported by the National Institutes on Drug Abuse, Grant #1RO1 DAO5847-O1.

2.   A fairly accurate image for thinking of the intersecting actions of scientists and arena participants is of several people traveling on separate roads that sometimes cross each other. What happens between travelers as they come to the intersections cannot be restricted to just horn honking, hand waving, or speeding up to get across the intersecting road first. Anything can happen—at least the range of possibilities is very great. The conditions affecting this are not hard to imagine.

To take this metaphor one step further: What takes place at the intersection is also profoundly affected by other interactional conditions. One condition is that more than two drivers may be arriving at the same moment, and none or only some are aware of this, or are not accurately judging the others' intentions, attentiveness, or their vehicles' rates of speed. Second, there may be other passengers within one or another automobile who react to the converging of moving bodies differentially, say, the driver's unconcerned reaction of "no danger" but a passenger's alarm and perhaps diverting scream of warning.

3.   See also Adele Clarke's (1993) comparable historical study of reproductive biology.

Chapter 11

Negotiated Order and Structural Ordering

Differential conceptualization of the "nature" of order and change and their relationships reflects one of the great divides between various sociological positions and traditions. Order translates easily and frequently into stability and structure, while change translates into instability and interaction. Every theory of action has pronounced implications for how such matters are conceived. So, in this concluding chapter I will first outline the Pragmatist/interactionist position on order and change, including my earlier extension of it through the concept of "negotiated order." Then I will suggest some implications of an interactionist theory of action for extending still further the position represented by what has come to be called "the negotiated-order approach." The detailing of these implications should also serve as a reminder of the materials and themes already presented. First, I will briefly summarize some matters discussed in the book.

After a deliberately autobiographical introduction to this Pragmatist-derived interactionist theory of action (acting), a lengthy list of assumptions behind that theory was presented. These assumptions are very useful for understanding the Chicago interactionist tradition as it has been influenced by Pragmatism, and lead to a theory of action that embodies them. My formal statement of this theory is built around the concept of trajectory and a set of related concepts. All of these, including also the methodological perspective and the concept of "conditional matrix," take into account the overwhelmingly important temporality inherent in courses of action. Major topics that were then discussed—always in terms of action and interaction—included work and its relations with other forms of action, the body, thought processes, symbolizing, social worlds and arenas, representation, the interplay of routine and creative action, and the relevance of the concept of social worlds to understanding and studying contemporary society. Consideration of these exemplifying topics provided an elaboration of the relatively spare initial presentation of the assumptions and theory of action.

THE INTERACTIONIST POSITION

When first reading Parsons during my graduate student years, I recognized an assumption of his that clashed head-on with my reading of Dewey. Parsons seemed to believe that stability—order—was primary and that change was secondary. For Dewey and other Pragmatists, change was taken for granted as central but the directions it would take were problematic. The direction and redirection of changed action were problematic in the sense that they were not strictly determined. However, they were affected by what Dewey and generally most people call "structure." This term stands for stability. In sociology it refers to the more or less stable or slowly changing social entities, such as institutions, organizations, social classes, stratification systems, and deep cultural or national values. But then again, those structural entities were regarded by the Pragmatists and the Chicago interactionists as neither unchanging nor unchangeable, because those structures themselves are constituted of action.

Here is Dewey's language for this:

> [T]he permanent and enduring is comparative. The stablest thing we can speak of is not free from conditions set to it by other things. . . . The rate of change of some things is so slow, or is so rhythmic, that these changes have all the advantages of stability in dealing with more transitory and irregular happenings—if we know enough. . . . A thing "absolutely" stable and unchangeable would be out of the range of the principle of action and reaction, of resistance and leverage as well as of friction. . . . [I]t would have no applicability, no potentiality of use as measure and control of other events. To designate the slower and the regular rhythmic events structure, and the more rapid and irregular ones process . . . expresses the function of one in respect to the other. [Also] by literalists [structure] is often conceived of as a rigid framework to which *all* changes must accommodate themselves. . . . Whatever influences the changes of other things is itself changed. The idea of an activity proceeding only in one direction, of an unmoved mover, is a survival . . . banished from science, but remains to haunt philosophy. (Dewey 1927, pp. 71–73)

To that statement of sixty years ago, now compare some sentences by a contemporary interactionist quoted more briefly earlier:

For interactionists, structures are the enduring temporal conditions of situations. They may be taken for granted by the actors and/or hidden from
them . . . but structures are obdurate and intrusive and must be studied and
"taken into account" in the pragmatist analyses along with social processes.
. . . [S]tructures are ultimately based in the commitments of individual
actors to collective action—to work of some kind—be it state-building,
international capitalist development, social movement organizing, drug
carteling, or doing sociology. That is . . . structures must have both a social
psychology (that is relentlessly sociological) and a larger-scale organization.
Neither is adequate without the other, and it is commitment to collective
action that ultimately structures social life. (Clarke 1991, pp. 129–30)

The Pragmatists gave to these early sociologists, and consequently their
descendants, a firm philosophic basis for an antideterminist sociology.
All forms of determinism (biological, cultural, economic, political, technological, etc.) are rejected in favor of a position somewhere between
extreme determinism and nondeterminism. Harvey Farberman (1991, pp.
481-82) has recently termed this a "soft determinism," citing Erving Goffman and Gregory Stone as advocates of this position. But the adjective
soft does not really capture the persistent Pragmatist/interactionist position on determinism across a century. This is better conveyed by the
words of an interactionist colleague of mine, Leonard Schatzman:

I hold to a non-mechanistic determinism for humans at least; a "determin-
ist" position in the sense that no action can occur without one or more
conditions for its occurrence. *There can be no science without conditioned action
or process.* Biological, class, geography etc. determinisms are old and conceptually crude. . . . That humans create action *under* some conditions and
in spite of other conditions is axiomatic with me. Is not human interpretation
also conditioned? (Personal communication)

In this sociological version of the enduring philosophic issue of constraint versus freedom of action, the action is shaped by conditions but in
turn is shaped by active actors. Thus, one can say yes, there definitely is
social structure, but it is not immutable, totally unshapable, and certainly
not entirely determining of action. This dominant interactionist perspective was expressed in a particularly apt phrase by one of the most important of second-generation Chicagoans, Everett Hughes ([1962] 1971),
who asserted that institutions should be regarded as "going concerns," in
terms of the changing interests and commitments of their members.
Therefore, although seemingly stable and ordered, institutions should not
be reified because they are subject to change through collective interaction. In a still later version of this perspective, Barney Glaser (1968) and
I wrote about "structural process" in order to suggest the interplay be-

tween structure and process. Or said another way, we were signaling that structural, including immediately contextual, conditions affected interaction but also the reverse. (See the discussion on the conditional matrix in Chapter 2.)

The inheritors of this sociological tradition still write in the same way about the relationships of structure and process, of stability and instability, of order and disorder. And these terms refer to any level whether societal, communal, organizational, suborganizational, or even interactional.

NEGOTIATED ORDER

In 1963, my colleagues and I published a paper (Strauss, Bucher, Ehrlich, Schatzman, and Sabshin 1963) about the "negotiated order" that we had noted in two mental hospitals. A year later we offered a more detailed version of this concept (Strauss, Bucher, Ehrlich, Sabshin, and Schatzman 1964). It is not surprising that the concept was quickly taken up by interactionists, especially those interested in organizations. I will quote some remarks about negotiated order made by an astute interactionist theorist, David Maines, in order to emphasize the concept's *continuity* with the Chicago tradition, begun around the turn of the century by Thomas's interest in "social organization" and later spelled out in monographic form by him and Znaniecki (1918–1920). Here is Maines's assessment:

The traditional source of strength in the symbolic interactionist perspective has been in the realm of social psychology. . . . By comparison, symbolic interactionists generally neglected the realm of social organization until the 1950s. To be sure, some individuals worked within that tradition on problems of social organization prior to the 1950s, but a basic conceptual scheme consisting of organizing concepts and statements about how organizations operate was lacking. Anselm Strauss' publication of *Mirrors and Masks* ([1959] 1969) may have marked a turning point. He candidly advocated the merging of social psychology and social organization, arguing, for example, that identities cannot be understood independently of the organizational contexts in which they exist and that social organization cannot be fully comprehended without an appreciation of the interpersonal dimension of human conduct. The merging of these two areas has been a central theme running through much of the subsequent work by Strauss and his collaborators. As a result of that work, a more focused perspective on social organization began to emerge in the 1960s. By the end of the 1970s, that perspective developed into a systematic framework for the study of organizations and social orders. It represents the currently dominant such perspective to have been born from the domain assumptions of symbolic interactionism, and its fertility can be measured by the rapidly increasing research activity generated by it.

The framework in question has been termed the "negotiated order perspective." It recognizes and attempts to take into account the importance of understanding interaction processes as well as the structural features of organizational life. It stresses the point of view that one of the principal ways that things get accomplished in organizations is through people negotiating with one another, and it takes the theoretical position that both individual action and organizational constraint can be comprehended by understanding the nature and contexts of those negotiations. (Maines and Charleton 1985, pp. 271–72)

The original formulation of the concept owed its origin to an interpretation of detailed field observations made in the two mental hospitals mentioned earlier (a private hospital and the acute wards especially of a state hospital). As researchers, we were attempting to capture the flexibility in the hospitals' division of labor and the surprisingly flexible governing rules of action in these institutions. A decade later, I summarized the original formulation of negotiated order in these words:

1. We stated that social order was negotiated order: In the organizations studied, apparently there could be no organizational relationships without accompanying negotiations.

2. Specific negotiations seemed contingent on specific structural conditions: who negotiated with whom, when, and about what. So the negotiations were patterned, not accidental. . . .

3. The products of negotiation (contracts, understandings, agreements, "rules," and so forth) all had temporal limits, for eventually they would be reviewed, reevaluated, revised, revoked or renewed.

4. Negotiated order had to be worked at, and the bases of concerted action needed to be continually reconstituted. Not only were negotiations continually terminated, but new ones were also made daily.

5. The negotiated order on any given day could be conceived of as the sum total of the organization's rules and policies, along with whatever agreements, understandings, pacts, contracts, and other working arrangements currently obtained. These include agreements at every level of the organization, of every clique and coalition, and include covert as well as overt agreements.

6. Any changes impinging on the negotiated order—whether something ordinary . . . or whether more unusual . . . —called for negotiation or reappraisal. This meant consequent changes in the negotiated order.

7. [The daily negotiation process] not only allowed the daily work to get done but also reacted on the more formalized and permanent organiza-

tional rules, policies, and established conventions and understandings. In turn, the latter served to set the limits and some directions of negotiation.

What was omitted [from our first formulation of the negotiated order was] *actors' theories of negotiation* [and] detailing of negotiation *subprocesses.* Hence . . . no explicit specifying of *conditions* and *consequences* associated with these subprocesses . . . no working out of a paradigmatic analysis in terms of *structural contexts* and *negotiation contexts* . . . virtually no references to the *options* for alternatives to negotiation: coercion, persuasion, manipulation of contingencies, and so on. Issues relating to rules, norms, and the like were handled explicitly, but others, relating to *power, coalition, politics,* and the like, were touched on only implicitly. (Strauss 1978, pp. 5–7)

With those quotations in mind, let us pose the following question: What has been added in the chapters of this book on a theory of action to the negotiated-order approach? A listing and brief discussion of some major points should serve to make more recognizable the implications of this theory of action for the issue of "order," at various levels of organizational and interactional complexity.

IMPLICATIONS CONCERNING ORDER AND CHANGE

1. Implications for Social Order. The various *interactional processes*—negotiation, persuasion, manipulation, education, threat, and actual coercion—will each have different salience, be of greater or less significance for *particular instances of any social order.* Thus, governments of some nation-states rely principally on various types of force and the threat of force, but even so they make much use of persuasion, propaganda, and education, including socialization of children. Also, certain forms of negotiation are absolutely requisite for the governance to be maintained with relative stability.

Conversely, even a "nation of laws" and relative democracy, such as the United States of America, obviously is not free of governmental use of coercion or manipulation of citizens and of institutions like the press. As is well understood by those who have battled to maintain the American Bill of Rights, the inevitably changing conditions of national and local life necessitate strenuous efforts and shrewd interactional strategies in order to maintain civil rights—let alone to extend these rights to groups previously denied or shortchanged: blacks, women, children, and more recently the disabled. What is true about the salience of different combinations of interactional processes for nations is equally so at other levels of organizational scale. As just one example: Goffman's "total institutions" (1961a) that are seemingly all coercion and manipulation turn out also to have negotiations over degrees of personal freedom. Goffman makes this clear in his discussion of "the underlife of a public institution" (1961b), although most readers seem to have missed the import of his qualification of total institutions.

2. *Implications for Arrangements and the Shaping of Conditions.* In theoretical terms, what is the primary significance of these interactional processes? First of all, they constitute necessary bases for making the *arrangements* that allow continued interaction to take place. Without arrangements, there would be no routines, no standardized modes of collective action, whether recurrent or episodic. Innovation is made possible by such arrangements, fashioned either on an ad hoc or more long-range basis. The various interactional processes are integral also to *shaping conditions* (the avoiding, preventing, adapting, manipulating, monitoring, changing) at every level of the conditional matrix. This is as true of the actions of persons, which after all do not take place in interactional vacuums, as of collective action. Insofar as conditions do not entirely constrain action but are reacted to, we need to persuade, teach, coerce, and/or negotiate with others, whether they are persons, groups, or organizations, including their representatives.

3. *Implications for Body Processes in Relation to Social Order and Symbolizing.* The bodies of actors are implicated in these interactional processes as objects as well as agents. So are the various *body processes.* Consequently there are no social orders at any level of organizational scale where bodies are irrelevant or unimportant. (Think of slavery and racial discrimination, or of the nearly universal societal dominance by males.) The concepts of "the body" and "body processes" include "the mental." No mind-body dualism can be countenanced. So *thought processes* and *selves* are included in this calculus of the body's continual significance. Moreover, selves exist in symbolic universes; that is, *symbolizing* is integral to action. Bodies ordinarily do not just react to stimuli; they act symbolically. To put this metaphorically, bodies survive only insofar as they breathe, more or less unconsciously, within an embracing symbolic atmosphere. An additional and related implication is that they exist and act and are acted upon historically. Individual and collective history affects current action and identities, affecting in turn their futures. So *biographies* are of crucial importance.

Symbolizing is integral to interaction around issues, as it is to all action. The primary *arena* process—"defining of issues"—immediately suggests contests over the rights of ownership over classifications and perspectives. Kenneth Burke (1937) some years ago offered a brilliantly conceived dictionary of terms to characterize the massive shifts in symbolization when large social orders undergo radical changes. He signalized the initial disaffection with the old order and then the development of new commitments and identities around new symbols. The same symbolic shifts occur on a less radical and massive scale when only parts of social orders change and are replaced by newer perspectives, stances, vocabularies, and different emphases on interactional forms, and with appearance of different generational, gender, racial, ethnic, and other identities.

4. *Implications for the Several General Orders.* In the second chapter, I briefly discussed the concept of "orders" and their subtypes: spatial, temporal, technological, work, sentimental, moral, and esthetic orders. These are convenient analytic terms for conceptualizing clusters of *general* conditions that actors have to take into account when interacting—or do not, to their peril. Action and interaction are played out, for instance, over time and in certain spaces. However, the *specifics* of space, time, work, sentiment, and other types of conditions vary locally in accordance with precisely when, where, how, and why the interaction occurs. In some situations, it is the scheduling that is irritatingly constraining and in other situations it is the deadlines or the pacing of actions that need to be managed. Locally, too, one or another order may be highly significant, if only temporarily: too small a space to work in, too much oversensitivity of your co-workers, or too great a moral hazard to risk. Interactional processes are necessary for shaping any of these clusters and subclusters of conditions.

5. *Implications for the Multiplicity of Perspectives and Resulting Contingencies.* Endemic to interaction is the probability of discrepancies between the perspectives of some participants in any interaction. This *multiplicity of perspectives* derives from differential statuses, experiences, and memberships in groups, organizations, and social worlds. Perspectives profoundly influence the actions and interactions, the stances taken with respect to the making and discarding of arrangements, and the preferred forms of interactional process (which anyhow are perceived as strategies by the interactants), be they manipulation, negotiation, persuasion, or the threat of coercion. In and of itself, the multiplicity of perspectives ensures a richness of interactional flow, because representativeness varies from interaction to interaction and within the interaction itself. Multiplicity also guarantees that courses of action, except perhaps quite brief ones, will have elements of surprise, will produce their own *contingencies* quite aside from the external ones.

6. *Implications for Social Worlds and Their Members.* With respect to perspectives and *representativeness* in contemporary society, the partici-

pations in *social worlds* and subworlds are particularly significant. Organizations are usually composed of members who are drawn from more than one social world or perhaps even more than one subworld. As we have seen, the social-world bases are often explicit but they can also enter into interaction implicitly, silently, unnoted. This can be all the more so, since each interactant belongs to and is oriented toward various social worlds and subworlds, some of them unknown to the other interactants. It follows that arrangements and modes of interaction can be deeply affected by those memberships and the corresponding identities of the members.

7. Implications for Arenas. Multiplicity of perspectives about courses of action is likely to bring about discussion and debate, if not downright argument. When disagreements are on a large scale, with many issues open to contest, then this interaction is likely to be referred to as an *arena*. In this book, I have extended that concept to cover conflicts over issues arising at any scale of organization. For example, families and friendships founder over persistent differences of issues; they also manage to be maintained, and such disagreements are surmounted through one or another or combinations of interactional processes.

8. Implications for Order and Disorder. The existence and evolution of multiple perspectives and consequently of arenas does not imply a totally changeable social unit. *Order and disorder exist coterminously.* Of course, order can be perceived from different standpoints, so that one person's order can be another's breakdown of order ("disorder" or "disorganization"). While some perceive disorder in American society because of widespread birth control and legalized abortion, others firmly believe societal order is enhanced *because* of those "humane practices." Or another example: The civil war currently raging in Yugoslavia represents to many non-Yugoslavs, and presumably to many Yugoslavian citizens also, a breakdown of the nation-state but to others the war represents a path to much preferred social orders in the form of several breakaway nation-states based in historically distinctive ethnic, religious, and political traditions. Even in the midst of a shattering event that most participants and observers might agree represents disorder, the mass flight from Paris as the Nazi army approached that city in 1941, even this seemingly complete collapse of civic order contained elements of order, albeit at different organizational levels. Surely it made sense for some people to flee Paris. Some Parisians wisely chose feasible destinations and made arrangements for meeting friends or kin in the event of getting separated, and so on. Interactional processes certainly were taking place then—some effectively resulting in the saving of lives, preserving of resources, and maintaining of family contact.

PROCESSUAL ORDERING

What then does all of this discussion add up to in terms of the concepts of order and change? Is order only "negotiated order" or is it something more? A quick review of the original usage of this term will show that it referred to the overall order of mental hospitals, and perhaps of most hospitals in general (Strauss et al. 1963, 1964). Later, in my book on negotiations (Strauss 1978), I was concerned with spelling out and arguing for the central place of negotiation in human affairs, and in relation to social order. This argument did not preclude the role of other processes, and indeed they could be seen operating in conjunction with negotiation in the various instances of types of negotiation explored in that book. Yet I did not there address analytically how the various processes combined or, as here, their relationships to other phenomena.

Meanwhile the term *negotiated order* has developed a career of its own, after some years of use, mainly by symbolic interactionists, coming to stand for flexible organizational arrangements, the fluidity of overall interactional patterns at any level of scale, and that social orders are forms of activity:

> Apropos, the astructural bias [of which symbolic interactionism is sometimes accused], and to the contrary, Symbolic Interaction . . . has created a negotiated approach to social order, at all levels of organizational scale, that fundamentally has changed the way we conceive of all institutions (see especially Strauss 1978). (Farberman 1991, p. 481)

Given the rhetorical history of the concept of negotiated order, it may be too late to substitute a new one, but I will attempt this. I suggest two new words in combination: *processual ordering*. My use of a verb—ordering—instead of the usual noun is meant to emphasize the creative or constructive aspect of interaction, the "working at" and "working out of" ordering in the face of inevitable contingencies, small and large. This same conception is embodied in Everett Hughes's imagery of institutions as "going concerns," noted a few pages ago, and of course by the Pragmatists. The German sociologist Hans Joas (1992) has recently highlighted this emphasis on creativity by the American Pragmatists and the early Chicago interactionists.

This concept of processual ordering of creativity is meant to embrace *every* main topic discussed in this book, and of course many more. If elaborated through further research and thought, this concept has the potential for developing what is manifestly still a very crude theoretical scheme for understanding what is involved in any type of ordering.

Yet this leaves unanswered the question of the relationships between this new concept (processual ordering) and the older one (negotiated order). It is still my belief that though negotiation is only one of the interactional processes, it must be a major contributor to any social ordering. As remarked earlier, even predominantly coercive orders ultimately require and produce negotiation, and lots of it. This takes place not only among the oppressors themselves as well as among the oppressed, but also between both. The same is true of predominantly manipulative orders, since the manipulators are likely to need allies who in turn will expect something in exchange for their services or support. Exchanging, trading off, bargaining, wheeling and dealing, compromising, power brokering, engaging in collusion, and even coercive negotiating are threaded throughout the interactions around space, time, work, sentiment—resulting in the reifications that are commonly referred to as civil or social orders.

However, more generally the concept of negotiated order was designed to refer not merely to negotiation and negotiative processes. It also points to the lack of fixity of social order, its temporal, mobile, and unstable character, and the flexibility of interactants faced with the need to act through interactional processes in specific localized situations where although rules and regulations exist nevertheless these are not necessarily precisely prescriptive or peremptorily constraining. My intent in coining the concept of processual ordering is not merely to capture the same attributes of interaction but to extend, deepen, and make possible a more detailed understanding of negotiated orders.

THE NECESSITY OF PROCESSUAL ORDERING AND THE FOUNDATIONAL ROLE OF MATRIX CONDITIONS

This section will consist of a simple example that is designed to be persuasively instructive and to lead to an additional and important theoretical point. Consider the characteristics of a more or less completely routinized though complex set of procedures: routine surgery. In this type of surgery, every procedure has been so often practiced that hazard is minimal and contingencies are prepared for with additionally well-tried procedures. The equipment is familiar and "in order." Before the actual surgery, patients have been prepared by standard procedures, and after surgery they are taken care of by equally routine procedures both in the operating room and in the postop ward. All the actors in this drama—physician(s), nurses, and others—know their well-rehearsed parts. Given no major contingencies, everything proceeds smoothly and there is no likelihood of disagreement over either medical or nursing care procedures.

This unruffled picture of a routinized order is completely deceptive. History is blotted out by a highly focused present. The contentious history of antisepsis is totally in the background, for antiseptic procedures are taken completely for granted. The jurisdictional arena battles over who should control the anesthesia also is shrouded in past history (perhaps remembered by the anesthesiologist from his or her student years when the legendary strife was invoked.) The surgical technology—both the procedures and the equipment—also have their histories: Sociologically these are relevant to the surgical action but ordinarily none of the actors notices them.

Backgrounded also are items from other levels of the conditional matrix: for instance, the differential training of each type of professional, or the usual high degree of status, privilege, and power of the surgeons within the hospital and the comparable accessibility of their resources. I could continue this list for quite a while—including, for instance, that surgery and surgeons are replete with symbolism (for instance, representing the epitome of skilled and life-saving medical work), imagery of magic, awe, anxiety, bodily vulnerability, and potential death heightened by frequent visibility in both common and media discourse. Each and every procedure taken for granted today has its history as do each of the participating professions and "the" hospital itself (see Wiener, Fagerhaugh, Strauss, and Suczek 1979).

So do a few imponderables that might just have entered this particular surgical episode. Suppose, for example, that the surgeon is Jewish or an African American. Today that makes no difference whatever in the interaction around the patient, but consider what that interaction might have looked like when Jews and African Americans were first becoming surgeons or as women now are increasingly doing. The point can be underlined by noting another status that is currently changing and entering the surgical theater and surgical wards: The status of patients and/or surgeons with HIV is an issue under debate and scrutiny, making many ordinarily routine operations anything but completely routine.

Also one more cluster of conditions of prime importance: the massive industrial enterprises—pharmaceutical, medical supply, and medical equipment especially—without which contemporary medical practice would be inconceivable. The industries are paralleled within the hospital by departments and specialized personnel: pharmacy, pharmacists, and pharmacologists; central supply departments and their workers; biotechnicians and their staffs. All play their background roles even when surgery and its treatment are uneventful and routine.

When surgery is more complex or exceedingly intricate, then the kinds of conditions and contingencies that can affect the course of interaction greatly increase and, analytically speaking, are much more visible. The processual ordering then is much more evident. It also exists for routine situations and actions; it is just less evident. If this is so for small projects like accepting a patient for surgery and seeing him or her through a course of surgical treatment, think of what is involved in the processual ordering of a large project, an organization of any size—or an entire nation-state!

An important implication of this example about surgery and its extension to less routine ordering is that the *conditional matrix* enters into the ordering in often completely unnoted but essential ways. Some are so indirect in their influence that perhaps only a researcher can take the time and energy and possess the requisite skills to track their conditional paths. In saying this, I am leading up to the point that *matrix conditions are foundational throughout the processual ordering that results in social orders.*

This is a somewhat different but related point that I have often made elsewhere (cf. Strauss 1985; Corbin and Strauss 1988; see also Becker 1982; Métraux 1991; Star 1991); namely, that actions essential to getting work accomplished are frequently invisible to anyone who is a bystander or who only sees part of the work process. This relative invisibility is sometimes deliberately furthered by those who receive or retain the most benefit from the invisibility, so that "this is a profoundly political process" (Star 1991, p. 281; see also Harroway 1989). In the example above, it is the surgeons who continue to get the most money and prestige rather than any of the many subsidiary workers who ultimately make recovery from surgery possible; but it is the political skills of the medical profession that have ensured continued economic and occupational dominance. Yet the emphasis on the power and dominance aspects of largely unrecognized actors, although useful, ought not to preempt the more inclusive issue—that to understand the creation-formation, maintaining-stability, and changing-changeable nature of any order, the interlocking impacts of conditions [including the moral (Addelson 1990)] at various matrix levels need to be recognized, or at least somewhat apprehended. Otherwise justice is not done to the complexity of the processual ordering of social orders.

The interactionist view of order is that it is *created*, and is *maintained* or *changed in desired directions* through *action*. Order(ing) is not something that is to be understood only in terms of concepts of effective communication (Lyotard) or the dominant influence of consensus (Habermas), and surely not by the people-less abstractions of various types of systems theory (Luhman). What I am asserting is necessary—at least implied in an interactionist theory of action—is consideration of the collective working out of ordering, involving self-interactive actors and the various interactive processes. [See Becker (1986, pp. 11–13) for another recent phrasing of this point; see also Gerson (Forthcoming) for a wonderfully detailed demonstration of it in his tracing of the evolution of biological theories and research.] Hence the term processual order*ing*. Hence also if we are to be accurate, we must think of a theory of act*ing* rather than a theory of action. In this book, trajectory has been the summarizing concept for this interactionist theory.

ORDER–DISORDER, STABILITY–INSTABILITY, AND CHANGE

This concept and the assumptions on which it rests (see, respectively, Chapters 2 and 1) have one last implication pertaining to the issue of order and change that was touched on above. There I noted the opposing stances of Parsons, the functionalist, and the Pragmatists/interactionists on that issue. If you examine closely Dewey's argument in those same pages, you can see the complexity of this issue. The opening phrase of Dewey's statement "the permanent and enduring is comparative" sets the frame of his argument. He is balancing the priorities of stability and those of change: sometimes there is an advantage in emphasizing stability, but not always or for all purposes. Dewey's Pragmatist perspective leads to a primary focus on the interaction between humans as active agents and relatively stable conditions (or "structure") and between the former and contingencies as well. So he is also emphasizing the interaction between the routine (stable) and the novel (change), the routine providing a nondeterministic framework for action, which in turn can be affected by actors and their actions. (This same position was explored in Chapter 8, concerning the interplay of the routine and the novel, but stated in sociological terms.) The early Chicago interactionists would not have read this particular passage of Dewey's but surely had absorbed its general thrust from a reading of his previous writings.

The analysis of Thomas and Znaniecki (1918–1920) centered around the conceptual couplet of social organization and social disorganization. This was their terminology for social order and social disorder. Both they and sociologists from other traditions have tended to equate stability with order and instability with change. (Though those same interactionist authors emphasized that social disorganization could be a condition for individual and collective creativity.) This seems reasonable, but this pairing does not fit well with my theory of action.

My reasoning is as follows. The basic interactionist assumptions, plus observations, suggest at least a preliminary line of thinking that refuses to reify any of these terms. In fact, it rejects the concept of "disorder" since then a dichotomy is assumed between order and change. This interactionist line of thinking emphasizes the activity of "defining." Whether events and institutions seem relatively unchanging or rapidly changing is surely a matter of differential perspectives that affect perceptions of particular actors at particular times and places and in particular situations. What is one actor's rapidly, even drastically changing world is another's relatively unchanging, stable world. If both actors agree, it may only be that although their experiences and perceptions do in fact differ markedly, nonetheless the convergence of definition is profoundly affected by perspective as related to the particularities of time, place, and situation.

Perspectives, experiences, and selective perception all have an interrelated bearing upon how persons and collectivities define and consequentially act toward events. You will undoubtedly find that last assertion noncontestable, if seemingly banal. A more radical statement might be that there is no surefire way to prove the degree of change or stability characterizing a given place, time, or situation, no matter how scientific the claim may be about the criteria for assessing or measuring it. Scientists also have perspectives and their definitions of change-stability are frequently found debatable by colleagues, suspect by laypersons, and later generations will surely revise their definitions and estimates.

Perhaps no one would disagree with the general statement that some things are changing rapidly while others are changing slowly—leaving aside which specific ones belong to each set. As Dewey wrote, "the rate of change of some things is so slow . . . that these changes have all the advantages of stability in dealing with more transitory happenings—if we know enough" (1927, p. 71). His statement applies not only to scientists but to every actor in this world of ours—though *not*, alas, his proviso.

The key questions then for every actor are, What is changing, what aspect of it, in what direction and at what rate? And so how do these affect me (or us) and how shall I (we) act? Is the world "going to hell in a handbag" or is it ravishingly and refreshingly changing for the better? The world referred to cannot mean everything but implies some implicit or explicit ranking: Some changes are viewed as more essential to the actor's definition of change or stability, and inevitably with reference to parts rather than the totality of the symbolized world.

So *the* issue is not whether social scientists, or anyone else, can assess change and its properties accurately or even approximately. Social scientists, I reason, do not have to solve the unsolvable—is the world changing rapidly or is it not, and which parts of it, etc.? Rather, our main issue is to study how specific institutions, organizations, social worlds, and other collectivities answer such key questions as were listed above.

Schatzman suggests that the idea of social order is so significant:

> [B]ecause of the nature of the stake people have in it—a stake in position, identity and its control—also a stake in its comfort—[if] one is uncomfortable, [then] one "calls for" changes. The irony is . . . that the call is almost always for particular changes which might affect an uncomfortable aspect of order that appears to exist. [So] On the one hand, order is ubiquitous: I live in it, find comfort, predictability or relative certainty in it. Change occasionally threatens my stake in it, . . . my sense of familiarity, knowing and control over my stake. On the other hand, at times, ideologically, I see order as affording low quality of life for self or others and so I want some change, but only the right kind. . . . So I try occasionally to ferment change or steer ongoing change in the *right* direction. (Personal communication)

Return now to the semantics of the usual pairing of the following sociological terms: stability-instability (or change) and order-disorder (or in Thomas and Znaniecki's lexicon, social organization and social disorganization). Is there only one dimension, running from very stable (order) to very unstable (disorder)? If so, where does change belong? Is it always destabilizing? Does it vary between only slightly destabilizing to very much so? Does it never promote stability? And is a high degree of order not also somewhat changeable in some of its components? Conversely, does so-called disorder (as during a social revolution) retain no elements of stability? (To quote Schatzman again: "If I can anticipate change and feel predictive [about it] then change is part of 'order.' If I am unhappy with some aspects of order, I 'call' for change—[but] certain kinds only.")

Where an interactionist theory of acting appears to lead is not merely to a social constructivist, and certainly not to a radically relativistic view of social order and social change. However, where it takes us needs to be clearly stated. At any level of analysis, from classical sociology's social order to Goffman's interactional order, *order* refers to relatively predictable events. These in turn are predictable because routines (whether simple procedures, or the rules and regulations and structures of complex organizations or of institutions) have been created by those who have enough power or influence to define them as so.

Now, the usual interactionist view about social *dis*order—and interactionists are not alone in this view—is that disorder is created by events that are either unpredictable or not predicted; hence routines are rendered problematic in greater or less degree. The events themselves largely occur because actors who are discontented with certain aspects of the order are attempting to bring about change. Whether they succeed or not, some measure of disorder is precipitated. (Of course, disorder can occur temporarily through physical disruption, as in earthquakes, or merely be the by-product of remote or external events such as wars or conquest.)

This perspective on order—a rather commonsense one—implies that disorder is a useful *analytic* concept, but I do not believe it is. There is always order; the world never does go completely to pieces, except perhaps briefly in total mass panics. Even in panics, however, complete disintegration is an illusion because in theater fire panics the mad rush is toward the exits and not to anywhere else; likewise when persons or families flee invading armies they some act irrationally but others act with full rationality. Such breakdowns as occur during periods of social disintegration consequently provide changed conditions that bear on subsequent actions, whether actors perceive this clearly or not. Order*ing* is ongoing. Whoever calls some aspect of the ordering by the name of disorder (or some synonym for it) does so from a perspective, one that we need to know for accurately accounting for this interpretative claim.[1]

In contrast, "social change" *is* a useful analytic concept, but only if we carefully separate the perspectival—social constructivist—issue from the one now being discussed, that is, How is change (or social change) related to (social) order and disorder? Change cannot possibly be either equivalent to disorder (assuming it exists) or antithetical to order because it can enhance or diminish the one or the other. Contributory to each, it is the servant of neither.

However, change and lack of change are perceived by actors as more or less relevant to themselves, and who act as appropriately as possible with regard to these according to their own lights. Sometimes their lights prove disastrous for themselves or for others.[2] Whether or not we would judge them by their results is, again, not the question. I maintain that our analytic task is clarified if the concept of change is distinguished conceptually from the order-disorder dimension, with *specific* questions to be asked about their perceived respective relationships as they emerge in particular times, places, and situations—and through particular interactions.

All of this is not to deny the ubiquitous nature of change. Change is ceaseless: Sometimes it is discernible (but to whom and when?) and sometimes not (likewise). An interactionist theory of acting follows through on its own assumptions, opting for the primacy of collective action. It therefore emphasizes contingencies and the inevitable changes brought about by them. But at the same time it cannot, must not, fail to link contingencies and action to the more slowly moving, more stable elements of the social environment created and maintained sometimes many generations ago.

To round off this chapter I offer: "A note to Shakespeare" written by an anonymous literary critic:

Hamlet: "To be or not to be, that is the question." . . . Oh, come now Shakespeare, you know very well that Hamlet's inaction is only another form of action. You are cleverly making us follow his inner debate, which of course mirrors the more visible interaction being played out among the full cast of characters—Hamlet's mother, stepfather, friends, Ophelia, the court, and Hamlet himself. *Therein* lies the question: practical for the Prince, seemingly philosophical but actually of significance for all of us, who generation by generation reinterpret his enigmatic answers. Canny Shakespeare to have presented us with such an ambiguous world: a created orderly structure—or perhaps a structured ordering of reality?

NOTES

1. A graphic illustration of this was Hedrick Smith's documentary portrayal of Russia, shown on TV some months post-Gorbachev. Viewers were shown a number of scenes reflecting intense anger at the enormous rise in prices and toward the avarice of private speculators, while several entrepreneurs with enthusiasm or in calm rational tones explained the many opportunities now opening both for themselves and the country through an emergent private economy. Respectively they were showing the two faces of the order/disorder, commonsense definition.

2. I borrow this usage from the historians Commager and Morrison, who once suggested about King George III's policy toward the American colonies that whatever his intentions, his lights were very dim.

References

Ablon, J. 1984. *Little People of America: The Social Dimensions of Dwarfism.* New York: Praeger.

Addelson, K. 1990. "Some Moral Issues in Public Problems of Reproduction." *Social Problems* 37:1–17.

Alexander, Thomas 1987. *John Dewey's Theory of Art, Experience, and Nature.* Albany, NY: State University of New York Press.

Bakhtin, M. [1968] 1984. *Rabelais and His World.* Translated by H. Iswolsky. Bloomington, IN: Indiana University Press.

Baszanger, I. 1992. "Les chantiers d'un interactionniste americain." Pp. 11–63 in *La Trame de la negociation: Sociologie qualitative et interactionnisme,* edited by I. Baszanger. Paris: L'Harmattan.

Becker, H. 1970. *Sociological Work.* Chicago: Aldine.

Becker, H. 1982. *Art Worlds.* Berkeley, CA: University of California.

Becker, H. 1986. *Doing Things Together.* Evanston, IL: Northwestern University.

Becker, H., Geer, B., Riesman, D. and Weiss, R. (eds.). 1968. *Institutions and the Person: Essays Presented to Everett C. Hughes.* Chicago: Aldine.

Berger, P. and Luckmann, T. 1966. *The Social Construction of Reality.* Garden City, NY: Doubleday.

Birrer, C. 1979. *Multiple Sclerosis: A Personal View.* Springfield, IL: Thomas.

Blumer, H. 1937. "Social Psychology." Pp. 144–98 in *Man and Society,* edited by E. Schmidt. New York: Prentice-Hall.

Blumer, H: 1946. "Collective Behavior." Pp. 170–200 in *New Outline of the Principles of Sociology,* edited by A. Lee. New York: Barnes and Noble.

Blumer, H. 1948. "Sociological Theory in Industrial Relations." *American Sociological Review* 12:271–78.

Blumer, H. 1969. *Symbolic Interaction.* Englewood Cliffs, NJ: Prentice-Hall.

Blumer, H. 1990. *Industrialization as an Agent of Social Change: A Critical Analysis,* edited with an Introduction by David R. Maines and Thomas J. Morrione. Hawthorne, NY: Aldine de Gruyter.

Bucher, B. and Schatzman, L. 1964. "Negotiating a Division of Labor among Professionals in the State Mental Hospitals." *Psychiatry* 27:266–77.

Burke, J. (ed.). 1991. *Morris Janowitz: On Social Order and Social Control.* Chicago: University of Chicago Press.

Burke, K. 1936. *Permanence and Change.* New York: New Republic.

Burke, K. 1937. *Attitudes Toward History.* New York: New Republic.

Burke, K. 1945. *A Grammar of Motives.* New York: Prentice-Hall.

Burke, K. 1950. *A Rhetoric of Motives.* New York: Prentice-Hall.

Busch, L. 1982. "History, Negotiation and Structure in Agricultural Research." *Urban Life* 11:368–84.

Callon, M. 1991. "Techno-economic Networks and Irreversibility." Pp. 132–61 in *Towards a Sociology of Monsters: Essays on Power, Technology and Domination*, edited by J. Law. London: Routledge.

Cassirer, E. 1944. *An Essay on Man*. New Haven, CT: Yale University Press.

Cassirer, E. 1953–1957. *The Philosophy of Symbolic Forms*. Three volumes. New Haven, CT: Yale University Press.

Chandler, A. 1977. *The Visible Hand*. Cambridge, MA: Belknap, and Harvard University Press.

Charmaz, K. 1975. "The Coroner's Strategies for Announcing Death." *Urban Life* 4:196–316.

Charmaz, K. 1991. "Turning Points and Fictional Identities." Pp. 71–86 in *Social Organization and Social Process: Essays in Honor of Anselm Strauss*, edited by D. Maines. Hawthorne, NY: Aldine de Gruyter.

Clarke, A. 1990a. "A Social Worlds Research Adventure: The Case of Reproductive Science." Pp. 23–50 in *Theories of Science in Society*, edited by S. Cozzens and Thomas Gieryn. Bloomington, IN: Indiana University Press.

Clarke, A. 1990b. "Controversy and the Development of Reproductive Sciences." *Social Problems* 37:18–37.

Clarke, A. 1991. "Social Worlds/Arenas Theory as Organizational Theory." Pp. 119–58 in *Social Organization and Social Process: Essays in Honor of Anselm Strauss*, edited by D. Maines. Hawthorne, NY: Aldine de Gruyter.

Clarke, A. 1993. "The Human Reproduction Domain, 1890–1990." In *Women's Health: Dynamics of Diversity*, edited by S. Ruzek, V. Olesen, and A. Clarke. Philadelphia: Temple University Press.

Clarke, A. and Fujimura, J. 1992. *The Right Tools for the Job: at Work in Twentieth Century Life Sciences*. Princeton, NJ: Princeton University Press.

Cohen, M. and Nagel, E. 1934. *An Introduction to Logic and Scientific Method*. New York: Harcourt, Brace.

Corbin, J. 1991. "Anselm Strauss: An Intellectual Biography." Pp. 17–42 in *Social Organization and Social Process: Essays in Honor of Anselm Strauss*, edited by D. Maines. Hawthorne, NY: Aldine de Gruyter.

Corbin, J. 1993. "The Caregiving Trajectory: an Interactive Processual Framework." *Revue Internationale d'Action Communautaire*.

Corbin, J. and Strauss, A. 1988. *Unending Care and Work*. San Francisco: Jossey-Bass.

Corbin, J. and Strauss, A. 1991. "Comeback: The Process of Overcoming Disability." Pp. 137–58 in *Advances in Medical Sociology: A Research Annual*, Vol. 2, edited by G. Albrecht and J. Levy. Greenwich, CT: JAI Press.

Corbin J. and Strauss, A. 1993. "The Articulation of Work Through Interaction." *Qualitative Sociology* 34:71–83.

Couch, C. 1992. "Toward a Formal Theory of Social Processes." *Symbolic Interaction* 15:117–34.

Dalton, M. 1954. *Men Who Manage*. New York: Wiley.

Davis, F. [1961] 1972. "Deviance Disavowal." Pp. 132–49 in *Illness, Interaction, and the Self*, edited by F. Davis. Belmont, CA: Waldmuth.

Davis, F. 1986. "Review of *The Social Organization of Medicine*, by Strauss et al." *Social Science and Medicine* 22:1370–71.

Davis, F. 1991. "Identity Ambivalence in Clothing: The Dialect of the Erotic and the Chaste." Pp. 105–16 in *Social Organization and Social Process: Essays in Honor of Anselm Strauss*, edited by D. Maines. Hawthorne, NY: Aldine de Gruyter.

Dawson, C. and Gettys, W. 1929. *An Introduction to Sociology*. New York: Ronald Press.

de Kruif, P. 1926. *Microbe Hunters*. New York: Harcourt Brace.

de Mille, A. 1981. *Reprieve*. New York: New American Library.

Dewey, J. 1896. "The Reflex Arc Concept in Psychology." *Psychological Review* 3:363–70.

Dewey, J. 1916. *Democracy and Education*. New York: Macmillan.

Dewey, J. 1920. *Reconstruction in Philosophy*. New York: Holt.

Dewey, J. 1922. *Human Nature and Conduct*. New York: Holt.

Dewey, J. 1927. *The Public and Its Problems*. New York: Holt.

Dewey, J. 1934. *Art as Experience*. Boston: Balach.

Dewey, J. 1935. *Liberalism and Social Action*. New York: Minton, Balach.

Dewey, J. 1938a. *Logic: The Theory of Inquiry*. New York: Holt.

Dewey, J. 1938b. *Experience and Education*. New York: Macmillan.

Doyle, B. 1937. *The Etiquette of Race Relations in the South*. Chicago: University of Chicago.

Dewey, J. and Bentley, A. 1949. *Knowing and the Known*. Westport, Ct: Greenwood Press.

Durkheim, E. 1915. *The Elementary Forms of Religious Life*. Translated from the French by J. Swain. New York: Macmillan.

Duster, T. 1990. *Eugenics through the Back Door*. Berkeley, CA: University of California Press.

Edge, D. and Mulkay, M. 1976. *Astronomy Transformed*. New York: Wiley.

Engestroem, Y. 1984. *Learning and Teaching on a Scientific Basis*. Aarhus, Denmark: Aarhus University, Psychological Institute.

Fagerhaugh, S. and Strauss, A. 1977. *The Politics of Pain Management*. Menlo Park, CA: Atherton-Westley.

Fagerhaugh, S., Strauss, A., Suczek, B. and Wiener, C. 1987. *Hazards in Health Care*. San Francisco: Jossey-Bass.

Fanon, F. 1968. *The Wretched of the Earth*. Translated from the French by C. Farrington. New York: Grove.

Farberman, H. 1991. "Symbolic Interaction and Postmodernism: Close Encounters of a Dubious Kind." *Symbolic Interaction* 13:471–88.

Fisher, B. and Strauss, A. 1978. "The Chicago Tradition: Thomas, Park and Their Successors." *Symbolic Interaction* 1:5–23.

Fisher, B. and Strauss, A. 1979. "George Herbert Mead and the Chicago Tradition of Sociology." Part 1: *Symbolic Interaction* 2(1):9–24; Part 2: *Symbolic Interaction* 2(2):9–20.

Flan, J. 1973. *Matisse on Art.*. New York: Phaidon.

Foote, N. 1951. "Identification as the Basis for a Theory of Motivation." *American Sociological Review* 16:14–22.

Frank, A. 1991. "For a Sociology of the Body: An Analytical Review." Pp. 36–102 in *The Body*, edited by B. Turner. Newbury Park, CA: Sage.

Freidson, E. 1976. "The Division of Labor as Social Interaction." *Social Problems* 23:304–13.

Fujimura, J. 1987. "Constructing Doable Problems in Cancer Research: Articulating Alignment." *Social Studies of Science* 17:257–93.

Fujimura, J. 1988. "The Molecular Biological Bandwagon in Cancer Research: Where Social Worlds Meet." *Social Problems* 35:261–83.

Fujimura, J. 1991. "On Methods, Ontologies, and Representation in the Sociology of Science: Where Do We Stand?" Pp. 207–48 in *Social Organization and Social Process: Essays in Honor of Anselm Strauss*, edited by D. Maines. Hawthorne, NY: Aldine de Gruyter.

Fujimura, J. 1992. "Crafting Science: Standardized Packages, Boundary Objects, and 'Translation.'" Pp. 168–211 in *Science as Practice and Culture*, edited by A. Pickering. Chicago: University of Chicago Press.

Fujimura, J. 1994 (forthcoming). *Crafting Science: The Case of Oncogen Research.* Cambridge, MA: Harvard University.

Fujimura, J. and Chou, D. Forthcoming. "Dissent in Science: Styles of Scientific Practice and the Controversy Over the Cause of AIDS."

Funk and Wagnalls. 1935. *The Practical Standard Dictionary of the English Language.* New York: Funk and Wagnalls.

Gasser, L. 1986. "The Integration of Computing and Routine Work." *ACM Transactions on Office Information Systems* 4:205–25.

Gerson, E. 1977. "Rationalization and the Varieties of Technical Work." Working paper, Tremont Research Institute, San Francisco.

Gerson, E. 1983. "Scientific Work and Social Worlds." *Knowledge* 4:357–77.

Gerson, E. Forthcoming. The American System of Research: Evolutionary Biology 1890–1950. Berkeley and Los Angeles, CA: University of California.

Gerson, E. and Star, S. L. 1986. "Analyzing Due Process in the Work Place." *ACM Transactions on Office Information Systems* 4:257–70.

Glaser, B. 1976. *Experts versus Laymen: A Study of the Patsy and the Subcontractor.* New Brunswick, NJ: Transaction Press.

Glaser, B. 1978. *Theoretical Sensitivity.* Mill Valley, CA: Sociology Press.

Glaser, B. and Strauss, A. 1965. *Awareness of Dying.* Chicago: Aldine.

Glaser, B. and Strauss, A. 1967. *The Discovery of Grounded Theory.* Chicago: Aldine.

Glaser, B. and Strauss, A. 1968. *Time for Dying.* Chicago: Aldine.

Goffman, E. 1959. *The Presentation of Self in Everyday Life.* New York: Doubleday.

Goffman, E. 1961a. "On the Characteristics of Total Institutions." Pp. 1–124 in *Asylums: Essays on the Social Situation of Mental Patients and Other Inmates*, edited by E. Goffman, Garden City, NY: Doubleday.

Goffman, E. 1961b. "The Underlife of a Public Institution: A Study of Ways of Making Out in a Mental Hospital." Pp. 171–320 in *Asylums: Essays on the Social Situation of Mental Patients and Other Inmates*, edited by E. Goffman. Garden City, NY: Doubleday.

Goffman, E. 1963. *Stigma: Notes on the Management of Spoiled Identity.* Englewood Cliffs: Prentice-Hall.

Goffman, E. 1963. *Behavior in Public Places.* New York: Free Press.

Goffman, E. 1967. *Interaction Ritual: Essays on Face-to-Face Behavior.* Chicago: Aldine.

Goffman, E. 1974. *Frame Analysis: An Essay on the Organization of Experience.* New York: Harper and Row.

Grathoff, R. 1970. *The Structure of Social Inconsistencies.* The Hague: Martinus Nijhoff.

Grathoff, R. 1978. *The Theory of Social Action: The Correspondence of Alfred Schuetz and Talcott Parsons.* Bloomington, IN: Indiana University Press.

Griffin, J. 1961. *Black Like Me.* Boston: Houghton Mifflin.

Gusfield, J. 1991. "Risky Roads." *Society* 28:10–16.

Halbwachs, M. 1950. *La Memoire Collective.* Paris: Presses Universitaires de France.

Harroway, D. 1989. *Primate Visions.* New York: Routledge.

Hayes-Bautista, D., Schink, W. and Chapa, J. 1988. *The Burden of Support: Young Latinos in an Aging Society.* Palo Alto, CA: Stanford University Press.

Hilgarten, S. 1990. "The Dominant View of Popularization: Conceptual Problems, Political Uses." *Social Studies of Science* 10:519–39.

Hoffman, E. 1989. *Lost in Translation: A Life in a New Language.* New York: Penguin Books.

Horowitz, I. 1980. *Taking Lives: Genocide and State Power,* 3rd edition. New Brunswick, NJ: Transaction Press.

Horowitz, I. 1988. "The Limits of Policy and the Purposes of Research: The Case of AIDS." *Knowledge in Society* 1:35–46.

Hughes, E. 1951. *Collected Papers of Robert E. Park, Vol. 1, Race and Culture.* Glencoe, IL: Free Press.

Hughes, E. 1952a. *Collected Papers of Robert E. Park, Vol. 2, Human Communities.* Glencoe, IL: Free Press.

Hughes, E. 1952b. "The Sociology of Work: An Editorial Foreword." *American Journal of Sociology* 57:298–303.

Hughes, E. 1955. *Collected Papers of Robert E. Park, Vol. 3.* Glencoe, IL: Free Press.

Hughes, E. [1962] 1971. *The Sociological Eye.* New Brunswick, NJ: Transaction Press.

Jackal, R. 1978. *Workers in a Labyrinth.* New York: Universe Books.

James, H. [1898] 1980. *The Turn of the Screw.* New York: New American Library.

Joas, H. 1992. "An Underestimated Alternative: America and the Limits of 'Critical Theory.'" *Symbolic Interaction* 15:261–76.

Klapp, O. 1962. *Heroes, Fools and Villains.* Englewood Cliffs, NJ: Prentice-Hall.

Klapp, O. 1964. *Symbolic Leaders.* Chicago: Aldine.

Kling, R. and Gerson, E. 1978. "Patterns of Segmentation and Intersection in the Computer World." *Symbolic Interaction* 1:24–43.

Langer, S. 1942. *Philosophy in a New Key.* New York: Penguin.

Lash, S. 1991. "Genealogy and the Body." Pp. 256–80 in *The Body,* edited by B. Turner. Newbury Park, CA: Sage.

Latour, B. 1988a. "Mixing Humans and Nonhumans Together: The Sociology of a Door-Closer." *Social Problems* 35:298–310.

Latour, B. 1988b. *The Pasteurization of French Society.* Cambridge, MA: Harvard University Press.

Latour, B. and Wolgar, S. 1979. *Laboratory Life*. Beverly Hills, CA: Sage.

Law, J. 1986. "Laboratories and Texts." In *Texts and Their Power: Mapping the Dynamics of Science and Technology*, edited by M. Callon, J. Law, and A. Rip. London: Macmillan.

Lazarsfeld, P. 1972. "Historical Notes on the Empirical Study of Action: An Intellectual Odyssey." Pp. 53–105 in *Qualitative Analysis*, edited by P. Lazarfeld. Boston: Allyn and Bacon.

Lear, J. 1978. *Recombinant DNA*. New York: Crown.

Levi, P. 1979. *Moments of Reprieve*. Translated by R. Feldman. New York: Simon and Schuster.

Levi, P. 1986. *Survival in Auschwitz*. Translated by S. Woolf. New York: Simon and Schuster.

Levi, P. 1988. *The Drowned and the Saved*. Translated by R. Rosenthal. New York: Summit Books.

Lewis, S. 1925. *Arrowsmith*. New York: Grosset and Dunlap.

Lindesmith, A. and Strauss, A. 1949. *Social Psychology*. New York: Dryden.

Lofland, J. (ed.) 1978. *Interaction in Everyday Life*. Beverly Hills, CA: Sage.

Luria, A. 1978. *The Selected Writing of A. R. Luria*. Edited by M. Cole. White Plains, NY: M. E. Sharpe.

Maines, D. 1978. "Bodies and Selves: Notes on a Fundamental Dilemma in Demography." In *Studies in Symbolic Interaction: A Research Annual*, edited by N. Denzin. Greenwich, CT: JAI Press.

Maines, D. 1982. "In Search of Mesostructure: Studies in the Negotiated Order." *Urban Life* 11:267–79.

Maines, D. 1991. "Reflections, Appreciations, and Framings." Pp. 3–9 in *Social Organization and Social Process: Essays in Honor of Anselm Strauss*, edited by D. Maines. Hawthorne, NY: Aldine de Gruyter.

Maines, D. 1992. "Life Histories." Pp. 1134–38 in *Encyclopedia of Sociology*, edited by E. Borgotta and M. Borgotta. New York: Macmillan.

Maines, D. and Charlton, J. 1985. "The Negotiated Order Approach to the Analysis of Social Organization." Pp. 271–308 in *Foundations of Interpretive Sociology: Original Essays in Symbolic Interactions*, edited by Harvey Farberman and Robert Perinbauayagam. Greenwich, CT: JAI Press.

McConnell, G. 1953. *The Decline of Agrarian Democracy*. Berkeley, CA: University of California Press.

Mead, G. 1934. *Mind, Self and Society*. Chicago: University of Chicago Press.

Mead, G. H. 1936. *Movements of Thought in the Nineteenth Century*. Chicago: University of Chicago Press.

Mead, G. 1938. *Philosophy of the Act*. Chicago: University of Chicago Press.

Mead, G. [1932] 1980a. *Philosophy of the Present*. Chicago: University of Chicago Press.

Mead, G. H. [1932] 1980b. "The Objective Reality of Perspectives." Pp. 161–73 in *The Philosophy of the Present*, edited by A. Murphy. Chicago: University of Chicago Press. [This paper was reprinted in 1932 from the *Proceedings of the Sixth International Congress of Philosophy*, circa 1925.]

Mead, G. H. 1982. *The Individual and the Social Self: Unpublished Work of G. H. Mead.* Edited by D. Miller. Chicago: University of Chicago Press.

Merleau-Ponty, M. 1962. *Phenomenology of Perception.* Translated by C. Smith. London: Routledge and Kegan Paul.

Merleau-Ponty, M. 1964. *The Primacy of Perception.* Edited by J. Edie. Evanston, IL: Northwestern University Press.

Métraux, A. 1991. "Reaching the Invisible: A Case Study of Experimental Work in Microbiology (1880–1900)." Pp. 249–60 in *Social Organization, and Social Processes: Essays in Honor of Anselm Strauss,* edited by D. Maines. Hawthorne, NY: Aldine de Gruyter.

Mills, C. 1940. "Situated Actions and Vocabularies of Motive." *American Sociological Review* 5:904–13.

Mura, D. 1991. *Turning Japanese: Memoirs of a Sansei.* New York: Anchor Books.

Nelkin, D. 1987. *Selling Science: How the Press Covers Science and Technology.* New York: Freeman.

Oestreich, James. 1991. "Is It Mahler? Or Is It Happy Talk?" *New York Times,* Section 2, p. 1.

Park, R. 1972. *The Crowd and the Public and Other Essays.* Edited by H. Elsner. Chicago: University of Chicago Press.

Park, R. and Burgess, E. 1921. *Introduction to the Science of Sociology.* Chicago: University of Chicago Press.

Park, R. and Miller, H. 1921. *Old World Traits Transplanted.* New York: Harper.

Parsons, T. 1937. *The Structure of Social Action.* New York: McGraw-Hill.

Peirce, C. 1958. *Charles P. Peirce Selected Writings,* edited by P. Weiner, New York: Dover.

Riemann, G. 1987. *Das Fremdwerden der eigenen Biographie: Narrative Interviews mit psychiatrischen Patienten.* Munich: Fink.

Riemann, G. and Schuetze, F. 1991. "'Trajectory' as a Basic Concept for Analyzing Suffering and Disorderly Social Processes." Pp. 333–56 in *Social Organization and Social Process: Essays in Honor of Anselm Strauss,* edited by D. Maines. Hawthorne, NY: Aldine de Gruyter.

Riemer, J. 1979. *Hardhats: The Work World of Construction Workers.* Beverly Hills, CA: Sage.

Riezler, K. 1950. *Man: Mutable and Immutable.* Chicago: Regnery.

Rochberg-Halton, E. 1986. *Meaning and Modernity: Social Theory in the Pragmatic Attitude.* Chicago: University of Chicago Press.

Rochberg-Halton, E. 1987. "Why Pragmatism Now?" *Sociological Theory* 5:194–200.

Ryan, C. 1974. *A Bridge Too Far.* New York: Simon and Schuster.

Sachs, O. 1989. *Seeing Voices: A Journey into the World of the Deaf.* Berkeley and Los Angeles: University of California.

Schegloff, E. 1972. "Notes On a Conversational Practice: Formulating Place." Pp. 267–89 in *Studies in Social Interaction,* edited by D. Sudnow. New York: Free Press.

Schlesinger, A. 1965. *A Thousand Days.* Boston: Houghton Mifflin.

Schneider, J. and Conrad. C. 1980. "In the Closet with Illness: Epilepsy, Stigma Potential and Information Control." *Social Problems* 28:32–44.

Schuetz, A. 1932. *Der sinnhafte Aubau der sozialen Welt.* Vienna: Springer.

Schuetz, A. 1966. *The Phenomenology of the Social World.* Edited by J. Wild. Translated by G. Walsh and F. Lehnert. Evanston, IL: Northwestern University Press.

Schuetze, F. 1981. "Prozess-Strukturen des Lebensablaufen." Pp. 67–156 in *Biographie in handlungswissenschaftlicher Perspektive,* edited by Matthes et al. Nuremberg: Verlag der Nuernberger Forschungsvereinigung.

Schuetze, F. 1983. "Biographieforschung und Narratives Interview." *Neue Praxis* 83:283–93.

Schuetze, F. 1992. "Pressure and Guilt: War Experiences of a Young German Soldier and Their Biographical Implications." *International Sociology* 7:187–208 (Part 1), 347–67 (Part 2).

Scott, M. and Lyman, S. 1968. "Accounts." *American Sociological Review* 33:46–62.

Shalin, D. 1992a. "Critical Theory and the Pragmatist Challenge." *American Journal of Sociology* 97:237–79.

Shalin, D. (ed.) 1992b. *Symbolic Interaction (Special Edition)* 15.

Shaw, C. 1930. *The Jack-Roller.* Chicago: University of Chicago Press.

Shaw, C. 1931. *The Natural History of a Delinquent Career.* Chicago: University of Chicago Press.

Shaw, C. 1936. *Brothers in Crime.* Chicago: University of Chicago Press.

Shibutani, T. 1955. "Reference Groups as Perspectives." *American Journal of Sociology* 60:522–29.

Shibutani, T. 1978. *The Derelicts of Company K.* Berkeley: University of California Press.

Shils, E. 1956. *Torment of Secrecy.* Glencoe, IL: Free Press.

Shilts, R. 1987. *And the Band Played On: Politics, People, and the AIDS Epidemic.* New York: St. Martins.

Singer, M. 1980. "Signs of the Self: An Exploration in Semiotic Anthropology." *American Anthropologist* 82:487–507.

Skolnick, J. 1966. *Justice Without Trial.* New York: Wiley.

Smith, H. 1990. *The New Russians.* New York: Random House.

Smith, W. 1939. *Americans in the Making.* New York: Appleton-Century.

Soeffner, H.-G. 1991. "'Trajectory' as Intended Fragment: The Critique of Empirical Reason According to Anselm Strauss." Pp. 359–71 in *Social Organization and Social Process: Essays in Honor of Anselm Strauss,* edited by D. Maines. Hawthorne, NY: Aldine de Gruyter.

Soeffner, H.-G. 1992. "Stil und Stiliserung. Punk oder die Ueberhoehung des Alltags." Pp. 76–101 in *Die Ordungder Rituale,* edited by H.-G. Soeffner. Frankfurt-am-Main: Surkamp.

Star, S. L. 1983. "Simplification and Scientific Work: An Example from Neuroscience Research." *Social Studies of Science* 13:205–28.

Star, S. L. 1985. "Scientific Work and Uncertainty." *Social Studies of Science* 15:391–427.

Star, S. L. 1989a. *Regions of the Mind: Brain Research and the Quest for Scientific Certainty.* Palo Alto, CA: Stanford University Press.

Star, S. L. 1989b. "The Structure of Ill-Structured Solutions: Boundary Objects and Heterogeneous Distributed Problem Solving." Pp. 37–54 in *Distributed Artificial Intelligence,* Vol. 3, edited by M. Huhns and L. Gasser. Menlo Park, CA: Morgan Kauffmann.

Star, S. L. 1991. "The Sociology of the Invisible: The Primacy of Work in the Writings of Anselm Strauss." In *Social Organization, and Social Processes: Essays in Honor of Anselm Strauss,* edited by D. Maines. Hawthorne, NY: Aldine de Gruyter.

Star, S. L. and Gerson, E. 1987. "The Management and Dynamics of Anomalies in Scientific Work." *Sociological Quarterly* 28:147–69.

Star, S. L. and Griesmer, J. 1989. "Institutional Ecology, 'Translations,' and Boundary Objects: Amateurs and Professionals in Berkeley's Museum of Vertebrate Zoology, 1907–39." *Social Studies of Science* 19:387–420.

Stein, J. and Urdang, L. (eds.) 1981. *The Random House Dictionary of the English Language.* New York: Random House.

Stelling, J. and Bucher, R. 1972. "Autonomy and Monitoring on Hospital Wards." *Sociological Quarterly* 13:431–46.

Stevenson, W. 1976. *A Man Called Intrepid: The Secret War.* New York: Ballantine Books.

Stone, G. 1962. "Appearance and the Self." Pp. 86–118 in *Human Behavior and Social Processes,* edited by A. Rose. Boston: Houghton Mifflin.

Strauss, A. [1959] 1969. *Mirrors and Masks.* San Francisco: Sociology Press.

Strauss, A. 1970. *The Contexts of Social Mobility.* Chicago: Aldine.

Strauss, A. [1961] 1976. *Images of the American City.* New Brunswick, NJ: Transaction Press.

Strauss, A. 1978. *Negotiations.* San Francisco: Jossey-Bass.

Strauss, A. 1982. "Social Worlds and Legitimation Processes." Pp. 171–90 in *Studies in Symbolic Interaction,* Vol. 4, edited by N. Denzin. Greenwich, CT: JAI Press.

Strauss, A. 1984. "Social Worlds and Their Segmentation Processes." Pp. 125–139 in *Studies in Symbolic Interaction,* Vol. 4, edited by N. Denzin. Greenwich, CT: JAI Press.

Strauss, A. 1985. "Work and the Division of Labor." *Sociological Quarterly* 26:1–19.

Strauss, A. 1987. *Qualitative Analysis for Social Scientists.* New York: Cambridge University Press.

Strauss, A. 1988. "The Articulation of Project Work: An Organizational Process." *Sociological Quarterly* 29:163–78.

Strauss, A. [1978] 1990a. "A Social World Perspective." Pp. 233–44 in *Creating Sociological Awareness,* edited by A. Strauss. New Brunswick, NJ: Transaction Press.

Strauss, A. [1978] 1990b. "The Chicago Tradition's Ongoing Theory of Action/ Interaction." Pp. 3–32 in *Creating Sociological Awareness,* edited by A. Strauss. New Brunswick, NJ: Transaction Press.

Strauss, A., Bucher, R., Ehrlich, D., Sabshin, M. and Schatzman, L. 1964. *Psychiatric Ideologies and Institutions*. New York: Free Press.

Strauss, A., Bucher, R., Ehrlich, D., Schatzman, L. and Sabshin, M. 1963. "The Hospital and Its Negotiated Order." In *The Hospital in Modern Society*, edited by E. Freidson. New York: Free Press.

Strauss, A. and Corbin, J. 1990. *Basics of Qualitative Method*. Newbury Park, CA: Sage.

Strauss, A., Fagerhaugh, S., Suczek, B. and Wiener, C. 1985. *The Social Organization of Medical Work*. Chicago: University of Chicago Press.

Strauss, A. and Glaser, B. 1970. *Anguish*. San Francisco: Sociology Press.

Strauss, A. and Glaser, B. 1975. *Chronic Illness and the Quality of Life*. St. Louis, MO: Mosby.

Sutherland, E. 1937. *The Professional Thief*. Chicago: University of Chicago Press.

Suttles, G and Zald, M. (eds.) 1985. *The Challenge of Social Control: Citizenry and International Building in Modern Society*. Norwood, NJ: Ablex.

Takagi, R. 1989. *Strangers from a Distant Shore: A History of Asian Americans*. New York: Little Brown.

Thomas, W. and Znaniecki, F. 1918–1920. *The Polish Peasant in Poland and America*. New York: Knopf.

Turner, B. (ed.) 1991. *The Body*. Newbury Park, CA: Sage.

Turner, R. and Killian, L. 1987. *Collective Behavior*, 3rd edition. Englewood Cliffs, NJ: Prentice-Hall.

Turner, V. 1982. *Celebration, Studies in Festivity and Ritual*. Washington, DC: Smithsonian Institution.

Van Doren, M. 1939. *An Anthology of World Poetry*. New York: Cornwall Press.

Vaughan, D. 1986. *Uncoupling: Turning Points in Intimate Relationships*. Oxford: Oxford University Press.

Vizetelly, F. (ed.) 1935. *The Practical Standard Dictionary of the English Language*. New York: Funk and Wagnalls.

Vygotsky, L. 1939. "Thought and Speech." *Psychiatry* 2:29–52.

Vygotsky, L. 1962. *Thought and Language*. Edited by E. Hanfmann and G. Vakar. Cambridge, MA: MIT Press.

Vygotsky, L. 1978. *Mind in Society*. Edited by M. Cole. Cambridge, MA: Harvard University Press.

Warren, C. 1974. *Identity and Community in the Gay World*. New York: Wiley.

Watson, J. 1968. *The Double Helix*. New York: Atheneum.

Weber, M. [1922] 1957. *The Theory of Social and Economic Organization*. Translated by A. Henderson and T. Parsons. Glencoe, IL: Free Press.

Weinstein, E. and Deutschberger, p. 1963. "Some Dimensions of Altercasting." *Sociometry* 20:254–66.

Wenck, E. 1972. *The Politics of the Ocean*. Seattle: University of Washington.

Whitehead, A. 1923. *Process and Reality*. New York: Macmillan.

Whitley, R. 1985. "Knowledge Producers and Knowledge Acquirers: Popularization as a Relation Between Scientific Fields and Their Publics." Pp. 3–28 in *Expository Science: Forms and Functions of Popularization, Sociology of the Sci-*

ences Yearbook, Vol 4, edited by T. Shinn and R. Whitley. Dordrecht and Boston: Reidel.

Wiener, C. 1981. *The Politics of Alcoholism.* New Brunswick, NJ: Transaction Press.

Wiener, C., Fagerhaugh, S., Strauss, A. and Suczek, B. 1979. "Trajectories, Biographies, and the Evolving Medical Scene: Labor and Delivery and the Intensive Care Nursery." *Sociology of Health and Illness* 1:261–83.

Wittgenstein, L. 1953. *Philosophical Investigations.* Translated by G.E.M. Anscombe. New York: Macmillan.

Woolf, V. 1946. *Orlando.* NY: Penquin Books.

Woronov, N. 1985. "A See-By-Logic-Life." Pp. 159–72 in *With the Power of Each Breath: A Disabled Women's Anthology,* edited by S. Brown, D. Conners and N. Stern. Pittsburgh: Cleis Press.

Wright, R. 1945. *Black Boy: A Record of Childhood and Youth.* New York: Harper.

Zald, M. and McCarthy, J. (eds.) 1979. *The Dynamics of Social Movements.* Cambridge, MA: Winthrop.

Zald, M. and McCarthy, J. (eds.) 1987. *Social Movements in an Organizational Society.* New Brunswick, NJ: Transaction Press.

Znaniecki, F. [1919] 1983. *Cultural Reality.* Houston, Texas: Cap and Gown Press.

Index